Sir Francis Dra
The Construction of a Hero

For four hundred years Sir Francis Drake's exploits have fascinated, inspired and entertained. Every age has sought to reconstruct the narrative of the great Elizabethan seafarer: the basis of his fame has shifted continually over the years, from single-handed victor over the Spanish Armada, to hero of commerce, explorer, and ruthless entrepreneur. In each incarnation, however, he has always been portrayed to answer the demands and anxieties of each new era.

Here, for the first time, the history of Drake as a cultural icon, and of his myth, is explored, from his appearances in West Country folklore to Elizabethan poetry, from eighteenth-century garden architecture to Victorian pageants and twentieth-century films. There is a particular focus on the `long' nineteenth century, during which Drake's reputation underwent a rigorous reconstruction to present him as a hero of empire.

BRUCE WATHEN gained his PhD from Exeter University.

Sir Francis Drake
The Construction of a Hero

Bruce Wathen

D. S. BREWER

First published 2009
D. S. Brewer, Cambridge

ISBN 978-1-84384-186-9

D. S. Brewer is an imprint of Boydell & Brewer Ltd
PO Box 9, Woodbridge, Suffolk IP12 3DF, UK
and of Boydell & Brewer Inc.
668 Mount Hope Ave, Rochester, NY 14604, USA
website: www.boydellandbrewer.com

A CIP catalogue record for this book is available
from the British Library

The publisher has no responsibility for the continued existence or accuracy of URLs for
external or third-party internet websites referred to in this book, and does not guarantee that
any content on such websites is, or will remain, accurate or appropriate.

This publication is printed on acid-free paper

Text pages designed by Tina Ranft
Printed in Great Britain by CPI Antony Rowe, Chippenham, Wiltshire

Contents

List of Illustrations

For Annette, Dora and my parents

Acknowledgements

'There must be a beginning to any great matter', and for that I need to thank the late Chris Brooks whose enthusiasm for all things Victorian was inspirational. I would like to thank the librarians at the Caird Library, Greenwich, for their assistance and efficiency. Also thanks to the staff at the University of Exeter Library and the Devon and Exeter Institution for their help and co-operation. I am particularly grateful to James Turner for his continued good humour while locating obscure and often disintegrating texts.

I am indebted to the picture researchers at Plymouth City Museum and Art Gallery, The Print Libraries at the British Museum and National Maritime Museum, Greenwich; the National Trust, The National Portrait Gallery and to the curatorial staff at the palace of Westminster. Thanks too to Angela Blaen for assistance with the study of folklore.

Finally, thanks to Annette and my parents for their help in so many ways.

Introduction

In a recent biography of Sir Francis Drake the author noted that, 'In all more than one hundred original books, fact and fiction, have dealt at full length with Drake's career.'[1] Perhaps surprisingly, this is probably a conservative estimate. The lives of few historical characters have received more intense investigation than that of Francis Drake. His fantastic sea-faring exploits have long exerted a great fascination and a multi-layered mythology has built up around him. Undoubtedly his reputation owes much to the Victorians who looked to an idealized Elizabethan past when constructing their imperial history. And yet Drake had survived (or had remained vigorously alive) in the popular imagination for almost three hundred years before the nineteenth-century myth-makers began to manipulate his exploits for their own ideologically motivated purposes. For this reason alone he is worthy of our attention. Familiarity with the unfashionable Victorian version of the Elizabethan should not disguise the fact that Drake is a significant historical figure whose afterlife deserves fuller examination.

Drake was not, of course, the only historical figure to be 'revived' and reconstructed during the Victorian period. The lives of other Elizabethan seafarers (Froude's 'forgotten worthies' including Frobisher, Hawkins and Grenville) received similar attention. Sir Walter Raleigh, to whom Drake is often compared, was another important figure in the nineteenth-century history of Empire. Millais's painting *The Boyhood of Raleigh* (1870), with its depiction of the young Walter listening captivated by an old sailor's tales of the sea, is perhaps the best-known portrayal. In many ways the cultural construction of Raleigh has paralleled that of Drake. Both have been celebrated as Elizabeth's seadogs impatient to be loosed against Spain; both have been constructed as pioneers of Empire and their stories used to encourage overseas expansion. But Raleigh has sometimes been portrayed as a tragic figure, an imperial visionary whose schemes were thwarted by the need to appease Spain. On the other hand, Drake's robust manliness (and enviable record of success) was rather more suited to the Victorian idea of Englishness, and he had loomed somewhat larger in the popular imagination.

The present work is not intended as yet another interpretation of the Drake narrative – a subject that has probably received quite enough attention.[2] Perhaps unsurprisingly Drake scholarship continues to be concerned with issues of truth, with revealing the 'real' Sir Francis Drake or the 'real' purpose behind his voyages. Since the 1950s subverting the Victorian version of Drake has been a preoccupation. Kenneth R Andrews's work *Drake's Voyages: A Reassessment of their Place in Elizabeth Maritime Expansion* (1967) is still one of the most successful revisionist works. Harry

Kelsey's more recent biography *Sir Francis Drake: The Queen's Pirate* (1998) is perhaps the most thorough in its overturning of the nineteenth-century construction. No doubt further works will appear all of which will claim to reveal the authentic Drake but, unless previously unknown sixteenth-century documents come to light that expand our knowledge of Drake's motives and actions, they will almost certainly reveal more about current attitudes than they do about Drake. It is the attitudes that have produced each version of Drake over the centuries in which I am interested.

Clearly, this work is not intended as a history of sixteenth-century expansionism or even a naval history (although I hope it may be of interest to those working in such areas). Instead I shall concentrate on an area that, when compared with Drake's life, has barely been touched upon by academic research: the ways in which Drake has been represented over the last four hundred years. I am not concerned with the issues that continue to preoccupy both naval and amateur historians such as what latitude Drake reached upon what date but rather with how and why he has been represented – or why he has not been represented – in certain ways during particular historical periods. Some work has been done in this area already. W.T. Jewkes has produced a useful introduction to the literary treatment of Sir Francis Drake.[3] More recently both John Cummins and John Sugden have included chapters on the 'Drake legend' in their biographies[4] but this is not their prime concern, and a fuller analysis of the determinants that lie behind each version of Drake is required. In a persuasive work concerned with the religious origins of the British imperial imagination Christopher Hodgkins dwells upon Drake's encounter with Native American Indians. He argues that the apparent desire of the Indians to worship the English (and, just as importantly, the English refusal of that worship) initiated a pattern of representing the relationship between colonizer and colonized that justified imperial possession and stayed current in historical and literary works for centuries.[5] Perhaps the finest work on the afterlife of Drake is provided by Mark Netzloff who concentrates on Drake's afterlife to explore the possibility of oppositional or alternative varieties of national sentiment in the early modern period.[6] My aim is to expand upon the beginnings provided by all these works but to move away from the early modern period and dwell on the nineteenth century in order to provide, for the first time, a full-length analysis of the Victorian version of Sir Francis Drake.

Of course, representations of Drake have not remained static since the late sixteenth century; the way he was portrayed during his own lifetime differs significantly from the way we regard him now. I have attempted to chart the emerging constructions and to unravel the layers of the Drake mythology. The method used to pursue this research is centred on cultural materialism, the investigation of cultural products representing Sir Francis Drake from his own day until the present. By 'representing' I mean products that imagine, describe or stand for Francis Drake. This cultural materialistic approach is combined with semiotics. When read textually each product becomes a sign structure that I have interpreted for evidence of cultural construction. In this way statues, paintings, novels and so on are shown to be not simply the work of individual imaginations but the products of the dominant cultural/historical developments of their time and of the ideological formations that both accompanied these developments and were generated by them. Whether represented by historical narratives, pageants, poems or plays, Sir Francis Drake has always been constructed in a way that makes sense at the time of production. The range of material under discussion is extremely varied and includes paintings, engravings, poems, songs, dramas, statues, architecture, medals, postage stamps, folk-tales, films and exhibitions. Perhaps unsurprisingly, historical narratives and biographical accounts form a large proportion of the research. Many of the cultural products I discuss originated in Drake's native Devon and have never been the subject of critical enquiry, although some works – Henry Newbolt's poem 'Drake's Drum' is the obvious example – were, until relatively recently, very well known. As the preceding list suggests, the research is not concerned solely with the products of 'high' culture. My position is very firmly that ordinary people have been involved in the production of their own culture and ideas; these are generated independently and not imposed from above. Consequently I have focused on popular culture whenever possible. When dealing with constructions of Drake produced in the nineteenth century this is unproblematic as the material is abundant. But, because of the largely oral nature of popular culture before the nineteenth century, few early popular representations have survived.

The bulk of the book (Chapters Five to Eight) is concerned with representations of Drake that appeared during the long nineteenth century. The reasons for this are twofold; first, the cultural products dealing with Drake that were produced in the late sixteenth and early seventeenth centuries have already received a disproportionate amount of scholarly attention. Historians and biographers searching for the 'real' Francis Drake have frequently consulted contemporary narratives in the mistaken belief that, because of their age, these texts have an inherent authenticity. Second, the nineteenth century was responsible for a vigorous reconstruction of the Drake narrative – a rewriting that was much broader in scope than all previous manipulations of the story. This reconstruction was facilitated by the great historical disjunction that occurred in the early part of the century. The huge economic and social changes wrought by the agrarian and industrial revolutions effectively severed the past from the present and made it available for imaginative reconstruction. In Drake's case, this reconstruction took the form of a specific causal narrative – the Elizabethan sea-faring past could be used to explain the origins of the British Empire. In contrast to the early work on Drake, nineteenth- and early twentieth-century cultural products have often been ignored by scholarly analyses. In these politically sensitive times the Victorian construction of Drake as a hero of empire is likely to involve features that cannot be accommodated within contemporary dominant ideology. Yet constructing the origins of the nation's naval power was an important cultural project in the nineteenth century – not least because it provided ideological justification for imperial possession. Until now this significant influence on national self-image has not been the focus of academic research.[7] This is despite the fact that the popular version of Sir Francis Drake and the Spanish Armada that emerged in the mid-

Victorian period remains familiar today: Drake is still the jovial, bowls-playing victor over the Spanish fleet.

Before discussing the Victorian version of Drake and how it marked a departure from previous portrayals, it is, of course, necessary to look at the representations produced by earlier centuries. Chapters One and Two are concerned with contemporary constructions and representations that appeared in the seventeenth century. Chapter Three deals with the eighteenth century – particularly the influence of the cult of commerce – while the fourth chapter investigates the construction of Drake during the Napoleonic wars, a crucial time in the repositioning of Drake. I aim to show that before the middle decades of the nineteenth century a different aspect of the Drake narrative was being emphasized. From his triumphant return to Plymouth in 1580 until the mid-Victorian period Drake's fame was derived principally from the circumnavigation of the globe. Whether his achievements were recorded in contemporary portraits by Marcus Gheeraerts or Jodocus Hondius, or in John Barrow's biography produced two hundred and fifty years after his death, the voyage was the defining element when constructing Drake. The significance with which the 'famous voyage' was invested was determined by contemporary concerns. For Richard Hakluyt writing in the late sixteenth century the voyage was a great feat of navigation skill and a worthy expansionist endeavour. For the author of *The World Encompassed* published in 1628, recalling the circumnavigation was a means of inspiring military and nautical endeavour at a time of high anti-Spanish feeling. Drake's identity as a circumnavigator was the dominant representation across all areas of English culture. As we will see, Daniel Defoe makes reference to a folk tradition concerning Drake in one of his lesser-known stories.

Broadly speaking, recalling the circumnavigation and Drake's other privateering exploits – most frequently the raid on Nombre de Dios and the Panama mule trains – in what we may term the 'pre-Armada' phase of his construction was a strategy employed when England was seeking to expand or when the nation was furthering her economic interests through foreign wars. The primary purpose of 'reviving' Drake was, then, to inspire patriotism and naval enterprise. For instance, William Davenant's opera *The History of Sir Francis Drake*, which was based upon the 1572 voyage, appeared during a war with Spain in 1659. Of course, 'offensive' conflicts were often subject to ideological manipulation. A war with Spain could be presented as another episode in the ongoing struggle between embattled Protestant England and the mighty Catholic foe that had its origins in Drake's day. But recalling Drake as an inspirational figure was not confined to times of conflict. Sir Francis was often used as an exemplum, a corrective figure from a previous age whose chivalrous conduct and moral qualities were an example for a degenerate present. Both Michael Drayton in *Poly-Olbion* and Samuel Johnson in 'The Life of Admiral Drake' look back to an Elizabethan golden age and identify Sir Francis as a figure worthy of emulation.

Notably, the cultural products of the seventeenth and eighteenth centuries seldom see Drake as the single-handed Armada victor. In direct contrast to Drake's privateering exploits, the failed Spanish invasion was recalled when Britain was on the defensive. The story of the Armada provided an historical precedent and appeared to demonstrate that God was watching over his chosen race whenever an invasion of the British mainland seemed a genuine possibility. The representation of Drake as the Armada victor was, in fact, a popular cultural tradition that provided a counterpoint to the literary version of the Drake narrative and its emphasis upon the circumnavigation. Initially the tradition was found in contemporary ballads and later, in the eighteenth century, appeared in entertainments intended for a popular audience such as the sea songs of Charles and John Dibdin.

Although the wars with Revolutionary and Napoleonic France produced relatively little written material dealing with Drake, the period from 1790 to about 1830 was nevertheless a crucial time in terms of representing Sir Francis. The military/nautical motivation that had lain behind the construction of Drake was gradually overtaken by a Romantic imperative. Southey's recording of folk-tales and the interest shown in the Drake relics found at Buckland Abbey, a specific Drake 'site', point towards a Drake broadly positioned across English culture. Here we find evidence of a popular Sir Francis Drake with a vigorous existence outside naval history. His presence in folk-tales (made available to the literate classes through Southey's activities) reveals Drake to be a figure firmly embedded in English culture, and it was perhaps this close identification with Englishness that facilitated his reconstruction as a hero of empire later in the nineteenth century.

As Chapter Five will demonstrate, it was during the middle years of the nineteenth century that the popular cultural tradition of Drake as the Armada victor began to be widely disseminated in written form. Indeed, the defeat of the Spanish Armada was elevated above the circumnavigation as Drake's greatest achievement. Historical works placed great importance on the Armada; the popular cultural tradition had clearly been embraced by literary culture. This transition was achieved only gradually, and one element of the circumnavigation narrative, Drake's knighthood, remained a powerful image. At a time when the economic well-being of the nation was increasingly coming under the control of middle-class merchants and industrialists, Drake's rise to distinction provided a historical precedent for the possibility of upward social mobility.

The precedence given to the Armada narrative with its enhanced role for Drake was the direct result of Britain's imperial status. Although there was no realistic prospect of a foreign power attempting an invasion of England, the potent image of a small nation peacefully going about its business but besieged by foreign aggressors could be mobilized in the colonial theatre, which was steadily increasing in size. This type of mythologizing deflected attention from Britain's own aggression. By the 1850s Drake's status as a hero of empire, what we might term the 'Armada' phase of his construction, was beginning to blossom. His new significance in terms of imperial history was achieved largely through the work of two men: James Anthony Froude and Charles Kingsley. They provide the focus for Chapter Six. Froude's great narrative of causation, *History of England from the Fall of Wolsey to the Defeat of the Spanish Armada*, marked the turning point in the construction of Sir Francis. For

Froude, the Reformation was secured by the activities of the Elizabethan mariners, 'England's forgotten worthies', and foremost among them was Sir Francis Drake. The reconstructed version of Sir Francis Drake that emerged was disseminated to a huge audience by Charles Kingsley's patriotic novel of sea-faring adventure *Westward Ho!* Kingsley was largely responsible for shaping the attractive notion of Drake as a bluff sea-dog with little regard for 'book learning'.

Sir Julian Corbett, whose biography of Drake was published in 1890, steered the construction of Sir Francis in a new direction. For Corbett Drake was a pioneer of offensive naval strategy. It was Drake, he argued, who developed the practice of seeking out the enemy and blockading his ports. In this way he was portrayed as a forerunner of Nelson. Corbett's ideas proved extremely influential. But while Corbett was content to dwell on the continuity between the two commanders in terms of naval strategy, Henry Newbolt was keen to show that Drake and Nelson were linked at a deeper level. For Newbolt, Drake's independent spirit and devil-may-care attitude had been inherited by Nelson. Although on the surface self-congratulatory, Newbolt's 'Drake poems' are in fact the product of a new anxiety that emerged in the 1890s. The cause of this fear was the armament of Britain's rivals – particularly Germany – in the final years of the nineteenth century. Sir Francis Drake became a figure to look to for reassurance about England's vulnerability. Far from being a display of triumphalism, the construction of Drake in the 1890s was actually impelled by deep anxiety. This is the subject of Chapter Eight.

The full patriotic potential of the myths of the drum and Nelson as a reincarnation of Drake was realized during the First World War. The myth of the drum was used as a rallying call for Englishmen. For intellectual culture at least the Great War did much to undermine the mythology of empire. Popular culture on the other hand continued to promote the image of Drake as the hearty, bowls-playing victor over the Spanish Armada. Chapter Nine discusses Drake in the twentieth century, and argues that the real turning point in Drake's construction was not the Great War but the Second World War. It was during the 1950s that historical accounts intended for a popular audience began to question the old myths. Drake was no longer the founder of the Royal Navy or the British Empire. The 1960s in particular were a time of cultural neglect for Sir Francis Drake.

However, the anniversaries of Drake's achievements in the 1970s and 1980s saw a revival of interest in the Elizabethan admiral. In an age of post-colonial sensitivity and supposed European political and economic co-operation, the Drake narrative needed some reconstruction. Plymouth's quadricentennial celebrations of the circumnavigation saw Drake as an explorer and great navigator rather than a privateer and feared opponent of Spain. Appropriately for a circumnavigator, the construction of Drake seemed to have turned full circle – Hakluyt may well have recognized the Drake being celebrated. The 1988 Armada celebrations in particular were marked by political sensitivity. Yet in Plymouth the celebrations bore a remarkable similarity to those that had taken place in 1888. The perpetuation of the old construction of Drake is explained by looking at the decline of Plymouth as a ship-building city and naval base and at the economic problems this has brought with it. In an effort to compensate for this loss the city has attempted to package its maritime heritage for tourist consumption. This heritage includes the well-known nineteenth-century version of Sir Francis Drake. It becomes apparent that, although the empire has disappeared, the representation of Drake that helped sustain it has survived as a signifier of Plymouth.

Quite clearly this book has emerged from an awareness of the malleable nature of the past. As David Lowenthal observes,

> The past is always altered for motives that reflect present needs. We re-shape our heritage to make it attractive in modern terms; we seek to make it part of ourselves, and ourselves part of it; we conform it to our self-images and aspirations. Rendered grand or homely, magnified or tarnished, history is continually altered in our private interests or on behalf of our community or country.[8]

This is not a modern phenomenon; the present work demonstrates that every age has manipulated the Elizabethan past for its own ends – to inspire endeavour in times of conflict or to reinforce certain ideologies. Nor is creative reconstruction confined to popular treatments of history. We might expect folk-tales or novels to present us with fanciful or fabulous versions of past events – the detailed discussion of folk narratives in Chapter Four shows that this is very much the case – but traditional historical discourse (what we may, perhaps, term History), which purports to concern itself with issues of truth and authenticity, is equally creative in shaping the past. The notion that History provides us with a 'correct' or 'ultimate' version of the past is problematic. First, we need to recognize that the objectives of history writing have not remained the same through the ages. Only in the nineteenth century did the cult of authenticity, the desire to tell the past as it really was, begin to preoccupy historians. Heavily influenced by empirical science – particularly its emphasis on cause and effect – a methodology emerged that foregrounded original documents as the starting point for the construction of 'scientific' history or seemingly objective narratives. Before the nineteenth century, however, historical scholarship 'was based more on creative observation, or some master plan (such as the presence of God's will on earth and the perfectibility of the human spirit), than upon the rigorous interrogation of primary materials'.[9] The past was often an exemplary tale – particularly so in the case of the Spanish Armada – that could be related without recourse to documentary evidence. For many people the past was little different from the present, human nature the same in all ages. As David Hume wrote, 'Mankind are so much the same, in all times and places, that history informs us of nothing new or strange in this particular.'[10]

In more recent times the past has become contested territory. Although faith in 'true' history still lingers, a proliferation of theoretical approaches (not least Marxist history) has undermined the dominance of the empirical tradition. Secondly, confronted with the fact of historical manipulation that Lowenthal summarizes above, we must recognize that there is no 'correct' or 'true' version of the past to be discovered. Nor is there a 'real' Sir Francis Drake. The misconceived idea of an authentic past ignores the fact that 'reality' is culturally constructed, that every purportedly accurate historical account is an interpretation formed by the prejudices of its author who, in turn, is formed by a particular culture and its values. Even the most impartial historian (or biographer) must exclude from their narrative material what seems irrelevant or makes little sense in contemporary terms. On the other hand, they may need to speculate when data is insufficient. This speculation will almost certainly reflect modern concerns. According to Hayden White,

> A historical narrative is thus necessarily a mixture of adequately and inadequately explained events, a congeries of established and inferred facts, at once a representation that is an interpretation and an interpretation that passes for an explanation of the whole process mirrored in the narrative.[11]

It soon becomes apparent that the present has traditionally been the most significant factor when constructing the past. Yet History has not been without its critics who have accused it of dealing in anachronisms.[12] It is precisely these anachronisms, this reshaping of the past for present needs, in which I am interested. Despite its critics, the traditional approach to history writing remains influential and is standard for popular histories. Raphael Samuel notes that 'Even if it [history] dispenses with notions of "destiny", it is still governed by an unspoken teleology, in which the past is a prelude to the present, and the present is the focal point on which lines of development converge.'[13] This explains the obsession of traditional History with the essential continuity of events – the past must be constructed so as to make the present seem inevitable, the only possible outcome of a series of occurrences. But because the present is changing constantly it is necessary to alter the past to keep pace or to maintain the feeling of continuity. Lowenthal again: 'To span the mental gulf between past and present, to communicate convincingly, and to invest historical accounts with interpretive coherence requires their continual reshaping.'[14] Simply because certain events are deemed important in one age, it does not follow that their significance will survive the passage of time. Reading the past in terms that make sense for the present is not, of course, an activity restricted to academic history; I shall demonstrate how the present informs almost all interpretations of the past.

★

Finally, to assist the reader it seems appropriate to provide a brief outline of the main events in Drake's life. Of course, in recounting these events I am also engaged in an act of cultural construction. This summary should not be read as an authentic life of Drake. Rather it should be regarded as a narrative framework, the components of which are variously stressed, ignored and rearranged by the texts I discuss.

Francis Drake was born near Tavistock in west Devon around 1540. His parents were not wealthy; the traditional narrative asserts that his father, who was a strict Protestant, was forced to flee his native county with his family in 1549 because of the Prayer Book Rebellion, a series of West Country uprisings occasioned by the imposition of Thomas Cranmer's new Prayer Book. Drake's formative years were spent apprenticed to the master of a ship operating from the River Medway in Kent where his father was employed as a lay preacher. Drake's youthful appetite for hard work displayed a Puritan zeal; this so impressed his employer that when he died he left Drake his first bark. For a time he continued to ship merchandise to Zeeland and France. However, in 1567 Drake sailed on John Hawkins's third slaving voyage to the West Indies, which appeared to guarantee a healthy return for Drake's investment. Although in the late 1560s King Philip had outlawed commerce between Spanish colonists and English traders, this did not prevent trade from taking place. National commitments could take second place when Spain and her colonies were separated by the Atlantic Ocean, and John Hawkins was more than willing to supply slaves. During the course of this voyage, bad weather forced Hawkins's fleet to put in at San Juan d'Ulua, Mexico. After the arrival of a new viceroy, the Spanish broke an uneasy truce – hostages had been exchanged and the English given control of the harbour battery, a measure of the distrust between the two nations even in peacetime – and attacked the English fleet in the crowded harbour. A desperate fight ensued during which all but two of the English ships were destroyed or captured. Drake and Hawkins were lucky to escape with their lives and, after a torturous journey during which the *Judith* captained by Drake appears to have deserted the *Minion*, arrived back in England.

The desire for retribution following the incident at San Juan persuaded Drake to give up the merchant trade and turn to privateering. He made two voyages to the Caribbean between 1569 and 1571, but little is known of their purpose. In 1572 Drake undertook the first of his famous exploits when he raided the town of Nombre de Dios in Panama and ambushed a mule train carrying gold to the port for shipment back to Spain. The success of this voyage made Drake a hero in the West Country. Shortly after his return he faded from public view and appears to have been engaged in ferrying troops across the Irish Sea during Essex's campaign in Ireland. In 1577 he embarked on his greatest voyage: the circumnavigation of the globe. In 1580 Drake returned to Plymouth the first Englishman to sail around the world. The aim of the voyage – perhaps with secret royal backing – seems to have been to capture Spanish treasure in the Pacific. The profits realized by the expedition were vast and Drake was knighted aboard his ship, the *Golden Hinde*, at Deptford in 1581. During the course of the voyage he executed Thomas Doughty, a gentleman adventurer, on what were possibly false charges of mutiny. He also claimed Nova Albion (an unknown location on the west coast of North America) in the name of Elizabeth and negotiated a treaty with the Sultan of Ternate in the Spice Islands.

In 1585/6 Drake led an expedition to raid Spanish settlements in the Caribbean. Santo Domingo and Carthagena were taken but the expedition was not considered a success; the anticipated treasure was not captured, disease depleted the troops and the investors in the voyage – including the Queen – lost considerable sums. His next exploit was a pre-emptive strike against an invasion fleet being assembled at Cadiz for the invasion of England in 1587. There were several reasons for the intended invasion: to curtail supplies to the Protestant rebels in the Spanish Netherlands, to eliminate privateering in the Caribbean, and to expand the

Habsburg empire while at the same time re-establishing Catholicism as the religion of England. Following the execution of Mary, Queen of Scots, in February 1587, Philip could put himself forward as the legitimate heir to the English throne once the heretic Elizabeth had been ousted. Drake's raid destroyed about twenty Spanish ships in the harbour together with a substantial amount of supplies; this was a serious disruption to the Spanish invasion plans and gave the English time to prepare their defences. When referring to the success of the raid Drake claimed that he had 'singed the king of Spain's beard'.

In the following year when the Spanish fleet, known as the Armada, came, Drake was appointed vice-admiral under Charles Howard. Details of Drake's precise role in the victory are sketchy but he seems to have led the bulk of the English fleet into the final battle off Gravelines after Howard and about twenty other ships veered off in an effort to capture a galleass stranded on the French shore. Drake also demonstrated a keen interest in taking prizes: he deserted his position to capture the Spanish *capitana* or flagship the *Rosario*, which was left helpless after colliding with another vessel. By 1589 Drake's fortunes had changed: a plan to elevate the pretender Dom Antonio to the throne of Portugal and to destroy the surviving Armada vessels anchored in the Tagus went disastrously wrong. The expedition was commanded jointly by Drake and Sir John Norris, two experienced generals. However, a combination of poor provisions, confused objectives and disagreements between the commanders meant that little was achieved for the loss of many lives. In disgrace until 1593, Drake embarked upon a new treasure-raiding voyage to the Indies in 1595, this time in the company of John Hawkins. The voyage was not a success; the towns that Drake had raided with such ease twenty years earlier were now much stronger and capable of resisting English aggression. Aboard the *Defiance* Drake died of dysentery and was buried at sea off Porto Bello in January 1596. It is important to remember that every element of this narrative, every 'fact' has been, at different times, qualified, emphasized, denied, adjusted, ignored, celebrated.

Notes

[1] John Sugden, *Sir Francis Drake* (1990; London, 1996), 321 note 1.

[2] The best modern biographical accounts are John Cummins, *Sir Francis Drake: The Lives of a Hero* (London, 1995); Sugden, *Sir Francis Drake*; and Harry Kelsey, *Sir Francis Drake: The Queen's Pirate* (New Haven, 1998). For an account of the place of Drake's voyage in relation to Elizabethan expansion, see Kenneth R. Andrews, *Trade, Plunder and Settlement: Maritime Enterprise and the Genesis of the British Empire 1480–1630* (Cambridge, 1984) and *Drake's Voyages: A Reassessment of their Place in Elizabethan Maritime Expansion* (London, 1967).

[3] W. T. Jewkes, 'Sir Francis Drake Revived: From Letter to Legend', in Norman J. W. Thrower, ed., *Sir Francis Drake and the Famous Voyage, 1577–1580* (Berkeley, 1980), 112–20.

[4] Cummins 315–24, and Sugden 258–302.

[5] Christopher Hodgkins, *Reforming Empire, Protestant Colonialism and Conscience in British Literature* (Columbia, 2002).

[6] Mark Netzloff, 'Sir Francis Drake's Ghost: Piracy, Cultural Memory, and Spectral Nationhood', in Claire Jowitt, ed., *Pirates? The Politics of Plunder, 1550–1650* (Basingstoke, 2007), 137–50.

[7] One of the few modern works on nineteenth-century myths of the sea is Cynthia Fansler Behrman's *Victorian Myths of the Sea* (Ohio, 1977), which contains a useful chapter on the Spanish Armada.

[8] David Lowenthal, *The Past is a Foreign Country* (1985; Cambridge, 1997), 348.

[9] Jeremy Black and Donald M. MacRaid, *Studying History* (London, 1997), 24.

[10] Quoted in W. H. Walsh, 'The Constancy of Human Nature', in H. D. Lewis, ed., *Contemporary British Philosophy* (London, 1975), 274.

[11] Hayden White, *Tropics of Discourse: Essays in Cultural Criticism* (1978; Baltimore, 1995), 51.

[12] Perhaps the best known is Herbert Butterfield who complained that 'The study of the past with one eye, so to speak, upon the present is the source of all sins and sophistry in history, starting with the simplest of them all, the anachronism.' See Herbert Butterfield, *The Whig Interpretation of History* (1931; London, 1951), 63.

[13] Raphael Samuel, 'Grand Narratives', *History Workshop*, vol. 29 (1990), 126.

[14] Lowenthal, 235.

CHAPTER ONE

Auxilio Divino

Sir Drake, whom well the world's ends knows
Which thou dids't compasse round,
And whom both poles of Heaven once saw,
Which North and South doe bound;
The starres above will make thee known,
If men here silent were,
The sunne himself cannot forget
His fellow-traveller.

(Anon. 1581)

This epigram was one of several written by the scholars of Winchester School and pinned to the main mast of the *Golden Hinde* shortly after her arrival at Deptford in 1581.[1] Here she was laid up in dry-dock on the queen's orders to act as a permanent monument to Francis Drake's circumnavigation of the globe. The ship and her captain generated a huge amount of public interest and the poem is a prophetic statement of eternal fame for Drake. A failure to recognize the achievement of sailing around the world would result in the stars of both the northern and southern skies – which Drake had seen and which had guided him on his voyage – commemorating the feat. In the event the stars were not needed; neither the circumnavigation nor any of Drake's other voyages would be forgotten. In this first chapter I shall explore the ways in which Drake was represented during the final twenty years of the sixteenth century and discuss the cultural implications of these constructions.

There is little doubt that Sir Francis Drake was a legend in his own lifetime. Writing in the early years of the seventeenth century, Edmund Howes claimed 'He was as famous in Europe and America as Tamberlaine in Asia and Africa.'[2] But when did Drake's dramatic rise to fame begin? He certainly gained renown locally when the *Judith* arrived back in Plymouth, having escaped the Spanish attack in the harbour at San Juan d'Ulua in 1568. His 1572 raid on Nombre de Dios and the Panama mule trains made Drake a hero in the West Country and provided the wealth required to establish himself as a prominent property-owning figure in Plymouth. But it was the circumnavigation of the globe undertaken between 1577 and 1580, the first by an Englishman and only the second ever,[3] that spread the name Francis Drake throughout England, Europe and the Spanish empire, and which facilitated Drake's meteoric ascent of the Elizabethan social ladder. The voyage was clearly an immense feat of navigational skill; no Englishman had sailed across the Pacific Ocean before let alone navigated the Magellan Strait. Recognizing his unrivalled seamanship, Howes claimed 'he was more skilful in all points of navigation than any that ever was before his time, in his time, or since his death'.[4] He went on to note the popular reaction to Drake's return: 'Books, pictures and ballads, were published in his praise, his opinion and judgement, concerning marine affaires stade currant.'[5] Regrettably, none of these books (presumably chapbooks or pamphlets) has survived.

But to understand fully the significance of the circumnavigation for Drake's contemporaries it cannot be viewed in isolation and must be set within the broad context of Elizabethan maritime endeavour and the political and economic determinants that propelled it. Conventional chronology – popularised by nineteenth-century historians intent on constructing a past for the Second British Empire – located the nation's imperial origins in the expansionist enterprises of the Elizabethan seafarers. This led to the latter part of Elizabeth's reign being portrayed as a 'Golden Age' of maritime endeavour during which an empire of the seas was forged, and this was a powerful image that endured.

> The myth was persistent not least because it enshrined an inescapable truth: the British Empire [after Trafalgar] *was* an empire of the seas, and without the Royal Navy's mastery of the oceans, it could never have become the global empire upon which the sun never set.[6]

Maritime enterprise driven by commercial interests – and the lure of easy plunder – certainly was a characteristic of the late sixteenth century and yet, as Kenneth Andrews has observed, endeavour was seldom matched by success. The Elizabethans attempted to plant colonies in North America and, with their activities underpinned by the concept of *mare liberum* (free sea),[7] made strenuous efforts to break into the trans-Atlantic slave trade. None of these endeavours was successful in Elizabeth's lifetime.

> Behind the glory of Elizabethan legend and nationalist propaganda lay a long and painful series of failures and disasters, only occasionally relieved by some brilliant feat such as Drake's voyage around the World.[8]

Here we begin to understand just why the voyage captured the Elizabethan popular imagination with such force. Circumnavigating the globe was a stunning achievement in itself. Returning with a hold crammed with Spanish treasure made the feat even more admirable. But set against a backdrop of thwarted endeavour – most notably Frobisher's failed attempts at locating the fabled North West Passage – the achievement was magnified tenfold and acted as a spur to the ambition of other venturers. (As we will see, recourse to the Drake narrative to inspire endeavour became a familiar motif in the seventeenth century.) Unlike so many of his contemporaries, Drake returned to England in triumph and immediately became a popular hero despite fierce attacks from his detractors both at Court, where his piracy was seen by some as dragging England closer to a costly war with

Spain, and in the mercantile community. It was the London merchants who dominated Anglo-Iberian trade that stood to suffer should Philip seize their goods in reprisal for Drake's Pacific raids. But for the masses,

> He now became the greatest of the pirate-heroes of English folklore, a perfect image of the wronged, righteous, magnanimous lawbreaker, embodying as common mariner made knight, the social aspiration of the masses.[9]

The primary purpose of the circumnavigation continues to be contested: was it an attempt to find the elusive North West Passage or a reconnaissance mission along the eastern coast of North America with the aim of locating possible sites for settlement, or was it simply a treasure-raiding voyage on a grand scale?[10] With a little manipulation the voyage can be constructed as being concerned principally with each of these things. It certainly represented the zenith of that piratical strand of English maritime endeavour that grew out of the mid-century Anglo-French wars and which, in line with the changing political situation during the 1560s, had turned its attention to Spain. Crucially, however, its greatest achievement was a by-product of Drake's piracy for the voyage 'promoted confidence in the maritime forces of the nation, for it seemed to lay open the western and eastern worlds to English enterprise'.[11] Its importance, then, lay not in what it achieved (which was considerable in terms of navigation and geographical discovery alone) but in the maritime potential that it served to reveal, what Kenneth Andrews has termed 'economic nationalism'.

Whether Drake had a serious interest in trade or not, his stay at Ternate represented the first English contact with the East Indies, and this was significant. In the 1550s the decline in the cloth trade, the so-called Old Draperies, had encouraged merchants to seek out new, more distant markets. Attempts were made to find a North East passage to Cathay that would link 'the attempt to seek out new outlets for cloth with a long standing desire to capture the rich eastern trade in spices and silks'.[12] Although unsuccessful in locating a sea passage, this quest led to English contact with Russia and the eventual formation of the Muscovy Company. Stories of Drake's sojourn in the Moluccas had the effect of reinvigorating interest in exploration of the East during the early 1580s. Schemes were put forward in a fever of excitement; two years later Edward Fenton set sail on an unsuccessful attempt to capitalize on Drake's contact with the ruler of Ternate. Similarly, Drake's encounter with the Native American Indians of Nova Albion prepared the way for attempts at settling colonies in North America well away from areas controlled by Spain.

Impeccable timing also had a role to play in securing Drake's fame. In 1574 Richard Grenville petitioned the queen to be allowed to undertake a voyage similar to Drake's. After initially approving the scheme, Elizabeth withdrew her consent for fear of the damage the venture might do to relations between England and Spain. However, when Drake came to propose a venture three years later things had changed. Anglo-Spanish relations had deteriorated and the prevalent mood at Court and in the country as a whole was distinctly anti-Spanish. If good timing played a part in allowing Drake to set forth, it also intervened on his behalf when he returned. In September 1580, the very month that he sailed into Plymouth, a papal expedition comprised partly of volunteers recruited in Spain had been sent to Ireland by Pope Gregory XIII to organize a rebellion against England. Although this force was soon defeated anti-Catholic feeling was running high. Writing of the Spanish reaction to Drake's predation in his biography *Sir Francis Drake: The Queen's Pirate* Harry Kelsey argues that

> Philip was annoyed, but less so than we now tend to think. The attacks made on Spanish Pacific ports were really minor matters when viewed in the context of Spain's other interests in Europe and around the world.[13]

This may well be true, for Philip certainly had more to fear from an English attack on his own coast while the Spanish army was engaged in the Netherlands yet, in England, the propaganda value of Drake's activities cannot be underestimated. With the Counter Reformation fully active and West Country sailors falling prey to the Inquisition, Drake 'the personification of holy wrath emerged as the hero of the nation',[14] The traditional narrative stresses Drake's devout Protestantism and, indeed, he may well have believed that 'it was the shipment of treasures from the New World that sustained Philip's standing in Europe and facilitated the suppression of Protestantism by fire and sword'.[15] He always carried John Foxe's *Book of Martyrs*[16] on his expeditions. This work fuelled the notion of England as the 'elect nation'[17] and 'popularized a national historical myth which saw Englishmen from Wyclif's day (at least) fighting against Antichrist, who in the sixteenth century was represented by the Pope and Spain'.[18] Did Drake see himself as part of this tradition? Kelsey suggests that Drake was indifferent to religious commitment and that his ostentatious show of piety was designed purely to impress and control others, his fellow countrymen as much as his Spanish adversaries.[19] Those engaged upon creating the Drake myth in later years would, of course, make the most of Drake's religion. It provided a noble cause that acted to legitimise his piracy. But whether Drake was as puritanical as he has been portrayed does not really matter; he rapidly became one of the great heroes of the Reformation. A quarter of a century after his death his own image appeared in Henry Holland's *Herwolgia Anglica*, a volume in celebration of well-known opponents of the Catholic Church.[20] Curiously, pre-empting a construction of Drake that would emerge in the late nineteenth century, the image was accompanied by a short poetic epitaph that hinted Drake would one day return and save the country from a new threat. But much more of this in later chapters.

The success of the circumnavigation was often attributed to the intervention of a benevolent and, of course, Protestant God. This is reflected in the device assigned to Drake as the crest for his coat of arms. This comprises a globe surmounted by the *Golden Hinde*; hawsers attached to the bow of the ship loop beneath the globe encircling it – a symbol of Drake's encircling voyage – and these are grasped by the hand of God appearing from a cloud that guides the *Hinde* on her journey. A motto reads 'Auxilio Divino', 'By divine Help'. So great was Drake's fame and so great was the impact of this voyage on the Elizabethan mind that six years after its completion the divinely guided ship device appeared in the first English emblem book, Geoffrey Whitney's *A Choice of Emblemes*,[21] a collection that has been termed 'a storehouse for Elizabethan commonplaces'.[22] The picture was accompanied by an explanatory poem or motto.

> *By gapinge gulfes hee pass'd, by monsters of the flood,*
> *By pirates, theeves, and cruell foes, that long'd to spill his blood.*
> *That wonder greate to scape: but, God was on his side,*
> *And throughe them all, in spite of all, his shaken shippe did guide.* (3–6)

An examination of contemporary portraiture reveals that the circumnavigation was the determining element in the construction of Sir Francis Drake. For a modern audience probably more familiar with the nineteenth-century construction of Drake as the Armada victor, this semantic emphasis may seem strange. In fact the victory over the Armada was incorporated as an explicit part of the portrait iconography of only two figures: the queen and her Lord High Admiral, Charles Howard.[23] David Cressy hints at one possible reason for the omission of Armada emblems from the portraiture of all other combatants. 'All credit for the victory was given to God. The celebrations were not for the triumph of English arms but for the signal mercy shown to England by an anglophile divinity.'[24] While it is undoubtedly true that the failure of the Spanish invasion proved to the Elizabethans that God was watching over them, Cressy's assertion needs some qualification. Church sermons and the official day of thanksgiving certainly credited God with the victory but at least one popular cultural product was also keen to promote Francis Drake as the key figure in the defeat of the Armada. The ballad 'Eighty Eight, or Sir Francis Drake'[25] conveniently ignores the fact that it was Charles Howard who organized the fireship attack off Gravelines.

> *Our Queen was then att Tilbury,*
> *What could you more desire-a?*
> *For whose sweete sake, Sir Francis Drake*
> *Did sett them all on fyre-a.* (29–32)

Drake was one of four squadron commanders worrying the Armada as it progressed along the English Channel, and even at the time there was a lack of unanimity about the merits of his actions.[26] This raises an important question: if Drake was only one player in the Armada engagements, why was he popularly credited with the victory? Without doubt Drake was Elizabeth's most famous admiral; he had captured the *Rosario*, the first real evidence of English success, but were fame and popularity enough to account for the elision of Howard, Frobisher and Hawkins? For a possible answer we need to turn our attention to the effects of the Reformation on the way people worshipped, more specifically on the effect of the abolition of mediating saints. Although the practice of invoking saints as part of the system of Christian belief had been officially abandoned, their absence seems to have led to an imaginative lack within English consciousness. The desire for a mediating figure to fulfil the imaginative need saw the healing or other thaumaturgic powers of the old saints gradually transferred to secular figures. The monarch was the obvious focus for this transforming pattern of worship; Helen Hackett has shown how Queen Elizabeth was often presented as a Marian intercessor figure.[27] However, it is quite possible that other prominent figures were also absorbed. Despite the fact that many sources – including the day of thanksgiving – identify Providence as the force behind England's deliverance, the popular cultural construction of Drake as the agent of the defeat suggests that he may have become a mediating figure enabling God's will to be carried out. Of course, the ballad is simply one example of Drake's portrayal as the Armada victor and cannot be taken as proof of a widespread practice of 'substitution'. However, calling upon Drake to intercede on the nation's behalf during England's darkest hours was a practice that continued throughout the following centuries, and it is worth speculating on its early emergence.

The art historian Roy Strong has argued that 'to the Elizabethan mind the recording of human likeness was connected to the concept of fame and social rank'.[28] Thus,

> [G]orgeous gem-encrusted costumes, richly inlaid armour, and multi-coloured plumes, wands of office and batons of command, the robes and orders of chivalry and the presence of coats of arms proclaim to every onlooker that these people are superior beings.[29]

And, of course, the images of Francis Drake are no exception. Indeed, the signs of his status would be even more obvious to a contemporary viewer aware of Drake's humble origins – for a man of Drake's status to receive a knighthood was almost unprecedented. An exquisite head and shoulders miniature by Nicholas Hilliard painted in 1581 is the earliest authenticated image of Drake. Dressed in an intricate ruff and fine doublet, a massive gold chain around his neck, *Sir* Francis is every inch a courtier. One version was painted on the back of an ace of hearts playing card owned by the Earl of Derby: what could be more fitting than to play the hero of the Protestant cause as your trump card?

Art (and naval) historians have spent a great deal of time and energy in attempting to unravel the complex relationships between images of Drake.[30] The existence of a large number of related images suggests a great demand for portraits of Drake in the late sixteenth century – and not only in England. Edmund Howes tells us that 'many princes in Italy, Germany, and others, as well enemies as friends in his lifetime desired his picture'.[31] As Garrett Mattingly has suggested, this trade in portraits is an indication of the way in which Anglo-Spanish hostilities were coming to be perceived, 'as if it [the naval war] were a personal duel between King Philip and Francis Drake'.[32] A portrait of Drake was a potent symbol of defiance in Protestant countries. More surprising perhaps was the distribution of portraits among Catholic rulers. Both Archduke Ferdinand of Tyrol and Henry III of France are said to have possessed images of Francis Drake.

Another image displays a whole wealth of devices that signify Drake's social status and the means by which he attained that rank: the half-length engraving usually – if questionably – attributed to the Dutch engraver Jodocus Hondius,[33] produced around 1583 (PLATE 1). Inscribed 'Franciscus Draeck Nobilissimus Eques Angliae an Sue 43' ('Francis Drake Most Noble English Knight Aged 43'), a rather plump-looking Drake stands with eyes turned toward the spectator, right hand resting on a plumed helmet and left hand holding a baton. The coat of arms to the right of Drake is improperly quartered with a wyvern – which also serves as the crest – appropriated from the unrelated Drakes of Ashe in East Devon. In a display of typical Drakean audacity, the purloined wyvern is positioned in the first and fourth quarters, those usually reserved for the chief arms. This quartering serves to connect Drake with the Devon gentry and so hide or distance his humble origins. The baton signifies command or generalship while the ornate helmet in the foreground confirms that the subject of the engraving is a knight. The richness of Drake's dress is a sign of his recently acquired and considerable wealth while the sword represents service for his country. Just what service is symbolized by a globe suspended in front of an arched window – the semiotic emphasis is placed very firmly on Drake's identity as a circumnavigator. The Latin inscription on a scroll draped over a ledge in the foreground confirms this reading.

> The most noble English knight Sir Francis Drake in the 43rd year of his life. Gentle reader the gallant and Invincible Knight Drake done from life. With favourable winds he circumnavigated the whole globe in the space of two years and ten months having left his English port on the ides of December 1577 returning to the same on the 4th of the calends of October in the same year 1580.

Importantly, the engraving contains another element passed over by all other Drake images. The distant view from the window is of a town, and it has been suggested that this is Plymouth.[34] The buildings are certainly huddled on the banks of a river: perhaps they represent the cluster of buildings around Sutton Pool that was Plymouth in the sixteenth century. Like the Ashe quartering, this serves to connect Drake with the West Country. If the buildings are taken to represent Plymouth, then the engraving is a complete picture of Drake's achievements at that time. Plymouth was, of course, the point of departure and return for the circumnavigation – the presence of the suspended globe partially obscuring the town certainly links the two. Furthermore, we should not forget that Drake became mayor of the town in the year after his return from the famous voyage.

Even after Drake's exploits in the West Indies in 1585/6, the daring raid on Cadiz in 1587 and the defeat of the Spanish Armada in 1588, the voyage around the world was still being presented as Drake's greatest achievement. This is illustrated by two portraits of Drake in later life: one after Marcus Gheeraerts the Younger is the so-called 'Greenwich Portrait' of 1594; the other is the half-length portrait certainly by Gheeraerts the Younger (after 1590) that now hangs in Buckland Abbey, Drake's country house just north of Plymouth. The former, three-quarter length portrait, shows Drake dressed almost entirely in black. He holds his right arm akimbo, which

PLATE 1. Attributed to Jodocus Hondius (retouched by Geore Vertue), *Sir Francis Drake*, c.1583. A complete representation of Drake's achievements at this time.

serves to draw the spectator's attention to the 'Drake Pendant', the jewelled locket containing a miniature of Elizabeth I by Hilliard that was presented to him by the queen sometime during the winter of 1586/7. This is very much a part of the chivalrous ethos of the late Elizabethan Court, which was calculated to show the power of an idealized queen over her subjects. With the other hand Drake holds his hat, the red glove just touching and so emphasizing the hilt of a sword. Once more the sword represents service to his country – the reference is all the more pointed because the image was produced during Drake's period of deep disgrace following the failure of the 'counter-Armada' in 1589. The painting acts, then, as a reminder of past service, and again it is the presence of a globe in the left foreground that provides explicit evidence of Drake's outstanding contribution: the circumnavigation.

While still displaying the symbolic globe, the Gheeraerts portrait is in marked contrast to the other images. It does more than display the wealth and achievement of its subject. It provides a clear illustration of what Strong describes as the 'new mood pervading late Elizabethan and Jacobean society which saw itself besieged by "sable coloured melancholy"'. This introduced a 'new world of pensive gloom and psychological introspection'.[35] Of course, it would be going too far to attempt to connect what was a widespread fashion in portraiture with specific events in an individual's life. However, in Drake's case the sense of melancholy and introspection that the painting conveys seems wholly appropriate when viewed in relation to the Portugal project of 1589. The attempt to elevate Dom Antonio to the throne of Portugal was marred by disease, ill planning and lack of provisions, and represented Drake's first taste of failure. John Cummins suggests 'perhaps Drake, older now and in poorer health was sickened by the loss of so many men in an enterprise for whose lack of success he was widely blamed'.[36]

More curious are a series of related engravings the earliest of which is by French printmaker Thomas de Leu (PLATE 2). This oval head and shoulders engraving is supposedly a copy of a now lost portrait by the Flemish artist Jean Rabel. The Latin inscription around the border reads 'Francis Drake Noble English Knight Aged 43 Years', which suggests that the engraving was completed shortly after the circumnavigation, probably in 1583. Like the Hilliard miniature, de Leu's Sir Francis certainly seems to be basking in the glory that the famous voyage brought him. Of great significance is the decorated shield that Drake wears on his left shoulder. The reference is to the shield of Aeneas, the hero of Virgil's *Aeneid*. This work constructs Aeneas as the founder of Rome and its empire – he is a Trojan prince who, with his followers, escapes the Greek destruction of Troy and devotes himself to his divine mission: the unification of the Trojan and Latin peoples. Aeneas was possessor of a shield that depicted presciently the events of Roman history culminating in the victory of Augustus over the forces of Anthony and Cleopatra at the Battle of Actium. This naval battle had taken place in Virgil's own lifetime and formed the central ornament of the shield. The shield Drake carries also depicts a naval engagement. It seems entirely plausible that the circumnavigation facilitated this prescient construction of Drake as the divinely inspired founder of an English maritime empire. The naval engagement is, perhaps, a representation of some future

PLATE 2. Thomas de Leu (after Jean Rabel), *Sir Francis Drake*, 1583. A prescient depiction of Drake as founder of a maritime empire.

sea-fight that will secure England's greatness. In the 1570s an ideology of maritime empire began to emerge propelled by the works of John Dee and Richard Hakluyt. Dee it was who first used the term 'Brytish Impire' in this context. Kenneth Andrews and John Appleby both make the point that the monarch and the people were largely unreceptive to imperial rhetoric and ideology.[37] Yet if we take care to read the signifiers contained in this image – of which the original artist would have been fully aware – then we can conclude that the idea of empire *was* gaining ground at a relatively early date.

The next image is pasted alongside an engraving of Thomas Cavendish, the second English circumnavigator, on the reverse of Jodocus Hondius's map of their voyages. The engraving is signed by Hondius, and the image is undoubtedly copied from the work by de Leu. In the foreground is a double hemispheric world map depicting the track of Drake's circumnavigation. The fleet that was shown on Drake's shield in the earlier image is reduced to a single ship, perhaps the *Golden Hinde*, which fires a broadside. The image is concerned, then, with commemorating a past event rather than predicting great things for the future. The original signifying function of the shield is lost. Drake rests his hand on the left hemisphere of the map and points at his name in the border. Beneath the map is a small shield containing the pole stars and fesse wavy from the Drake arms.

The final engraving is by Crispin van de Passe and is taken from an anonymous volume called *Effigies Regum ac Principum*[38] printed in Cologne in 1598. Van de Passe was clearly familiar with the Spanish idea of Drake as *draco*, the dragon. The image is accompanied by a Latin verse that reads:

> *Had Ovid known my life as well*
> *True tales there would have been to tell:*
> *How Neptune's son had spread his wing*
> *And round the oceans drawn a ring;*
> *Then into Drake, this Dragon-Knight,*
> *Transformed was he (amazing sight!)*
> *Thus was I always armed for wars*
> *With tail and talons wings and jaws.*[39] (1–8)

Ovid was, of course, the author of *Metamorphoses*, a collection of tales with a common theme of bodily transmutation. The Drake/Dragon transformation would have provided Ovid with a fruitful source of material.[40] The posthumous image is a very close copy of the Hondius map engraving except that the map shows Cavendish's route around the globe. This is placed above a Latin inscription reading 'Fortune Favours the Bold'. The border reads 'Francis Drake Noble English Knight, Great Navigator and Expert Warrior. 1598'. This time Drake points at the word 'warrior', and signifiers of Drake's role as expert warrior and great navigator are displayed in the corners of the engraving. In the top left is a compass and in the top right an astrolabe: the emphasis is firmly on Drake as navigator. Two oars continue the maritime theme while in the bottom left corner a shield and gauntlets and in the right a sword and dagger place the emphasis on Drake the expert warrior.

Although images of Drake were becoming known throughout Europe, English poets were slower to sing his praises. One of the first works in verse (other than popular ballads) to celebrate Drake was Henry Robarts's poem *A Most Friendly Farewell, Given by a welwiller to the right worshipful Sir Francis Drake Knight*.[41] Published in 1585, this poem was produced on the occasion of Drake's departure for the West Indian raids. In a rather rambling prose address Robarts laments the failure of scholars to provide Drake with the customary poetic farewell.

> Seeing none of the learned sort have undertaken to write according to custome, I being the unworthyest, yet the most willing was loathe good knight that you should depart our Englishe coastes without some rembery to be published in prayes both to your worshippe, and the rest of your gentlemen followers.[42]

Robarts is determined to correct this literary neglect. In Robarts's hands Drake becomes a paragon of patriotic virtue. Of his motivation the poet writes, 'for it is seene that the desire of honour and not of wealth doeth move him to these enterprises, but the desire to doe his countrey good'.[43] Foregrounding service for his country facilitates a comparison with Mucius Scaevola who thrust his hand into the fire to prove his loyalty in the defence of Rome. Further comparisons include Hannibal and Curtius for their military service, Ulysses for his policy and Alexander for his valour. But Robarts's complaint is not directed solely at the lack of material concerning the present voyage. The ballad makes it clear that the circumnavigation had been similarly neglected.

> *When true report had blased abroad ye iii yeres taken toile,*
> *Of that rare knight Syr Francis Drake though many a foraine soile,*
> *Who by his travaile on the Seas unto his endlesse fame,*
> *Did purchase for his countrey's wealth, and credit to his name.*
> *I did expect some Ovids pen to paint his worthy praise.* (1–5)

The present work will, according to its title page, make amends. The subtitle reads 'Wherein is briefly touched his perils in his last daungerous voiage'. Reference to the famous voyage is indeed brief; the poem contains no details and there is little indication that the expedition was a circumnavigation. We can speculate that the poem contains no precise information because Robarts may have been unfamiliar with the details of the voyage. It is important to realize that no full account of the circumnavigation was published until the first edition of Richard Hakluyt's *Principal Navigations, Voyages, Traffiques and Discoveries of the English Nation* in 1589 – nine years after Drake's return – and then as an unnumbered six-leaf insert, which may have been added to the volume at an even later date.[44] As I have already indicated, portraits constructing Drake as circumnavigator were already in wide circulation and these could be read by even the illiterate. So how are we to account for the delay in printed narratives? Any detailed description of the circumnavigation was certain to contain sensitive information about Drake's privateering activities – far more specific than any portrait. This information would further damage the already fraught relationship between England and Spain, and it would certainly suggest that Drake acted with Elizabeth's approval. It is probable that there was an official ban on the publication of circumnavigation narratives in the years following Drake's return. That the voyage appeared in the *Principal Navigations* as an insert certainly suggests that any prohibition on publication was lifted only after the collection was complete – perhaps after the Spanish Armada when news of Drake's activities on the voyage would have provided excellent propaganda. It is likely, therefore, that Robarts's ignorance of the details of the circumnavigation is the result of an official policy of secrecy.

Yet this does not account fully for Drake's poetic neglect. There is some evidence that right up until his death the poets had largely ignored Drake. In 1596 Charles Fitzgeffrey published a long poem entitled *Sir Francis Drake, his Honourable Lifes Commendation and his Tragicall Deathes Lamentations*.[45] The poem was prefaced with several Latin verses 'partlie to supplie the superfluitie of vacant paper, partlie to upbraid our *English*-men, whose negligence hath left him unremembered'.[46] At first this seems strange, particularly when we consider that the heroic was considered 'not only a kind, but the best and most accomplished kind of poetry'.[47] Undoubtedly many of Drake's exploits displayed the values of courage, honour, endurance and leadership that heroic poetry sought to celebrate. Or at least Drake made sure that they did when he regaled his listeners with embellished tales of her activities. But there were considerations that impeded the celebration of Drake. As John Cummins observes:

> During his lifetime England had a reality to set against the myth. … There
> were plenty of people in England who had small cause to worship Drake:
> the widows and orphans of the men who died in the voyages which
> enriched him; soldiers and sailors long unpaid, ranging the countryside
> and the streets of London; more orthodox and less rewarded officers such
> as Borough; aristocratic adventurers such as Doughty's brother and Francis
> Knollys; diplomats walking a tightrope during the cold war with Spain;
> not least the Queen herself, for long periods, and therefore anyone seeking
> the Queen's favour.[48]

There were certainly people who had no time for Drake. Of John Winter's assumption that Drake had died in the South Seas, Robarts writes: 'Which newes to some right ioyful was ye [sic] wished him no good' (28). Similarly, Camden records that Drake was upset by the Courtiers who refused the gold he offered them because, they said, it was gained by piracy. Deeds of the past could be idealized but Drake's exploits were too immediate to be celebrated in heroic terms, the full extent of their repercussions was yet to become apparent. The system of Court patronage meant that if the Admiral was out of favour with the queen, as was the case after the failure of the Portugal expedition, no-one attempting to gain Royal favour would want to eulogize Drake in verse. Netzloff argues that in the late sixteenth century Drake embodied an urban, mercantile model of adventure which was distinct from that of the aristocratic, knightly quest. His neglect by the literary elite did not result from his privateering exploits in themselves but from the fact that 'this form of commercial piracy was a domain unsuitable for gentlemanly adventure'.[49] As such it would not be celebrated in epic poetry. This may be so, but it does not take into account the trade in portraits of Drake including those imagining Drake as the epic hero Aeneas. Kelsey concludes that when Drake died his reputation in England was in eclipse.[50] That might have been the case as far as 'high' culture was concerned, but it is rather more problematic to assert that all levels of culture were united in their neglect of Drake. Owing to the ephemeral nature of popular cultural material (much of it communicated orally) we cannot state with any certainty that Drake had become a marginal character in the popular imagination or whether he was still regarded as the Armada hero and held in high esteem.

Robarts's lone celebration was joined in 1589 by George Peele's 'A Farewell intitled to the Famous and Fortunate Generals of our English Forces by Land and Sea, Sir John Norris and Sir Francis Drake, Knights'.[51] This optimistic work is a product of the anti-Catholic fervour brought to a pitch by the defeat of the Spanish Armada the previous year and subsumes the military objectives of the Portugal expedition – principally to destroy the surviving Armada vessels – beneath a religious motivation. Drake and Norris are the agents 'To propagate religious piety' (26); they will 'deface the pride of Antichrist,/ And pull his paper walls and popery down' (35–6). But by far the finest poem to be produced during this period was Fitzgeffrey's lamentation on Drake mentioned above. Published shortly after Drake's death, the poem comprises 279 stanzas of rhyme royal – the form generally reserved for matters of a tragic nature. The tragedy is not so much that Drake is dead but that he has not received sufficient poetic recognition. Fitzgeffrey puts this down to envy.

> *Some such there are (O shame! Too great a summe!)*
> *Who would impeach the worth of worthy DRAKE,*
> *With wrongful obloquies sinister doome,*
> *And eagerly their serpent-tongues they shake,*
> *And sith they cannot sting, a hissing make.* (358–62)

Fitzgeffrey laments the fact that Drake and his exploits are not sufficiently distant to be celebrated by heroic poetry.

> *Had he beene borne in* Agamemnons *age,*
> *When stout* Achilles *launce scourg'd* Troies *proud towers:*
> *When men gainst men, and Gods gainst Gods did rage,*
> Aneas, Achilles, *nor* Ulysses *powers,*
> *Had been so famous in this age of ours.* (204–8)

For Fitzgeffrey, then, Sir Francis Drake is a hero to rank with and even surpass those mythical figures of the ancient world. Clearly inspired by patriotism and fierce loyalty to his subject, Fitzgeffrey invokes a whole host of classical heroes and gods with whom Drake is favourably compared. 'DRAKE did *Ulysses* worth exceede so farre' (1051) and 'Which, when he list, could make great Neptune quake' (505). Sir Francis is a figure who deserves to take his place in the national epic: 'Let famous RED CROSSE yield to famous Drake,/ And good sir Guion give to him his launce' (197–8). The reference is, of course, to Edmund Spenser's *The Faerie Queene* which, with its allusions to Elizabeth and the Tudors, can be read as an epic of the English nation. Like Red Crosse (or, perhaps, St George), Drake is a figure of virtue. Indeed, Fitzgeffrey sees him as a martyr of the Protestant cause. Sir Francis is elevated to the status of a (non-Catholic) saint – and even a god. Fitzgeffrey calls on personified posterity, 'Be thou religious to renowned DRAKE,/ And place him in thy catalogue of saints;/ Instead of *Neptune*, God of sea him make' (456–8).

The poem concludes with Drake being transported to the heavens to become the constellation Draco. However, it is Fitzgeffrey's concentration on one of Drake's non-military (and less well-known) endeavours that is, perhaps, most intriguing. The part played by the seafarer in the construction of a leat bringing fresh water to Plymouth from Dartmoor prompts Fitzgeffrey to compare Drake with Hercules. This feat of civil engineering is an achievement comparable to Hercules' cleansing of the Augean stable, one of his twelve exploits.

> *Equall with* Hercules *in al, save vice,*
> *DRAKE of his country hath deserved grace,*
> *Who by his industrie and quaint devise*
> *Enforc'd a river to leave his former place,*
> *Teaching his streames to runne an uncouth race:*
>
> . . . .
>
> *Her now-bright face, once loathsomely defiled,*
> *He purg'd and clensed with a wholesome river:*
> *Her, whom her sister-cities late reviled,*
> *Up-braiding her with unsavory favor,*
> *DRAKE of that opproby doth now deliver.* (897–901, 911–15)

Here we find a new and significant element in the construction of Drake. Until this point Fitzgeffrey has sung of Drake's military and nautical prowess, he is very much a hero in the traditional sense, a man of action and of courage. Yet Drake is not compared with Hercules for any act of expiation that he undertakes or for any feat of arms but for his part in a commercial enterprise.[52] This conjunction of the commercial and the heroic prefigures the celebration of British commerce that, as we shall see later, became widespread in the eighteenth century.

Fitzgeffrey produced another poem on Drake early in the seventeenth century. His sonnet 'Upon the Discoverie of the Little World by Mister John Davies'[53] appears as a preliminary poem to John Davies's *Microcosmos* (1603). Fitzgeffrey uses Drake and the circumnavigation for a metaphysical speculation on the relationship between the microcosm and macrocosm. Drake's encompassing of the earth was still, it appears, the achievement to inspire poetic sensibilities. The conceit equates Davies with Drake who, through the *Microcosmos* or 'Paper-Bark', will enable the reader to discover great truths about themselves. Addressed to Drake and that other great explorer, Columbus, the sonnet reads

Go Drake *of England,* Dove *of Italie,*
Unfolde what ever Neptune's armes infolde,
Travell the Earth (as Phoebus does the skie)
Till you begette new Worlds upon this olde.
Would any wonders see, yet live at rest,
Not hazard life upon a dangerous shelfe?
Behold, thou bear'st a World within thy breast,
Take ship at home, and sayle about thy selfe.
This Paper-Bark may be the Golden-Hinde,
Davies *the* Drake *and true discoverer is,*
The end, that thou thy-selfe thy-selfe maist finde;
The prize and pleasure thine, the travel his:
See here display'd as plaine as knowledge can,
This little World, this Wondrous Ile of Man.

The first collection of Drake narratives appeared in Richard Hakluyt's *Principal Navigations* published in 1589. Drawing upon the Aristotelian concept of self-sufficiency, Hakluyt's Classically influenced works were concerned with the benefits that would accrue to the nation through the establishment of colonies in North America. This was a subject he had first approached in *A Particuler Discourse Concerninge the Greate Necessitie and Manifolde Commodyties That Are Like to Growe to This Realme of Englande by the Westerne Discoueries Lately Attempted* (1584). Overseas possessions, he reasoned, would ease overpopulation in England and counter the effects of contracting English markets abroad, as well as providing new materials and products for the English economy. In short,

> The overall aim of the new colonies would be to return the economy of England to its self-sufficiency by balancing its production, consumption and population. This could only be achieved by the export of people, and the institution of new markets, all of which would be conceived as parts of the commonwealth, albeit across an ocean, rather than new commonwealths in themselves.[54]

Clearly influenced by John Foxe's treatment of personal narratives the *Principal Navigations* represent an early attempt at adding chronology to geography. The first edition contained three accounts of Drake's voyages: Hawkins's third voyage (during which Drake captained the *Judith*), the raid on Nombre de Dios and the circumnavigation or 'Famous Voyage', which may have been added to the volume some years later. Drake's later endeavours are not included. They fell outside Hakluyt's parameters being 'neither of remote length and spaciousness, neither of search and discoverie of strange coasts'.[55] Drake's voyage to Nombre de Dios certainly provided information on where a new market could be found but its wealth could only be acquired through piracy. Unusually for the first edition of the *Principal Navigations*, Hakluyt uses a foreign account of the voyage, a short narrative by the captured Portuguese pilot Lopez Vaz. This may explain why it is hard to find anything heroic in the account: having captured the Nombre de Dios fort, Drake and his men flee 'in so great feare, that leaving their furniture behind them, and putting off their hose, they swam and waded to their Pinneses'.[56]

More revealing is the account of the famous voyage compiled by Hakluyt from (at least) two narratives; one by John Cooke, a sailor aboard the *Elizabeth*, and the other the so-called 'Anonymous Narrative' titled *A Discourse of Sir Francis Drakes iorney and exploytes after he had passed ye Straytes of Magellan into Maer de Sur, and throughe the rest of his voyadge afterward till hee arrived in England. 1580 anno.*[57] Here we get a clearer view of Drake, or rather how Hakluyt thought he should be regarded. Drake's honourable behaviour is emphasized as much as his skill in navigation. He never takes supplies from natives without repaying them in some way: on the island of Mogador, Drake 'bestowed amongst them [the natives] some linen cloth and shoes, and a javelin, which they joyfully received'.[58] Drake's treatment of the Coast Miwok Indians of Nova Albion – particularly his attempt at converting them to (Protestant) Christianity – would have been considered exceptionally fair at the time. Spanish or Portuguese captives are also treated humanely: off Santiago Drake took a 'good prize' but sent the crew away in a pinnace with supplies. The significance of this would not be lost on a contemporary audience only too aware of the treatment of captured English seamen by the Inquisition.

Even if Drake received a hostile reception from natives – as was the case at the island of La Mocha off Chile where two men were killed when sent ashore to fill barrels with water – the narrative assures us that this was a case of mistaken identity. 'The people taking them for Spaniards (to whom they use to show no favour if they take them) laid violent hands on them, and, as we think, slew them.'[59] Drake's treatment of natives is in marked contrast to that of the Spaniards who are presented as particularly cruel. This moral superiority serves to make the English rather than Iberian nations seem worthy of a New World empire. (Of course, this conveniently ignored Drake's earlier involvement with John Hawkins's slaving voyages.) Indeed, Drake seems to have achieved the success that George Chapman predicted for Sir Walter Raleigh in his poem 'De Guiana, Carmen Epicum'[60] published in 1596. The actions of the Coast Miwok are interpreted as a desire to worship the Europeans and to 'resign unto him [Drake] their right and title of the whole land, and become his subjects'.[61] The parallel with Guiana 'Kissing her hand, bowing her mightie breast,/ And every sign of submission making' (21–2) is noticeable. Drake, it seems, has achieved what the Spanish could not – '*Conquest* without blood' (15)

The notion of submission is significant in terms of legitimizing settlement in the Americas in the early seventeenth century. In contrast to the Spanish *conquest*, England's overseas possessions could be presented as the result of peaceful, almost invited settlement. In an insightful work on the religious origins of the British imperial imagination Christopher Hodgkins has traced the beginnings of what he terms the 'White Legend' of the British Empire to Drake's encounter with the Californian Indians. This sustaining myth is summarized neatly as 'pious English self-restraint merits possession'.[62] Drake may have accepted what interpreted as the Indians offer of their land but, in contrast to the Spanish conquistadors, he refused their worship. Indeed, while the Indians prostrated themselves on the ground Drake ordered the ship's chaplain to read from the Bible while the crew sang psalms and he pointed away from himself to the sky. It was this inherent Protestant humility that made the English worthy of empire. Hodgkins argues that Drake was fully aware of this and was

> not unconsciously working to construct what we might call a reformed imperialism, both in the sense that the English were to see it as morally better than earlier 'cruel and bloody' Iberian imperialisms, and in the sense that they saw it as spiritually better because it was specifically Protestant – in other words, Reformed.[63]

It is worth noting that the pattern set up by Drake's encounter with the Miwok would be repeated in some of the great works of English literature from Shakespeare to Defoe's *Robinson Crusoe*. Shakespeare may well have used the incident as source material for *The Tempest*. Caliban's lines gain resonance when one is familiar with the Drake narrative, 'These be fine things, an if they be not sprites./ That's a brave god, and bears celestial liquor:/ I will kneel to him' (2.2.116–18).

The second, greatly extended edition of the *Principal Navigations* was printed in three volumes between 1598 and 1600. In the dedicatory epistles Hakluyt defends England's failure to establish an overseas empire in the face of continued Iberian success. 'True it is, that our successe hath not been correspondent unto theirs: yet in this our attempt the uncertaintie of finding was farre greater, and the difficultie and danger of searching no whit lesse.'[64] It is this edition that provides accounts of Drake's later exploits, and it is the section on the defeat of the Spanish Armada that is most significant. In Hakluyt there is no hint of the strident nationalism that was to be associated with the Armada in later centuries. Nor is there any attempt to portray Drake as the sole victor over the Spanish. Indeed, in the Preface to the second edition Hakluyt wrote humbly, 'But why should I presume to call it our vanquishing; when the greatest part of them escaped us, and were onely by God's out-stretched arme overwhelmed in the Seas.'[65] However, Emanuel van Meteran's narrative does dwell on Drake's capture of Pedro de Valdez and the *Rosario*, the Spanish *capitana* or flagship. Doubtless it was this incident that fuelled still further the popular myth of the victory as Drake's alone. Sir Francis is constructed as a man of great honour, always fair to the vanquished. Valdez surrenders after learning that his assailant is Drake whose humane treatment of captives is assured. And, indeed, once the Spaniard is taken Drake 'gave him very honourable entertainment, feeding him at his own table and lodging him in his cabin'.[66]

Strikingly, what this exploration of cultural products reveals is that during his lifetime Drake's fame rested principally on the circumnavigation of the globe. This is reflected very clearly in contemporary portraiture. The voyage was often portrayed as divinely guided, a demonstration of the favour of a benevolent Protestant God. There is some evidence, however, that popular culture sought to portray him as the sole victor over the Armada. Although Drake was a popular hero and presented as a man of great honour, he was not without his detractors. The complaints of Robarts and Fitzgeffrey provide evidence that Sir Francis and his exploits were not engaging the attention of the finest poets. After Drake had been laid to rest in the Caribbean, however, there was no reality to temper the myth: in the seventeenth century Drake's reputation would flourish.

Notes

[1] See William Camden, *The Historie of the Most Renowned and Victorious Princess Elizabeth Late Queene of England* (London, 1630), 115. The translation from Latin is presumably Camden's.

[2] Edmund Howes, *Annales, or a General Chronicall of England* (London, 1631), 808.

[3] Drake was the first commander to complete the circumnavigation of the globe. Although some of Ferdinand Magellan's crew completed the voyage in 1522, Magellan himself was killed by natives in the Moluccas.

[4] Howes, 808.

[5] Howes, 808.

[6] David Armitage, *The Ideological Origins of the British Empire* (Cambridge, 2000), 100.

[7] The notion that the high seas (as opposed to coastal waters) were free for all nations to sail underlay much expansionist activity. For a detailed analysis see Armitage, 107.

[8] Kenneth R. Andrews, *Trade, Plunder and Settlement: Maritime Enterprise and the Genesis of the British Empire 1480–1630* (Cambridge, 1984), 1.

[9] Kenneth R. Andrews, *Drake's Voyages: A Reassessment of their Place in Elizabethan Maritime Expansion* (London, 1967), 82.

[10] Harry Kelsey argues that Drake's sole interest was plunder. See *Sir Francis Drake: The Queen's Pirate* (New Haven, 1998). An alternative theory is proposed by Samuel Bawlf who, in a detailed account of the circumnavigation, suggests that Drake's secret mission was to locate the North West Passage. See *The Secret Voyage of Sir Francis Drake* (London, 2004). Kenneth R. Andrews agrees that Drake's interest was in treasure but that colonization was also an important element of his design. See his *Trade, Plunder and Settlement*.

[11] Andrews, *Trade, Plunder and Settlement*, 36.

[12] John C. Appleby, 'War, Politics and Colonisation 1558–1625', in Nicholas Canny, ed., *The Origins of Empire: British Overseas Enterprise to the Close of the Seventeenth Century* (Oxford, 1998), 60.

[13] Kelsey, 208.

[14] Andrews, *Trade, Plunder and Settlement*, 36.

[15] John Sugden, *Sir Francis Drake* (London, 1996), 123.

[16] John Foxe's *Book or Martyrs*, correctly titled *Acts and Monuments Most Special and Remarkable, Happening in the Church*, was first published in English in 1563. A copy of the second edition (1570) was placed next to the Bible in all major English churches.

[17] Recent scholarship suggests that Foxe did not seek to promote the vision of England as the elect nation. For the debate concerning Foxe's universalism see Armitage, *Ideological Origins of the British Empire*, 78–9.

[18] Christopher Hill, *Reformation to Industrial Revolution: a Social and Economic History of Britain 1530–1780* (London, 1967), 28.

[19] See Kelsey, 170–1 and 393.

[20] Henry Holland, *Herwolgia Anglica* (London, 1620), 106. This contains a brief account of Drake's exploits in Latin, 106–10.

[21] Geoffrey Whitney, *A Choice of Emblemes*, 1586, ed. Henry Green (1866; Hildesheim, 1971), 203.

[22] Rosemary Freeman, *English Emblem Books* (London, 1948), 57.

[23] See particularly the 'Armada Portrait' of Elizabeth I, attributed to George Gower now at Woburn Abbey, and the full-length portrait of Charles Howard (c.1620) by Daniel Mytens held at the National Maritime Museum.

[24] David Cressy, *Bonfires and Bells: National Memory and the Protestant Calendar in Elizabethan and Stuart England* (London, 1989), 117.

[25] Anon., 'Eighty Eight, or Sir Francis Drake', in T. W. H. Crosland, compiler, *English Songs and Ballads* (London, 1907), 117–18.

[26] Sir Martin Frobisher complained of Drake's inactivity during the first Armada engagement:

> Sir Fra. [ncis] Drake reporteth that no man hath done anye good service but he, but he shall well understand that others hath done as good service as he, and better too. He came braginge up at the first, indeed, and gave them his prowe and hys broade side, and then kept his lowfe and was gladde that he was gone agyne, lyke a cowardly knave or traytor.

Quoted in John Cummins, *Francis Drake: The Lives of a Hero* (1995; London, 1997), 191.

[27] Helen Hackett, *Virgin Mother, Maiden Queen: Elizabeth I and the Cult of the Virgin Mary* (New York, 1995).

[28] Roy Strong, *The English Icon: Elizabethan and Jacobean Portraiture* (London, 1969), 29.

[29] Strong, 29.

[30] See Geoffrey Callender, 'The Greenwich Portrait of Sir Francis Drake', *Mariner's Mirror*, vol. 18 (1932), 359–62, and John Sugden, 'Sir Francis Drake: A Note on his Portraiture', *Mariner's Mirror*, vol. 70 (1984), 303–9.

[31] Howes, 808.

[32] Garrett Mattingly, *The Defeat of the Spanish Armada* (1959; London, 1988), 87.

[33] The quality of the engraving purportedly by Hondius is rather poor when compared to an image of Drake almost certainly by him that is attached to the reverse of Hondius's map of Drake and Cavendish's voyages. However, the plate was reworked by George Vertue in the eighteenth-century, and this may account for the quality.

[34] This suggestion is put forward by the National Trust, which displays a copy of the engraving at Buckland Abbey.

[35] Strong, 21.

[36] Cummins, *Sir Francis Drake*, 223.

[37] See Appleby, 62, and Andrews, *Trade, Plunder and Settlement*, 35.

[38] The engraving is reproduced as a frontispiece in Norman J. W. Thrower, ed., *Sir Francis Drake and the Famous Voyage, 1577–1580: Essays Commemorating the Quadricentennial of Drake's Circumnavigation of the Earth* (Berkeley, 1980).

[39] Translation by Neil Cheshire, in David B. Quinn, *Sir Francis Drake as Seen by his Contemporaries* (Providence, RI, 1996), 24.

[40] The notion of Drake as Draco the Dragon first appeared in a Spanish work, *La Dragontea* (1598) by Lope de Vega Carpio. The poem concentrates on Drake's final voyage and displays a fierce hatred of an enemy together with a grudging admiration for a valiant foe. For a discussion of the Spanish reaction to Drake, see Cummins, 258–83, and Nina Gerassi-Navarro, *Pirate Novels: Fictions of Nation Building in Spanish America* (Durham, NC, 1999).

[41] Henry Robarts, *A Most Friendly Farewell, Given by a Welwiller to the Right Worshipful Francis Drake Knight* (1585; Cambridge, 1924).

[42] Robarts, [3].

[43] Robarts, [6].

[44] The gathering is unnumbered and inserted between pages 643 and 644. See the British Library copy of Richard Hakluyt, *The Principal Navigations, Voyages, Traffiques and Discoveries of the English Nation* (London, 1589). There is some debate as to when the insert was actually written. Harry Kelsey argues that it was probably not produced until 1595. For a full discussion, see Kelsey, 85–6.

[45] Charles Fitzgeffrey, *Sir Francis Drake, his Honourable Lifes Commendations and his Tragicall Deathes Lamentations*, in Alexander Grosart, ed., *The Poems of the Reverend Charles Fitzgeffrey (1593–1636)* (Manchester, 1881), 1–107.

[46] Fitzgeffrey, *Sir Francis Drake*, 15.

[47] Philip Sidney, *The Defence of Poesie* (1595; Cambridge, 1901), 33.

[48] Cummins, 273.

[49] Mark Netzloff, 'Sir Francis Drake's Ghost: Piracy, Cultural Memory, and Spectral Nationhood', in Claire Jowitt, ed., *Pirates? The Politics of Plunder, 1550–1650* (Basingstoke, 2007), 141.

[50] Kelsey, 394.

[51] George Peele, 'A Farewell Intitled to the Famous and Fortunate Generals of Our English Forces by Land and Sea, Sir John Norris and Sir Francis Drake, Knights', in A. H. Bullen, ed., *The Works of George Peele*, 2 vols (London, 1888), vol. 2, 237–40.

[52] The building of Drake's Leat has often been seen as an act of philanthropy on the part of Sir Francis. This is not in fact the case. The plan to construct a leat was forwarded not by Drake but by the Plymouth Corporation. Drake's role in the enterprise was principally the allotment of compensation to landowners whose grazing the leat traversed. His enthusiasm for the project is, perhaps, explained by the fact that once completed, he was able to erect six corn mills on the new waterway. For the best accounts of Drake and the Leat, see Richard Nicholls Worth, 'Sir Francis Drake: His Origins, Arms and Dealings with the Plymouth Corporation', *Transactions of the Devonshire Association*, vol. 16 (1884), 505–52.

[53] Charles Fitzgeffrey, 'Upon the Discoveries of the Little World by Mister John Davies', in Grosart, ed., *Poems of the Reverend Charles Fitzgeffrey*, xxxviii–xxxix.

[54] Armitage, 75.

[55] Hakluyt, *Principal Navigations*, 1589 and 1598–1600, 12 vols (Glasgow, 1903–5), vol. 1, xxv.

[56] Hakluyt, *Principal Navigations*, vol. 10, 76.

[57] The 'Anonymous Narrative' and the Cooke narrative are included as appendices in William Vaux, ed., *The World Encompassed by Sir Francis Drake being his Next Voyage to that to Nombre de Dios* (London, 1854). For a full exploration of Hakluyt's sources, see Henry H. Wagner, *Sir Francis Drake's Voyage Around the World: Its Aims and Achievements* (California, 1926), 238–85 or Harry Kelsey, 85–9.

[58] Hakluyt, *Principal Navigations*, vol. 11, 102.

[59] Hakluyt, *Principal Navigations*, vol. 11, 113.

[60] George Chapman, 'De Guiana, Carmen Epicum', in Phyllis Brooks Bartlett, ed., *The Poems of George Chapman* (New York, 1962), 353–7.

[61] Hakluyt, *Principal Navigations*, vol. 11, 121.

[62] Christopher Hodgkins, *Reforming Empire: Protestant Colonialism and Conscience in British Literature* (Columbia, 2002), 78.

[63] Hodgkins, 85.

[64] Hakluyt, *Principal Navigations*, vol. 1, xl–xli.

[65] Hakluyt, *Principal Navigations*, vol. 1, lviii.

[66] Hakluyt, *Principal Navigations*, vol. 4, 214.

CHAPTER TWO

'Sir Francis Drake Revived'

'Recommended as an Excellent Example
to all Heroick and Active Spirits.'
(Robert Burton, *The English Hero*, 1687)[1]

The celebration of Drake in print during the seventeenth century was far more fulsome than anything that had appeared while Sir Francis was still alive. Material was also far more plentiful. But there were also periods when the production of Drake- related material dried up; these lacunae are as revealing as the cultural products themselves and suggest that far from acting as a simple signifier of English military prowess, the revival of Sir Francis was a complex and politically loaded activity.

The popular cultural construction of Drake as the hero of the Armada conflict, first seen in popular ballads, re-emerges in Thomas Heywood's play *If You Know Not Me, You Know Nobody. The Second Part*.[2] This work was first performed in 1606 and appeared in numerous versions, the final in 1632. The bulk of the play is a comedy concerned with Thomas Gresham's building of the Royal Exchange, but a final patriotic section is devoted to the defeat of the Spanish Armada. This section may seem entirely unrelated until we realize that during the spring and summer of 1588 192 merchant ships were mobilized in defence of the nation.[3] London merchants were also an important source of loans to the government. In Heywood's play a merchant named Hobson tells the queen, 'When thou seest money with thy grace is scant,/ For twice fiue hundred pound thou shalt not want.'[4] Noticeably, Drake's part in the defeat of the Armada is enhanced in the later edition. In the 1606 version the queen anxiously awaits the news of the sea-fight off Calais. She receives a reassuring message:

> … *the vndaunted worth*
> *And well known valour of your Admirall,*
> *Sir* Francis Drake, *and Sir* Martin Furbisher,
> *Gives vs assured hope of victory.*[5]

But almost immediately this confidence is shattered; a second messenger relates the details of Martin Frobisher's desperate clash with the Spanish off the Isle of Wight. Moved by the description of his furious defence, the queen prepares to lead her troops into battle but as they march about the stage Sir Francis Drake enters with Spanish flags '… to shew that Spaniards liues are in the hands/ Of England's soueraign'.[6] He relates the ebb and flow of the battle and even credits Howard with the capture of

Pedro de Valdez. God is praised and the play ends. By the 1632 version, however, things have changed; victory is less assured. Elizabeth receives a different message:

> *… but the vndaunted worth*
> *And well knowne valour of your admiral,*
> *Sir* Francis Drake, *and* Martin Furbisher,
> John Hawkins, *and your other English captains,*
> *Takes not away all hope of victory.*[7]

The account of the fight is extended but Heywood still finds time to celebrate Drake's other achievements; the messenger predicts continuing fame for Drake. 'This *Drake*, I say, (whose memory shall liue/ While this great world, he compast first, shall last).'[8] Heywood's Drake leads the first assault on the Armada off Gravelines (which is almost certainly true). But then dramatic licence takes over; in an act of selfless bravery Drake takes the full force of the enemy broadsides so that the ships following can return fire before the Spanish have time to reload. 'They shot, and shot, and emptied their broadsides/ At his poor single vessel.'[9] This is probably taken from van Meteran's narrative in Hakluyt, which claimed 'Sir Francis Drake's ship was pierced with shot above forty times.'[10] The section on Frobisher's action is slightly shortened, and it is Drake *and* Frobisher who enter carrying Spanish ensigns. But it is Drake who relays the details of the battle to an appreciative queen. *If You Know Not Me, You Know Nobody* provides compelling evidence that while others may have taken part in the action, Drake was still the popular hero.

How are we to account for Drake's enhanced role in the later editions of Heywood's play? To find an answer we must look at the dominant political and religious developments of the early seventeenth century. Firstly, James I's peace settlement with Spain in 1604 inevitably meant a reduction in naval forces. This has sometimes been portrayed as wilful neglect. Paul Kennedy notes,

> The fleet was laid-up and allowed to languish; corruption was rampant throughout naval administration; the merchant fleets were at the mercy of Dunkirk pirates and Barbary corsairs; and privateering was forbidden by the new monarch.[11]

Whether it is fair to blame the new king for the navy's decline is debatable – after all, parliament was unlikely to grant him the funds for a large fleet when the war with Spain was over. There can be no doubt, however, that this reduction in naval forces had an impact on national esteem, particularly when it came to England's attempts at intervening in European affairs as the ill-fated military actions of the 1620s were to prove. We must also be aware that James's foreign policy was far from universally popular. Although the peace was welcomed generally, there was a vocal minority, Sir Walter Raleigh among them, who were keen to prolong the conflict in an attempt to inflict maximum damage upon a weakened Spain. True, there had been a boom in trade, especially with the resumption of traffic to Spain and Portugal following the end of the war, and this was accompanied by a renewed interest in exploration. But economic downturn after 1614 dampened this enthusiasm and anti-Spanish feeling intensified during the 1620s. As David Armitage has observed, this 'was the period of James's policy of religious irenicism in Europe and comprehension in England was under greatest strain'.[12] The prospect of the Spanish Match[13] and the King's pro-Spanish stance – even after the outbreak of the Thirty Years' War in 1618 – outraged many powerful figures who sought to return England to its position as the champion of beleaguered Protestantism. Opponents of the Spanish Match were keen to invoke Protestant heroes and the supposed chivalry of the Elizabethan era as part of their anti-Spanish polemics. 'From their perspective, to be chivalric was to be generally anti-Habsburg, anti-Spanish, and of course anti-Catholic.'[14] Sir Francis Drake fitted these criteria perfectly. Heywood's treatment of Drake is almost certainly a product of this contemporary championing of an idealized past.

Mark Netzloff argues that early seventeenth-century nostalgia for the age of Elizabeth together with the 'revival' of Drake 'served as a mode of critique, as a way to intimate an underlying dissatisfaction with the Jacobean state'.[15] We can certainly locate implicit dissatisfaction with one aspect of the state, government policy, in the work of Michael Drayton. In the Preface to the first part of his long chorographical poem *Poly-Olbion* (1612), Drayton complained of the shift away from the unbounded enthusiasm and scope of Elizabethan poetry.

> In publishing this Essay of my Poemme, there is this great disadvantage against me; that it commeth out at this time, when Verses are wholly deduc't to Chambers, and nothing esteem'd in this lunatique Age, but what is kept in Cabinets, and must only passes by Transcription.[16]

Book XIX from the second part of *Poly-Olbion* (1622) celebrates English voyagers including Frobisher, Fenton, Gilbert, Raleigh and, of course, Drake. Sir Francis is praised for the circumnavigation and for annoying Spain generally. Drayton's intention become even clearer when we realize that the first 18 books of *Poly-Olbion* were dedicated to Prince Henry who, until his untimely death, was believed to be the next champion of the Protestant cause. Drayton's complaint about poetry, along with his celebration of Drake, reflects a discontent with the perceived degeneracy of the present – a degeneracy that was manifest in such diverse areas as literature and foreign policy. This short section of *Poly-Olbion* reveals a repining for the Elizabethan 'Golden Age' of literature, endeavour and, of course, Protestant heroes. Here we are faced with a different emphasis in the construction of Drake. Unlike Hakluyt, who uses Drake primarily to encourage further exploration and settlement, Drayton's poem revives the Elizabethan admiral as an exemplum, a corrective figure from a previous and supposedly superior age. Drake is well on the way to becoming a mythical figure: 'This more than man (or what) this demie-god at sea' (313).

All this would seem to overturn a recent suggestion that Drake's reputation was faltering during the early years of the seventeenth century and that it was only through the efforts of his nephew in the 1620s that he was 'revived'.[17] The mid-1620s saw a great outpouring of material on Drake. Long accounts of voyages were published individually for the first time. The published works included Samuel Purchas's *Hakluyt Posthumus or Purchas His Pilgrimes* (1625), William Camden's

Annales in English for the first time (1625), *Sir Francis Drake Revived* (1626 and 1628), *The World Encompassed* (1628 and 1635) and Edmund Howes's continuation of Stowe's *Annales* (1631). Patriotic fervour lay behind many of these works. The title page of *Sir Francis Drake Revived* continues: *Calling upon this Dull or Effeminate Age to follow his Noble Steps for Gold and Silver*. Following the failure of the Spanish Match in 1625 Charles I adopted an aggressive policy towards Spain. A fleet was sent to attack Cadiz but the raid proved a spectacular failure. This fiasco provided an obvious and embarrassing contrast to the highly successful Cadiz raids of Essex (1596) and Drake, and perhaps fuelled the notion of an effeminate and foppish present. Nevertheless, in the midst of the anti-Spanish clamour, to celebrate Drake was no longer to criticize the King and Privy Council but to support them. Of course, it could also be seen as an implicit criticism of Parliament that had clashed with the king over foreign policy – particularly the raid on Cadiz – and the funding of overseas campaigns.

Anti-Catholic and anti-Spanish sentiment soon found its way on to the London stage. Jacobean theatre was, of course, a commercial enterprise and a successful company of players needed to perform drama that would attract a large audience. With the Spanish Match capturing the attention of the capital, plays with a Spanish subject were clearly a major draw. A variety of 'Spanish' plays appeared in the early 1620s,[18] among them *Rule a Wife and Have a Wife* by John Fletcher,[19] first performed in 1624. This is a comedy that draws upon *El casamiento engañoso* by Cervantes and is concerned with the deceit that lies behind two marriages both of which are entered into out of greed and self-interest. Coming so shortly after the failure of the Spanish Match, the play is a clear attack upon the Spaniards who are portrayed as untrustworthy and morally lax. Indeed, the prologue warns any ladies watching not to be angry should they see a young woman 'Seek to abuse her husband, still 'tis Spain,/ No such gross errors in your Kingdom raign' (11–12). The implication is that the country had had a narrow escape. The play is of note because of the presence of a character named Cacafogo, a wealthy usurer who is tricked out of a large sum of money by one of the couples. While some characters are derived from those of Cervantes, Cacafogo is undoubtedly an invention of Fletcher's. His name is taken from that given by the English seamen to the richly laden-treasure ship captured by Drake during the circumnavigation. This is confirmed when Cacafogo announces, 'I am a man of war too' (1.1.48); the dramatic irony would not be lost on an audience familiar with the story of the capture of the *Cacafuego*. The ease with which both character and ship are relieved of their treasure is, of course, not coincidental. This suggests that knowledge of the Drake narrative, or at least certain parts of it, was still in wide circulation and that Drake remained the figure to invoke at times of anti-Spanish hostility.

Rather more direct in their anti-Spanish attitudes were the Drake narratives that appeared in the mid-1620s. Coming after hostilities with Spain had commenced, *Sir Francis Drake Revived*[20] is an attempt to stir up bold, patriotic feelings, as the address 'To the Courteous Reader' makes clear: 'My ends are to stirre thee up to the worship of God and service of our King and Country by his [Drake's] example.'[21] Published for Drake's nephew (another Sir Francis Drake), MP for Plympton and a strong supporter of Charles I, the work was entirely in keeping with contemporary anti-

Spanish feeling. Clearly, the 'revival' of Drake was far more than a whim on the part of his nephew, although making the most of a famous ancestor may well have been part of his design. The account of the 1572 raid on Nombre de Dios becomes a classic example of a David and Goliath contest as Drake seeks recompense from Philip II for his treatment at San Juan d'Ulua. Reference to Aesop on the first page of the narrative situates Drake's adventure within an explicitly moral framework.

> For as Aesope teacheth, even the Fly hath her spleene and the Emmet is
> not without her choler, and both together many times find meanes
> whereby though the Eagle lay her egges in Jupiters lap, yet, by one way or
> the other, she escapeth not of her wrong done the Emmet.[22]

Importantly, in this work Drake displays all the longed-for virtues of the age. He is constructed as a charismatic, determined, resilient and, above all, chivalrous leader of men. The concept of chivalry as seen at the tilt or tournament is reflected very clearly when Drake's fleet sails for home: 'Thus we departed from them, passing hard by Carthagena, in the sight of all the Fleete, with a Flag of Saint George in the maine top of our Fregat, with silke streamers and ancients downe to the water.'[23] In keeping with the chivalric code, Drake never ill-treats his captives – on the way from Carthagena to Saint Domingo he takes two vessels but sets free the 'common mariners' in a ship's rowing boat. As we saw in Hakluyt's account of the circumnavigation, this honourable behaviour is contrasted to that of the cowardly Spaniards who, at Carthagena, display a flag of truce and then pretend to flee when Drake is rowed towards the shore. This is a trick to lure the outnumbered English onto the beach, but Drake is aware of the Spaniards' intentions and is content to let them know that 'though hee had not sufficient forces to conquer them, yet hee had sufficient judgement to take heed of them'.[24]

Although chivalrous, Drake is no gentleman adventurer, he works closely with men of all ranks and manages to retain their loyalty – no small achievement after the raid on Nombre failed to yield any treasure. The attack on the treasure house is halted by a tropical storm that rendered bow strings ineffective; perceiving the growing anxiety of his men he rallies them. '[O]ur captaine ... told them that he had brought them to the mouth of the treasure house of the world, if they would want it, they might henceforth blame no bodie but themselves.'[25] Even in adversity Drake never contemplates defeat. It is his self-confidence and ingenuity when his troops begin to despair that secure the voyage's success. Believing that the Spaniards have captured their pinnaces, Drake constructs a raft in an effort to reach the English ships before the Spaniards find them. With his usual bravado he tells his men that 'he would, God willing, by one means or other get them all aboard, in despite of all the *Spaniards* in the Indies'.[26] Clearly, we are meant to admire Drake's determination to 'make' the voyage even after the failure of the treasure house raid. This determination is most evident when he ascends a tree and, for the first time, sees the Pacific Ocean. Our narrator tells us that 'hee besought Almightie God of his Goodnesse to give him life and leave to sayle once in an English ship in that sea'.[27] The circumnavigation provided that opportunity.

PLATE 3. Robert Vaughan, 'Sir Francis Drake', engraved frontispiece from *The World Encompassed*, 1628. The hand of God ensures the success of the voyage.

The World Encompassed,[28] a long account of the voyage around the world put together from the notes of Francis Fletcher the fleet's preacher and 'diverse others', continues the by-now familiar chivalrous construction of Drake. The voyage is not designed to increase Drake's already considerable wealth – it is for the benefit of his country. His delight in lavish ostentation is made to serve a national purpose. Drake carried with him 'expert musicians, rich furniture … and diverse shewes of curious workmanship, whereby the civility of his native countrie might, amongst all nations withsoever he should come, be the more admired'.[29] The notion of the voyage as divinely guided is made very apparent. The frontispiece (PLATE 3) is an adaptation by Robert Vaughan of an engraving by Robert Boissard. Drake rests his right hand on a globe; on a table to the right are an array of navigational aids including compass, cross-staff and astrolabe. Vaughan omits a flying genius that extends a laurel wreath towards Drake while also supporting his coat of arm but displays the coat of arms very prominently. The narrative itself tells us that the *Golden Hinde* escaped the storms in the Magellan Strait 'as it were by his holy Angels still guiding and conducting us'.[30] Indeed, God seems to have a special affection for Drake: the escape is made possible 'by the great and effectual care and travell of our Generall, the Lord's instrument therein'.[31] And Drake's faith in God remains unshakable; the storm that forces the ship southwards after leaving the Strait of Magellan is interpreted by Drake as part of God's master plan – a way of demonstrating to the English the previously unknown fact that there is ocean south of the Tierra del Fuego.

There is also a sense in which the narrative portrays Drake himself as somehow quasi-divine.

> Ever since Almighty God commanded Adam to subdue the earth, there have not wanted in all ages some heroical spirits which, in obedience to that high mandate ... have expended their wealth, imployed their times, and adventured their persons, to finde out the true circuit thereof.[32]

Mirroring Adam, Drake sails around a little known world naming capes, bays and even countries, which then burst into life – in the imagination of the seventeenth-century reader at least. This is particularly relevant when we consider the date of *The World Encompassed*. By 1628 the pace of Western colonization was beginning to gather speed after a faltering start. Virginia had supported a permanent colony since 1607, the Pilgrim Fathers had settled in Massachusetts in 1620 and plans were well under way for further settlements along the eastern seaboard. This expansionist endeavour in the late 1620s and 1630s was accelerated by religious dissidents seeking a new life free from oppression and, perhaps more importantly, by merchants intent on developing plantation production in both North America and the West Indies. We do not know the view of Drake's nephew concerning the colonization of the Americas (or indeed his economic involvement in any schemes), but it is quite possible that the 'herociall spirits' *The World Encompassed* aimed at stirring were those of potential settlers. Kenneth R Andrews has drawn attention to the lack of English colonial achievement in the first decades of the seventeenth century. He attributes the lack of success, in part, to the inability of the settlers to survive in a hostile environment.

> [T]hey found it hard to adapt because they began with false ideas about America itself and about the kind of life they could lead there. Such false ideas were in part the results of deliberately deceptive propaganda ... and in part the natural assumptions of men who had almost no means of imagining a world different from their own.[33]

While *The World Encompassed* could hardly be described as expansionist propaganda, anyone reading the account of Drake's time spent with the Miwok Indians would get a very false view of the life that awaited them. By the 1620s there would be very little worship to refuse.

Noticeably, there was a lull in the production of material on Drake between the mid-1630s and the 1650s. This was almost certainly the result of the Ship Money crises of 1634 to 1641 and ultimately the English Civil War. A struggle developed in the 1630s between Parliament and the Crown over economic control. During his period of Personal Rule Charles I revived a tax known as Ship Money traditionally levied on coastal areas to provide defence at times of national crisis. But Charles modified Ship Money and extended it to inland areas in 1635, arguing that as all subjects of the Crown benefited from the security of the nation's defences and as the sea was the greatest of those defences, all were liable to pay.[34] Fiercely opposed to Ship Money, Parliament argued that it was illegal for the king to levy a tax without calling a parliament. But it was not only the legality of the tax that caused discontent. Charles's pro-Catholic stance had led to the use of Royal Navy ships on the Spanish side in the Thirty Years' War. This was unacceptable to the Protestant-dominated parliament. Of course, Drake would have appreciated the need for a strong navy and, as we have seen, his loyalty to his monarch was unswerving. On the other hand, his actions were supposedly guided or justified by his burning Protestant faith. I suggest that it is the distancing of monarch from the English Church that prevented Drake from being appropriated as an inspirational figure by either Parliament or Crown.

Thomas Fuller's *The Holy and Profane State* provides the only substantial reflection on Drake from this period. The book is a product of Fuller's position in relation to the huge gulf that had opened up between Parliament and the Crown. *The Holy State* is a character, a popular literary form of the seventeenth century that set out the attributes of various 'types' (occupations or the possessors of dominant character traits). Fuller seems to have had Drake specifically in mind when he came to write the typical good sea captain. His religion is praised:

> In taking a prize he most prizeth the men's lives whom he takes; though some of them may chance to be Negroes or savages. It is the custom of some to cast them overboard, and there is an end of them: for the dumb fishes tell no tales. ... But our captain counts the image of God and nevertheless his image cut in ebony as if done in ivory, and in the blackest Moors he sees the representation of the King of heaven.[35]

Each character is followed by a short biography displaying Fuller's inventive wit. He is careful to make it clear that it was a minister who persuaded Drake that he could lawfully recover his losses sustained at San Juan d'Ulua. 'The case was clear in sea-divinity, and few are such infidels as not to believe doctrines which make for their own profit.'[36] It is Fuller who, in John Cummins's words, 'comes closest to medieval moralizing in his reflections on over-ambition and on the contrast between Drake's dashing early exploits and the long-planned but ill-fated Panama voyage'.[37] This is, perhaps, the inevitable result when Protestant self-restraint breaks down. Fuller sets aside Drake's successful endeavours and dwells on the 1595/6 expedition.

> Thus an extempore performance, was scare heard to be begun before we
> hear it is ended, comes off with better applause, or miscarries with less
> disgrace, than a long studied and openly premeditated action. Besides, we
> see how great spirits, having mounted to the highest pitch of
> performance, afterwards strain and break to go beyond it.[38]

To appreciate fully the significance of this extract, however, we must look at Fuller's
position in relation to the opposing sides in the Civil War. Although a Royalist at
heart, he was crucially placed between king and parliament with friends on both
sides, to whom he remained loyal throughout the war. This central positioning
reinforced the already moderate tone of Fuller's works and this is reflected in a
sermon he delivered in December 1642.

> Think not [he told his congregation] that the King's army is like Sodom –
> not ten righteous men in it; and the other army like Zion – consisting all
> of saints. No, there be drunkards on both sides, and swearers on both sides,
> and whoremongers on both sides, pious on both sides and profane on
> both sides.[39]

It is this sense of moderation that marks Fuller's biography of Drake. Drake may be
an English hero, but he is not perfect – perfection is reserved for God alone who
'often times leaves the brightest men in eclipse, to shew that they do but borrow
their lustre from his reflection'.[40]

The demand for narratives recommenced in the 1650s. In 1652 Walter Bigges's
Summarie and True Discourse was reprinted along with an anonymous account
entitled *A Full Relation of another Voyage made by Sir Francis Drake and others to the
West Indies.* The following year the first anthology of Drake's voyages appeared. This
was titled *Sir Francis Drake Revived. Who is or may be a Pattern to stirre up all Heroicke
and Active Spirites of these times, to benefit their Countrey and eternize their Names by like
Noble Attempts.*[41] The reason for this revival of Drake was twofold. In the years after
the Civil War the benefits of a strong navy came to be perceived (most of the
important naval towns including Plymouth sided with parliament), which is not a
little ironic given the role of Ship Money in the King's downfall. The war had
elevated to power a group with specific interests.

> [R]eligious zealots who had yearned to emulate Drake's exploits and to
> foil the Counter-Reformation … colonial enthusiasts who perceived the
> natural connection between maritime strength and overseas settlement …
> All of these came to regard the navy as a vital instrument of *national*
> policy, revealing thereby a fusion of their religious conviction and personal
> prosperity with a sense of insular patriotism.[42]

Who exemplified what could be achieved with maritime strength better than
Drake? Secondly, in 1652 England embarked upon the first of three naval wars that
it was to wage against the Dutch between 1652 and 1674. There were several
reasons for this conflict: a general distrust for Dutch support for Prince Charles and
the Dutch belief in free trade – a policy that resulted in aid being supplied to the

defeated Royalists. But, above all these were trade wars, with the United Provinces fighting to retain their economic dominance. While England and Spain were engaged in protracted wars, the Dutch had capitalized on trading opportunities that the warring nations could not seize. By the 1650s the United Provinces were Europe's leading commercial nation, carrying on a regular trade with the Orient. It was English envy of this success and a desire to protect the nation's commercial interests that led to the outbreak of the first Anglo-Dutch war. But although the Dutch were the immediate enemy, relations with Spain were far from stable. In a lull between the First and Second Dutch Wars, hostilities with Spain were resumed with a war lasting from 1655 to 1660. This conflict was fought largely in the Caribbean and represented the first stage of Cromwell's 'Western Design', which aimed at overturning the Spanish Empire in the Caribbean. This would have the effect of enriching England and forwarding the Protestant cause.

Although Jamaica was captured, the importance of this gain at the heart of Spanish Caribbean territory was not appreciated at the time and the war received little popular support. Nevertheless 1659 saw the first performance of *The History of Sir Francis Drake, Exprest by Instrumental and Vocal Musick, and by Art of Perspective in Scenes*,[43] a patriotic opera by William Davenant. Under the Lord Protector drama was forbidden; the theatres were closed in 1642 as places of depravity. Yet Davenant was able to exploit Cromwell's love of music by persuading him to sanction opera. By the time *The History of Sir Francis Drake* came to be performed, however, Davenant's productions had become increasingly dramatic. *Drake* in particular is 'much more of a drama, with several characters, some dialogue and a certain amount of action and plot – although it is still divided into entries and not Acts'.[44] The opera is certainly a product of the 'insular patriotism' mentioned above. Drake is a figure to inspire the nation: 'Our story, which shall their Example be,/ And make succession cry, To Sea, To Sea' (6.1.116–17). But striking a strong patriotic note was also a means of securing Cromwell's favour (or that of the Puritan government after Cromwell's death in 1658), thus ensuring a future for Davenant's productions. A Royalist general during the Civil War, Davenant took every opportunity to ingratiate himself with the new leader. Significantly *The History of Sir Francis Drake* makes no mention of Drake's loyalty to his monarch – Davenant clearly had no wish to antagonize those in power.

The opera is concerned with the 1572 voyage (hardly surprising given the contemporary military activities in the West Indies) and takes many details from *Sir Francis Drake Revived*. For instance, in the Fourth Entry Drake sees the Pacific Ocean and makes his vow. 'When from those lofty branches I/ The south Atlantick spy/ My vows shall higher fly' (4.1.44–6). Drake is celebrated as a pioneer of English expansion. 'For thou of all Britons art the first/ That Boldly durst/ This Western World invade' (4.1.53–5). Davenant's works with vocal music represent some of the first operas produced in English, and the use of 'perspective in scenes' marks a departure from the largely undecorated Elizabethan theatre. Drake's 1572 voyage evidently kept the scenery painters busy; the audience was treated to a harbour with two moored ships, the tree from which Drake saw the Pacific, a 'Symeron' village and a mule train laden with gold and silver. The use of perspectival scenes suggests that Drake's exotic adventure carried a strong visual appeal. Little would Drake have suspected that his voyage would provide material for a new and important development in English theatre.

Davenant chooses to concentrate on Drake's chivalrous behaviour. Sir Francis appreciates valour in all its forms and prevents his younger brother from killing a wild boar that Drake has wounded.

> When a courageous beast does bleed,
> Then learn how far you should proceed
> . . . .
> To courage even of Beasts some pity's due;
> And when resistance fails, cease to pursue. (4.1.14–15, 17–18)

Drake almost becomes the knight in shining armour from medieval romance when he rescues a damsel in distress. The stage directions refer to 'a beautiful lady tied to a tree, dressed as a bride, hair dishevelled and praying. Near her are Symerons who took her prisoner.'[45] No doubt this scene was inspired by the episode in *Sir Francis Drake Revived* when, at Venta Cruz, Drake finds a house sheltering women with young children – he instructs the cimarrones that they must not be harmed. In Davenant's opera Drake is appalled at the behaviour of the escaped slaves. 'Arm! Arm! The honour of my nation turns/ To shame, when an afflicted Beauty mourns' (5.2.19–20). But the woman is swiftly released and Drake is assured 'She is free and unblemisht too/ As if she had a pris'ner been to you' (5.3.1–2). Contradicting much evidence, Drake is not motivated by anything as base as gold – he craves only glory. There is no honour in overpowering a lightly guarded mule train, the glory comes when they defeat the Spanish troops sent to recover the treasure. Drake makes it clear that their fame will not rest on financial gain but on their bravery and resourcefulness.

> Our dang'rous course through storms and raging floods,
> And painful march through unfrequented woods,
> Will make those wings by which our fame shall rise.
> Your glory, valiant English, must be known,
>   When men shall read how you did dare
>   To sail so long, and march so far,
> To tempt a strength much greater than you own. (6.1.100–6)

In the following years several other works on Drake were produced. In 1671, the year before the Second Dutch War, Samuel Clark published an historical account, *The Life and Death of the Valiant and Renowned Sir Francis Drake*.[46] 1687 saw the publication of what was to be the most popular biography of Drake over the next eighty years, Robert (or Richard) Burton's *The English Hero: or, Sir Francis Drake Revived: Being a full Account of the Dangerous Voyages, Admirable Adventures, Notable Discoveries, and Magnanimous Atchievements of that Valiant and Renowned Commander*.[47] This was a small, relatively cheap book that ran to at least seventeen editions, the final one in 1777. The first edition was divided into four sections: the Nombre de Dios Voyage, the circumnavigation, the raid on the West Indies and Drake's final voyage.

The fourth edition (1695) is enlarged and includes an account of the Spanish Armada and the Portugal expedition. Again Drake is a figure to inspire endeavour – crammed on to the crowded title page is the recommendation that acts as the epigram for this chapter. Drake's exploits are an example of how active spirits can 'benefit their Prince and Country'. As we have seen, it is not unusual for Drake to be recommended as an example, but it surely is strange that Burton should suggest emulating the Protestant hero for the benefit of a Catholic king. James II had succeeded to the throne in 1685, two years before the first edition of *The English Hero* was published. His initial popularity lost, James had embarked on a programme of establishing absolute rule and the Catholic Church – this included the promotion of Catholics in the armed services. No doubt Drake would be turning in his watery grave.

The accounts themselves are largely reproductions of existing narratives and form what has been dismissively termed a 'rambling compilation'.[48] More interesting is Burton's conclusion to the circumnavigation section. Using details probably from Camden or Stowe, Burton informs the reader that the *Golden Hinde* was left at Deptford for many years and was held in great regard. Undoubtedly Drake's ship was a curiosity, and yet it was more than this. The very fact that the *Hinde* was 'preserved' suggests the existence of a cult of venerated relics. (Later centuries would, of course, rebuild *HMS Victory* but it is unusual to find such a desire as early as the 1580s.) Unlike the relics that formed the focus for the Catholic cult of saints, the *Hinde* was, of course, a purely secular object – it formed the tangible remains of Drake who, as we have seen, may have been manoeuvred into the imaginative space left by the old saints. The ship held such a fascination that souvenir hunters began to remove pieces from the rotting vessel. Before serious decay set in, however, the docked *Golden Hinde* was used for banqueting. At least, this is the function it performs in *Eastward Ho!*, a drama by Ben Jonson, George Chapman and John Marston that was first performed in 1605.[49] Sir Petronell Flash, a debauched knight, makes the following speech:

> [W]e'll have our supper brought aboard Sir Francis Drake's ship that hath encompassed the world, where, with full cups and banquets, we will do sacrifice for a prosperous voyage. (3.3.130–1)

Burton includes two poems by Abraham Cowley that meditate and play on the fact that a chair was made by John Davies, a master shipwright, from timbers removed from the decaying ship. Cowley lived in Deptford and was no doubt familiar with what remained of the *Golden Hinde* when the poems were written in the mid-1650s.[50] The first poem, titled 'Upon the Chair made out of Sir Francis Drake's Ship, Presented to the University Library in Oxford, by John Davies of Deptford, Esq,'[51] is concerned with the fact that the ship that had travelled so far is now at rest – as a place to rest.

> *Drake and his ship could not have wished from fate,*
> *A more blest station, or more blest estate.*
> *For Lo! A seat of endless rest is given,*
> *To her in Oxford, and to him in Heaven.* (7–10)

The longer poem, 'Sitting and Drinking in the Chair made out of the Reliques of Sir Francis Drake's Ships,'[52] one of Cowley's Pindaric Odes, is spoken by a Drakean sea-dog persona. 'Cheer up my mates, the wind does fairly blow./ Clap on more sail, and never spare' (1–2). The speaker continues by praising the chair that, because of its travels, is truly universal, unlike that of the pope, the original Universal Chair. It should come as no surprise to find an object connected with Drake surpassing its Catholic rival.

> In every air and every sea 't has been,
> 'T has compass'd all the earth, and all the heavens 't has seen.
> Let not the Pope's with this compare;
> This is the only universal chair. (26–9)

The third stanza compares the *Hinde*/chair favourably with Odysseus' fleet and Jason's 'first poetic ship of Greece' because it alone has found rest. The final stanza predicts continuing fame for the chair and for Drake's circumnavigation. Noticeably, the chair – with all its associations with the Protestant hero – is described as a relic.

> Great Relique! Thou too, in this port of ease,
> Hast still one way of Making Voyages;
> The breath of fame, like an auspicious gale,
> (The great trade-wind which ne'er does fail)
> Shall drive thee round the World, and thou shal't run,
> As Long around it as the Sun. (59–64)

Cowley's apostrophe to the chair suggests an ironic subversion of the Roman Catholic cult of relics. At the same time, however, he appropriates the imaginative resonance of the cult for purposes that are not only secular but also emphatically nationalistic.

Clearly the voyage around the world continued to form the basis of Drake's fame in the century after his death. The circumnavigation facilitated the construction of Drake as a pioneer of overseas expansion at a time when permanent colonies were being established in North America. Drake continued to be revived as an inspirational figure at times of national crisis or when the nation was perceived by some to be in decline. But appropriating Drake as an inspirational figure was not entirely unproblematic. The king's struggle with parliament led to a break in the production of Drake material during the 1630s and 1640s. A fierce Protestant and loyal servant of the Crown, Drake could not be appropriated easily by either side. Nevertheless, it was during the seventeenth century, particularly during the Commonwealth when the nation's maritime strength became the subject of renewed attention, that Drake was closely identified with national naval power. This identification continued in the eighteenth century when Britain's economic well-being depended very heavily on the Royal Navy, her wooden walls.

Notes

[1] From the title page of Robert Burton, *The English Hero: or, Sir Francis Drake Revived: Being a full Account of Dangerous Voyages, Admirable Adventures, Notable Discoveries, and Magnanimous Atchievements of that Valiant and Renowned Commander* (London, 1687).

[2] Thomas Heywood, *If You Know Not Me, You Know Nobody. The Second Part*, 1606 and 1632, in *The Dramatic Works of Thomas Heywood*, 6 vols (London, 1874), vol. 1, 249–351.

[3] These figures are quoted from M. J. Rodriguez-Salgado, et al., *Armada 1588–1988* (exh. cat., National Maritime Museum, London, 1988), 151.

[4] Heywood, 318. This edition does not divide the drama into acts and scenes therefore I have used page numbers.

[5] Heywood, 346.

[6] Heywood, 348.

[7] Heywood, 339.

[8] Heywood, 339.

[9] Heywood, 339.

[10] Richard Hakluyt, *The Principal Navigations, Voyages, Traffiques and Discoveries of the English Nation*, 1589 and 1598–1600, 12 vols (Glasgow, 1903–5), vol. 4, 225.

[11] Paul M. Kennedy, *The Rise and Fall of British Naval Mastery* (London, 1983), 38.

[12] David Armitage, *The Ideological Origins of the British Empire* (Cambridge, 2000), 83.

[13] The Spanish Match was the scheme for James I's son, Prince Charles, to marry the Infanta Maria (the second daughter of Philip III of Spain). This union would position James as a central figure in both Protestant and Catholic Courts and allow him to act as a mediator between rival dynasties. His daughter was already married to the Protestant Elector Palatine, Frederick V. The Match failed partly because of Buckingham's inept negotiations and partly because it became clear that Spain was forging threateningly powerful alliances across Europe over which James could exercise no influence. For a detailed account of these political manoeuvrings, see Roger Lockyer, *The Early Stuarts: A Political History of England 1603–1642* (London, 1989), 17–21.

[14] J. S. A. Adamson, 'Chivalry and Political Culture in Caroline England', in Kevin Sharpe and Peter Lake, eds, *Culture and Politics in Early Stuart England* (London, 1994), 169.

[15] Mark Netzloff, 'Sir Francis Drake's Ghost: Piracy, Cultural Memory, and Spectral Nationhood', in Claire Jowitt, ed., *Pirates? The Politics of Plunder, 1550–1650* (Basingstoke, 2007), 147. He goes on to suggest that works casting Drake as a pirate focused attention on the piratical origins of the nation's emergent empire and this revealed a repining for an earlier model of adventure that was being superseded by joint-stock companies. However, although Drake's endeavours were widely celebrated, very few works identified him as first and foremost a pirate. William Davenant's *The History of Sir Francis Drake*, which Netloff cites, certainly does not.

[16] Michael Drayton, *Poly-Olbion*, 1612 and 1622, in J. William Hebel, ed., *The Works of Michael Drayton*, 5 vols (Oxford, 1933), vol. 4, v.

[17] Harry Kelsey, *Sir Francis Drake: The Queen's Pirate* (New Haven, 1998), 398.

[18] For example, William Rowley *All's Lost by Lust* (1619), Thomas Middleton, *A Game of Chess* (1624), and Thomas Middleton and William Rowley, *The Spanish Gipsy* (1623).

[19] Traditionally attributed to Francis Beaumont and John Fletcher, the play is now usually thought to be the work of Fletcher alone. See John Fletcher, *Rule a Wife and Have a Wife*, in *The Works of Francis Beaumont and John Fletcher*, 10 vols (Cambridge, 1906), vol. 3, 169–235.

[20] Anon., *Sir Francis Drake Revived. Calling Upon this Dull or Effeminate Age to Follow his Noble Steps for Gold and Silver*, 1626, in Irene Wright, ed., *Documents Concerning English Voyages to the Spanish Main 1569–1580* (London, 1932), 245–326,

[21] Wright, ed., *English Voyages*, 245.

[22] Wright, ed., *English Voyages*, 253.

[23] Wright, ed., *English Voyages*, 323.

[24] Wright, ed., *English Voyages*, 284.

[25] Wright, ed., *English Voyages*, 265.

[26] Wright, ed., *English Voyages*, 320–1.

[27] Wright, ed., *English Voyages*, 300.

[28] Anon., *The World Encompassed by Sir Francis Drake being his Next Voyage to that to Nombre de Dios*, 1628, in William Vaux, ed., *The World Encompassed by Sir Francis Drake* (London, 1854), 1–162.

[29] Vaux, ed., *The World Encompassed*, 7

[30] Vaux, ed., *The World Encompassed*, 86.

[31] Vaux, ed., *The World Encompassed*, 86.

[32] Vaux, ed., *The World Encompassed*, 5.

[33] Kenneth R. Andrews, *Trade, Plunder and Settlement: Maritime Enterprise and the Genesis of the British Empire 1480–1630* (Cambridge, 1984), 338.

[34] For a discussion of Ship Money as an element in the definition of England as a maritime realm, see Armitage, 117.

[35] Thomas Fuller, *The Holy State and Profane State* (1642; London, 1840), 105.

[36] Fuller, *Holy State*, 107.

[37] John Cummins, *Sir Francis Drake: The Lives of a Hero* (1995; London, 1997), 285.

[38] Fuller, *Holy State*, 113.

[39] Quoted in William Addison, *Worthy Doctor Fuller* (London, 1951), 105–6.

[40] Fuller, *Holy State*, 113.

[41] Anon., *Sir Francis Drake Revived. Who is or may be a Pattern to Stirre up all Heroicke and Active Spirits of these Times, to Benefit their Country and Eternize their Names by Like Noble Attempts* (London, 1653).

[42] Kennedy, 46.

[43] William Davenant, *The History of Sir Francis Drake. Exprest by Instrumental and Vocal Musick, and by Art of Perspective in Scenes*, 1659, in *Three Centuries of English Drama: English 1642–1700* (New York, 1960), Microcard 9.

[44] Mary Edmond, *Rare Sir William Davenant: Poet Laureate, Playwright, Civil War General, Restoration Theatre Manager* (Manchester, 1987), 133.

[45] The stage instructions for the second scene of the Fifth Entry.

[46] Samuel Clark, *The Life and Death of the Valiant and Renowned Sir Francis Drake, His Voyages and Discoveries in the West Indies, and About the World, with his Noble and Heroicke Acts* (London, 1671).

[47] Burton, *The English Hero*.

[48] W. T. Jewkes, 'Sir Francis Drake Revived: From Letters to Legend', in Norman Thrower, ed., *Sir Francis Drake and the Famous Voyage, 1577–1580: Essays Commemorating the Quadricentennial of Drake's Circumnavigation of the Earth* (Berkeley, 1980), 117.

[49] Ben Jonson, *Eastward Ho!*, 1605, in G. A. Wilkes, ed., *The Complete Plays of Ben Jonson*, 4 vols (Oxford, 1981–2), vol. 2, 351–531.

[50] There is no record of when the *Golden Hinde* was finally broken up (or when she finally succumbed to rot). Neither Samuel Pepys nor John Evelyn saw fit to mention the ship in their diaries, which together cover the period 1650 to 1669. This does not, of course, mean that no remains existed.

[51] Abraham Cowley, 'Upon the Chair made out of Sir Francis Drake's Ship, Presented to the University Library in Oxford, by John Davies of Deptford, Esq.', in Alexander Grosart, ed., *The Complete Works in Verse and Prose of Abraham Cowley*, 2 vols (1881; Hildesheim, 1969), vol. 1, 169.

[52] Abraham Cowley, 'Sitting and Drinking in the Chair made out of the Reliques of Sir Francis Drake's Ships', in Grosart, ed., *The Complete Works*, vol. 1, 156–7.

CHAPTER THREE

'Behold the warrior dwindled to a beau'

The glorious reign of Queen Elizabeth opens to us a
large field of matter for this history and lays before us the
noble plans and ground-work, upon which the whole
superstructure of our Naval Glory is built.
(Thomas Lediard, *The Naval History of England*, 1735)[1]

With Protestant succession secured by the Glorious Revolution of 1688,
the problems surrounding the celebration of Sir Francis Drake, loyal
subject and Protestant hero, were at once removed. It was not long
before Drake was again 'revived' as an inspirational character at a time of national
crisis. The outbreak of the Nine Years' War[2] in 1689 provided the perfect
opportunity for Drake's exploits to be recalled. Drake was, in fact, a particularly
relevant figure when we consider the parallels between the Anglo-French conflict
and the war with Spain in the sixteenth century. Like Spain, France was a Catholic
country; it also posed a very real invasion threat if England lost control of the
Channel. Whether the similarities with the Elizabethan conflict were appreciated at
the time is open to question, but there can be no doubting the appeal of Sir Francis
Drake during the war years. Three more editions of Robert Burton's *The English
Hero* had appeared by 1695.

As the previous chapter sought to establish, *The English Hero* was the standard
work on Drake throughout most of the eighteenth century. Eleven editions
appeared at regular intervals between 1701 and 1777, and not necessarily at times
of armed conflict. While the sheer number of editions provides firm evidence of Sir
Francis Drake's continuing popularity, we need to question just why the
Elizabethan seafarer should still generate such interest. Linda Colley has shown how
Protestantism made sense of the world for a huge number of Britons and also the
way in which they marked their separate religious identity. The reasons for this
concentration on religious separateness are not hard to find.

> Eighteenth- and nineteenth-century Britons reminded themselves of their
> embattled Protestantism … because they had good cause to feel uncertain
> about its security and about their own. In 1707, the Counter-Reformation

was still very much in progress in parts of Continental Europe. France had attempted to expel its Protestant population in 1685.... In Spain, the Inquisition continued to take action throughout the eighteenth century.[3]

It was, perhaps, the continuing threat to Protestant hegemony that lay behind the popular interest in Drake. What better figure than Sir Francis Drake, the scourge of Catholic Spain, to remind the devout Protestant of the Catholic threat and the way it could be countered?

However, editions of Burton's book in 1701, 1706, 1710 and 1716 disguise the fact that during the first twenty years of the eighteenth century *literary* interest in Drake waned. He was ignored by dramatists, and only one substantial work in verse dealt with the Elizabethan hero: John Sadler's 'Loyalty, Attended with Great News from Drake's and Raleigh's Ghosts'.[4] Printed in 1705, this heroic poem presents 'the true means whereby Britain may be recovered from her maladies, and obtain a lasting happiness, honour, and renown'.[5] Without doubt Sadler's Drake is an exemplum, a heroic figure from an Elizabethan Golden Age, but the poem is not content to brood on the virtues of an idealized past as a means of correcting an indifferent present. The ghosts of the two Elizabethan heroes delineate a scheme that will create a new Golden Age. Drake's shade tells the reader how Britain may be recovered from her 'maladies'.

> *The British vessel shall through billows flee,*
> *Far from the prospect of the vultures eye;*
> *And, from the new world which I first survey'd,*
> *In gold and silver mines they soon shall trade.*
>
> *In this grand juncture of your state affairs*
> *Britain, with open eyes, and heart, and ears,*
> *That happiness shall seek, and seeking find,*
> *Which heals her maladies of every kind.* (63–70)

Significantly, the New World is seen as a place for commerce. The emphasis on commerce is more direct than that displayed by such seventeenth-century poems as Andrew Marvell's 'Bermudas', in which a benevolent nature lays her fruit at the feet of the colonists.[6] Sadler's verse is an early example of the enthusiastic promotion of commerce, which would develop into a vociferous cult as the century progressed: but much more of that later.

Having aroused the reader's curiosity, Drake's shade disappears and Raleigh's ghost continues to delineate the enterprise. Heaven decrees that Britain must colonize Darien, 'The place which heav'n to her has late assign'd' (99). Of course, Sir Walter Raleigh was directly involved with plans to colonize North America, and it seems wholly appropriate that he should propound an expansionist scheme in Sadler's poem. Drake's involvement with colonization, on the other hand, was far more marginal. He may have claimed Nova Albion for Queen Elizabeth but he was not concerned with the establishment of colonies. 'Great News, from Drake's and Raleigh's Ghosts' is perhaps the first instance of a new strand in the Drake mythology: Drake constructed as a deliberate empire-builder. This aspect of the mythology is distinct from the construction of Drake as circumnavigator and expert warrior and became hugely significant in the late nineteenth and early twentieth centuries when he was seen as a founding father of a benevolent British Empire.

But what lies behind Sadler's construction of Drake? At the time the poem was published, Britain was engaged with the War of the Spanish Succession (1702–13). As Linda Colley has noted, '[This] war had been fought, as far as Britain was concerned, in large part because the French monarch Louis XIV, had insisted on recognizing the exiled James II and his son as the only rightful kings [of Great Britain].'[7] If the Stuarts were going to recover the British Crown, it could only be with French military assistance. 'Britons had every reason to suppose, therefore, that a restored Stuart dynasty would operate, whether it wanted to or not, under the shadow of French power and in support of French interests.'[8] This would have serious consequences when it came to British commerce. For their part in restoring the Stuart monarchy, the French would demand trading concessions in the British colonies or, perhaps, a reduction in the number of Royal Navy ships. It becomes apparent that French support for the Jacobites was one element in an Anglo-French struggle for trade. Sadler's answer to the threat posed by France is to strengthen British commerce by colonizing Darien, 'The grand Emporium of the world for trade' (106). The scheme cannot fail because it is divinely sanctioned: heaven will protect the colony 'From Frenchified-Spanish insolence' (123), and the nation's newly acquired wealth will force Louis XIV to bow to Britain's 'rich imperial Crown' (140).

John Sadler was not the first exponent of a project to colonize the Isthmus of Panama, however. The original Darien Scheme was devised by William Paterson, founder of the Bank of England and a writer on finance. Paterson was concerned with expanding the trade of his native Scotland; his idea was to found a colony at Darien (which was crucially placed between the Atlantic and Pacific Oceans) where the newly formed African Company could trade with merchants from both the East Indies and Africa. The scheme received considerable support but, in practice, proved a dismal failure. Disease and Spanish raids – Spain claimed Darien as her territory – ensured that the colony, first settled in 1698, could not survive. Undeterred, Paterson revived his scheme in 1701 but this time the project received scant support. Little is known of John Sadler, but it is obvious that his belief in Paterson's scheme was absolute. The poem calls for a terrible vengeance on all opponents of the project.

> *Now let the dreadful doom of James the First,*[9]
> *(Who all his Popish successors sore curst)*
> *Light on those black infernal minds, who join*
> *This Enterprise to break; or shall repine*
> *Against this deed, which heav'n's broad seal does sign.* (146–50)

As the century progressed, Drake's adventures provided source material for the rapidly maturing literary form, the novel. Daniel Defoe's A *New Voyage Round the World, by a Course Never Sailed Before*[10] (1725) is not concerned with Drake directly, but it is almost certain that Defoe was familiar with accounts of Drake's adventures.

Several incidents – far too many to be coincidental – seem to be drawn from the narratives of Drake's voyages, particularly those concerned with the circumnavigation. The commander of Defoe's fictitious voyage has to suppress a mutiny occasioned by his plan to sail around the globe the 'wrong' way or via the Cape of Good Hope. The travellers are confronted and outnumbered by aggressive natives in a scene that recalls Drake's landing at Mocha Island. They also discover a peaceful race of Indians (the Coast Miwok); chase and board a treasure ship (the *Cacafuego*) and, in an episode that must have been inspired by Drake's 1572 Nombre de Dios voyage, march across Chile and Patagonia constructing a raft as they go. That the name Francis Drake was still associated with circumnavigating the globe is made clear by the first sentence of the book:

> It has for some time been thought so wonderful a thing to sail the tour or circle of the globe, that when a man has done this mighty feat, he presently thinks it deserves to be recorded like Sir Francis Drake's.[11]

It is revealing that although new literary work largely ignored Drake, Defoe's novel alludes to a widespread recognition of at least one of his achievements.

> Such a mighty and valuable thing also was the passing of this Strait [of Magellan], that Sir Francis Drake's going through it gave birth to that famous old wives' saying, viz., that Sir Francis Drake shot the gulf; a saying that was current in England for many years after Sir Francis Drake was gone his long[est] journey of all; as if there had been but one gulf in the world, and that the passing it had been a wonder next to that of Hercules cleansing the Augean stable.[12]

Here we find strong evidence of a folk–Drake tradition. It is not the commercial aspect of the voyage, the claiming of Nova Albion or the treaty with the Sultan of Ternate, that has lodged in the folk consciousness but the fact that Drake navigated the Magellan Strait. Probably the saying has its origins in the old 'flat earth' belief that to cross from one plane of the earth's surface to the other the intrepid sailor must traverse the roaring waters of a treacherous gulf. But no matter what its origins, that Drake shot the gulf proved a very enduring saying. Not only was it current in England during the later years of the sixteenth century but Daniel Defoe makes use of it and, in 1836, it resurfaced in a book concerned with the West Country. In *A Description of the Part of Devonshire Bordering on the Tamar and the Tavy* Anna Eliza Bray jokes that 'There is … one old picture of Drake at Oxford, representing him holding a pistol in one hand which … [a guide claimed] was the very pistol with which Sir Francis had shot the gulf.'[13] The painting to which Bray refers is undoubtedly the full-length portrait of Sir Martin Frobisher by Cornelius Ketel (held in the Bodleian Library), in which the subject brandishes a wheel-lock pistol in a rather aggressive pose.

Literary neglect of Drake found no equivalent in historical works where Sir Francis figured prominently. As the century progressed material concerned with Drake and his exploits appeared in the increasingly popular naval history. The primary cause of this sudden interest in the nation's maritime past was the growing importance of the Royal Navy. The power and wealth of Britain (as it became with the Act of Union in 1707), it was believed, was a direct result of its commerce. And, of course, commercial growth went hand in hand with colonial expansion. The wars fought during the first half of the eighteenth century saw Britain make great territorial gains at the expense of her colonial rivals – France and Spain. The War of the Spanish Succession (1702–13) brought Newfoundland, Nova Scotia and Hudson's Bay under British rule. In the Mediterranean the strategic naval stations of Gibraltar and Minorca were gained. The colonies gained as a result of victory in the hugely successful Seven Years' War[14] (1756–63) formed the basis of the First British Empire. At the conclusion of the war, the Paris peace settlement saw France lose its grasp on Canada, leaving Britain in virtual control of North America; it added Tobago, St Vincent and Dominica to the country's West Indian possessions and ended French involvement in India. Britain rapidly found itself Europe's foremost economic power.

Obviously the Royal Navy had made these far-flung colonial gains possible in the first place, but once won, trade routes had to be protected. Even during peacetime merchantmen needed protection from the predations of privateers and pirates. But the Royal Navy's role was not just to guard merchant shipping from pirates. We need to consider the naval requirements of the protectionist economic system known as mercantilism, which operated during the first part of the century. The term 'mercantilism' was first coined by Adam Smith,[15] although the economic system had been in existence since the sixteenth century. This system promoted governmental regulation of a nation's economic activities in order to increase the country's wealth at the expense of its European rivals. The principal objective of the mercantile system was, in its simplest form, the accumulation of gold and silver, the chief realizable assets in times of war. This treasure could be obtained by maintaining what was termed a favourable balance of trade or by ensuring that Britain's exports exceeded its imports. Charters were granted to companies to carry British trade to far-flung nations, and colonies came to play an important part in the system. They provided a monopoly for the country that established them – British territories could only sell their produce to British merchants. This was particularly true of what Smith calls enumerated goods, those, such as sugar, that could only be produced in specific locations. After arriving back in the mother-country these products could then by re-exported to eager continental markets. It was the task of the Royal Navy to prevent foreign merchants from trading with the colonies and upsetting Britain's favourable balance of trade.

The British reminded themselves continually that their greatness was built upon trade. Histories, political speeches, songs and poems all dwelt on the subject, and this predominantly Whig 'cult of commerce'[16] was well aware of the inseparable relationship between the country's wealth and its navy. Perhaps the symbiotic link between naval strength and commerce was best summed up by Lord Haversham in a speech to the House of Lords in 1707:

> Your trade is the mother and nurse of your seamen; your seamen are the
> life of your fleet, and your fleet is the security and protection of your trade,
> and both together are the wealth, strength, security and glory of Britain.[17]

The exploits of the Elizabethan sea-dogs inevitably attracted the attention of naval historians. Indeed, John Sinclair, MP for Caithness and notable for his interest in all matters nautical, argued that it was unnecessary to look at maritime history before the reign of Elizabeth because, although the first naval commissioners were appointed in 1512, the country had engaged in no 'remarkable sea exploits'.[18] Here we must assume that Sinclair means voyages of discovery in order to secure overseas markets. The prefaces of many naval histories placed great emphasis on the belief that it was the activities of the Elizabethan sea-dogs that laid the foundation of Britain's flourishing trade. The quotation from Thomas Lediard's *Naval History of England* that opens this chapter is just one example.

While not strictly speaking a naval history, probably the most influential new work in terms of the construction of Drake to appear during the early part of the century was Awnsham Churchill's *A Collection of Voyages and Travels* (1704). Importantly, the third volume contained for the first time the *Naval Tracts* of Admiral Sir William Monson.[19] Monson, who had known Drake, devoted the last years of his life to writing this semi-autobiographical narrative. By his own admission, Monson's intent was to 'set down mistakes and oversights committed as a warning to others to prevent similar errors'.[20] Consequently, Drake is criticized on two points in connection with the 1585 West Indian raids. Firstly, that the voyage was badly victualled and it was only with luck that a fully laden Newfoundland fishing vessel was taken on the return journey. Secondly, that Drake failed to keep Hispaniola, Santa Domingo and Santa Justina, which, because of English naval superiority, should have been an easy task. This, Monson argues rather optimistically, would have kept the Anglo-Spanish war out of Europe. Of the Portugal expedition Monson states 'These two generals never overshot themselves more.'[21] Nevertheless, while condemning Drake for his failure to meet Norris at Lisbon, he does not hold the General responsible for the expedition's lack of success. This is blamed on poor provisioning of the fleet. The stress placed on the victualling of ships is, perhaps, connected to the failure of the raids organized by Charles I and Buckingham in the 1620s. Monson had been consulted about the expeditions but given the poor provisioning of the fleets it is doubtful whether his advice was taken.

The Tracts influenced many naval histories – Lediard's *Naval History of England* borrows extensively from Monson and reproduces his specific criticisms. But by 1742, when John Campbell came to publish *Lives of the British Admirals*,[22] the attitude towards Drake seems to have changed. Again Monson's list of logistical mistakes is included, but now Drake's 'failings' are excused. It was impossible to keep Hispaniola and Santa Domingo, argues Campbell, because sickness had depleted Drake's troops; Portugal was not a failure because the country had been 'crossed' by English soldiers. But what lay behind this desire to free Drake of any blame? We can certainly detect the influence of the cult of commerce in Campbell's history. He ponders on the significance of Drake's capture of the carrack *San Felipe* on the return from the Cadiz raid:

> It was in consequence of the journals, charts and papers taken on board his East India prize, that it was judged practicable for us to enter into that trade … To this we may also add, he first brought in tobacco, the use of

which was much promoted by Sir Walter Raleigh. How much this nation
has gained by these brands of commerce, of which he was properly the
author, I leave to the intelligent readers' consideration.[23]

And the intelligent reader would be well aware of the money that was being made
from tobacco – a product that was no longer a luxury but a necessity. More
revealing, however, is this extract from Campbell's preface:

> Our own privateers were allowed to pass into the West Indies, where they
> carried on an illicit trade, not more to their own benefit than the public
> benefit; for by this means they gained a perfect acquaintance with the
> ports, rivers, and fortresses in the West Indies, with the nature of the
> commerce transacted there, the method of sharing by fair means, or by
> destroying it by force.[24]

By 1737 Britain was again at war with Spain. The cause of this conflict was
Britain's determination to gain commercial access to the Spanish Caribbean. While
prepared, if grudgingly, to buy slaves from British slavers – even though the Treaty
of Utrecht that concluded the War of the Spanish Succession allowed one British
ship per year to sell its goods at Porto Bello – the desire to maintain a trade
monopoly in the colonies was very strong. Alongside the sanctioned traffic there
existed an unofficial trade, and it was the treatment of Captain Robert Jenkins, an
illegal trader, at the hands of the Spanish coastguards that pushed Britain towards
war. Famously, Jenkins's ear was severed and his ship looted and set adrift. This
combined with the (more important but less well-known) Spanish seizure of five
British vessels, provoked outrage in the Commons. Demands for compensation were
not met and a reluctant Robert Walpole was forced into the War of Jenkins's Ear.

The parallels between Elizabethan traders (including Drake and Hawkins)
illegally supplying slaves to Spanish planters, and British merchants attempting to
end the Spanish monopoly in the eighteenth century, is striking. Similar, too, were
the outrages perpetrated by Spain in defence of her monopolies. In a statement
recalling Elizabethan anti-Spanish rhetoric, the *Gentleman's Magazine* declared:

> At a time when the nation is engaged in a War with an enemy, whose
> insults, Ravages and Barbarity have long called for vengeance, an account
> of such English commanders as have merited the acknowledgement of
> posterity, by extending the power, and raising the honour of their country,
> seem to be no improper entertainment for our readers.[25]

There followed a life of Admiral Robert Blake, the successful English commander
of the Anglo-Dutch wars. But recourse to Sir Francis Drake was inevitable –
especially when we consider the ideological manoeuvring that a war with Spain
facilitated. 'In the campaign for tougher measures the merchants and their allies in
the press had regularly appealed to England's Protestant destiny and to the
buccaneering spirit of the Elizabethan and Cromwellian eras.'[26] The war was never
presented solely as a trade conflict but as the latest episode in the continuing
struggle between Protestantism and its Catholic foe. In 1739 one incident above all

thrust Drake back into the public mind: Vernon's capture of Porto Bello. This town was an obvious target, being the port from which those obstacles to British commerce, the Spanish coastguards, sailed. News of the capture of Porto Bello caused 'the people of England to go mad with excitement and joy'.[27] Vernon became a national hero to rank alongside Sir Francis Drake. Like Drake in 1585, he had taken positive action against the Spanish in the Caribbean and, for the opponents of the prime minister, his success served to expose the weakness of Walpole's non-aggressive foreign policy. In 1741 (following Vernon's return to England), the *Gentleman's Magazine* printed an anonymous poem titled 'On Vernon's Success in America'.[28] It celebrates Drake and Raleigh as great opponents of Spain and Vernon as their natural successor.

> *To humble Spain three heroes born,*
> *Drake, Raleigh, Vernon, Britain's Isle adorn,*
> *The first in Courage and success surpast,*
> *The next in well plann'd schemes; in both the last;*
> *Drake had all honour valour could obtain,*
> *But Raleigh fell a sacrifice to Spain:*
> *With happier fate we see our Vernon rise,*
> *As Drake Courageous and Raleigh wise:*
> *The heroes and Patriots worth to show,*
> *To make a third, Heav'n joined the former two.* (1–10)

Another product of the 1740s anti-Spanish patriotism is a volume entitled *The Heads and Characters of Illustrious Persons of Great Britain*,[29] which was published in two volumes in 1743. Sir Walter Raleigh and Sir Francis Drake are among a host of celebrated figures whose images were calculated to remind the patriotic Englishman of past successes against Spain, France and foreign powers in general. With the inclusion of Hampden, Locke and Milton, the book is a pretty complete representation of the Whig version of history, which is discussed later in this chapter. The engraving of Drake[30] (PLATE 4) is by the well-respected Dutch portrait engraver Jacobus Houbraken. Although it is impossible to identify the image from which Houbraken worked, it is almost certainly one of the engravings based upon that by Thomas de Leu (PLATE 2). A rather mild-looking Drake (when compared to de Leu's Sir Francis) stares from a rococo frame, which is raised on a plinth supporting a trophy or representation on the paraphernalia of navigation and naval warfare. The whole image is based upon funerary monuments of the seventeenth century, and this accounts for its architectural design. A cartouche depicting a naval engagement may seem to provide the strongest link to the original de Leu engraving but such decorations are a common feature of funerary monuments commemorating admirals.

There can be little doubt that the War of Jenkins's Ear played a huge part in reviving interest in Drake during the early 1740s. But to assume that the proliferation of Drake material was solely the result of the Anglo-Spanish war would be to ignore an important underlying political motivation. To fully appreciate Drake's role we need to understand the significance of Gothic history and how the prime minister, Robert Walpole, was seen as betraying this version of national identity. Antiquarians during the Reformation had constructed a Gothic history that accounted for the origins of the English race.[31] The Goths were just one Germanic tribe at the time of the Roman Empire, but in the hands of the antiquarians many separate races including the Anglo-Saxons came to be subsumed beneath the title. From the Roman historian Tacitus it was discovered that these Germanic peoples possessed many admirable attributes; these included robustness, honesty, a lack of false sophistication and, above all, a love of liberty. A continuity between the Gothic past and the present was carefully constructed. The Goths had overthrown the corrupt and decadent Roman Empire, and it was the Gothic legacy, the perpetuation of Gothic virtues, that facilitated the casting off of the Catholic Church in the sixteenth century. A central element of Gothic theory was an opposition to the absolute power of kings – Saxon kings were elected by an assembly and held limited powers. Parliament had used Gothic history in an attempt to find a precedent for its opposition to Charles's attempt at Personal Rule. With some modification to account for private landownership, Gothic theory – particularly the defence of liberty – was absorbed into the political beliefs of the Whigs, the party of government for most of the eighteenth century. It is no surprise, therefore, that historical figures who displayed great patriotism or had fought to keep the nation free should be appropriated and celebrated by the Whigs. In 'Summer' from his long poem *The Seasons* first published in 1727, James Thomson 'Introduces a panegyric on Britain'.[32] He celebrates the country's 'sons of glory' (1479) including Alfred, Sir Walter Raleigh, Philip Sidney and Drake. He writes 'A Drake, who made thee mistress of the deep,/ And bore thy name in thunder round the world./ Then flamed thy spirit high' (1495–7).

Yet celebrating Whig heroes was not as simple as it may seem. The Whigs themselves were far from united. During the late 1720s and 1730s, the revival of patriotic figures from history could be used by an opposing faction of the Whig party as a means of attacking Robert Walpole, particularly his non-aggressive foreign policy and his closeness to the Court. With British trade flourishing in the 1720s – despite the exclusion from the Spanish Caribbean – Walpole was unwilling to get involved in a war of commerce with Spain. Thomson's poem *Britannia*[33] (1729) is, in part, a condemnation of Walpole's perceived weakness. For Thomson and many others, the outrages suffered by British merchants at the hands of the Spanish were a shocking violation of British liberty. The days when Britain was able to act against the 'insulting Spaniard' (23) are recalled with reference to the Spanish Armada. In this poem Britannia sits on the shore lamenting the lost age, 'When all the pride of Spain, in one dread fleet' (64) was destroyed by a few stout-hearted Britons. Whig opposition to Walpole was centred on Lord Cobham. He had opposed Walpole's Excise Bill in 1733 – which was considered another violation of British freedom – and as a consequence lost control of his regiment. Incensed, Cobham and his supporters – dismissively termed the 'Boy Patriots' by Walpole – mounted a concerted attack against the prime minister. As George Clark has noted:

PLATE 4. Jacobus Houbraken, 'Sir Francis Drake' from Thomas Birch, *The Heads and Characters of Illustrious Persons of Great Britain*, 1743. Drake recruited to the Whig version of history.

PLATE 5. Peter Scheemakers' bust of Drake. The Temple of British Worthies, Stowe, Buckinghamshire. A personification of Gothic virtue.

Their campaign was concentrated against Walpole who had raised himself
to an improper position of 'prime' minister for selfish ends neglecting
England's true destiny by sacrificing her interests to Hanover and by
allowing her traditional enemies, France and Spain, to imprison her
seamen and strangle her trade.[34]

Stowe, Cobham's landscaped garden in Buckinghamshire, contains a classical
building known as the Temple of British Worthies. This is by William Kent and was
erected in 1735. The temple comprises a semi-circular exedra with curving wings
either side of a central pyramid. Each wing contains eight busts, each in a slightly
projected bay with its own pediment. These busts, by Michael Rysbrack and Peter
Scheemakers, are an extremely important piece of political iconography. They are
the British Worthies: patriotic men (and one woman – Queen Elizabeth) of action
and of contemplation who personify Gothic virtues. In 1748 William Gilpin wrote
of the men of action: 'Inspired by every generous sentiment, these gallant spirits
founded constitutions, stemmed the Torrent of corruption, battled for the state,
ventured their lives in the Defence of their country, and gloriously bled in the cause
of Liberty.'[35] Here we find a neat summary of all the things that Robert Walpole was
not doing while he supposedly subsumed national interest beneath personal
advancement. The busts include several of the figures celebrated by Thomson in
'Summer': Drake, Raleigh, the merchant Thomas Gresham (the City opposed
Walpole), and John Hampden the celebrated parliamentarian. Hampden had
opposed Charles I's non-parliamentary imposition of Ship Money and died, a martyr
to the Parliamentary cause, of wounds sustained during a Civil War skirmish. Sir
Francis Drake (PLATE 5) is undoubtedly modelled on the half-length engraving
usually attributed to Jodocus Hondius. Importantly, eight of the figures, including
Drake, signify an area on which Walpole could be attacked. Above each bust is a short
inscription, some classical and some by either Alexander Pope or George Lyttleton
(both, along with Thomson, frequent guests at Stowe). Attention had been drawn to
the satirical nature of these inscriptions.[36] The wording above Drake reads, 'Who
thro many perils, was the first of Britons, that adventured to sail round the globe,
and carry into unknown seas the knowledge and Glory of the English name.' The
emphasis is firmly placed on Drake's identity as explorer, a figure who had opened
up new lands and new markets for English commerce. Similarly, the 'Boy Patriots'
were keen to extend Britain's colonial empire but at the cost of France and Spain.
The irony is that, from a Whig opposition perspective, Walpole would not defend
even existing commercial rights. But the work also functions on another, more
general level. It draws attention to the perceived degeneracy of Britain, its lack of
heroic spirit. Originally, the Temple of British Worthies faced the Temple of Modern
Virtue (sometimes called the Temple of Vanity), which was symbolically designed as
a ruin. This contained a headless statue said to represent Walpole.

The most revealing celebration of Drake to emerge from this period – and one
that develops the theme of a degenerate present – is the biographical account by
Samuel Johnson that appeared in the Gentleman's Magazine in 1740 and 1741.[37] The

bulk of material is drawn from Burton's biography, which had been republished in 1739, almost certainly as a result of the surge in interest in Drake after Vernon's capture of Porto Bello. Johnson uses the past to explain the present: it was during the reign of Elizabeth that 'our long continued wars with the Spaniards laid the foundation of that settled animosity which yet continues between the two nations'.[38] The cult of commerce is never far away: 'and we are more indebted to the Discoverer than the Soldier, as the Nation owes less of its wealth and Power to its Arms than to its navigation'.[39] For Johnson, Drake is primarily the self-made man as hero. Johnson's Drake embodies the moral qualities – especially determination and resilience – that (he believes) are necessary for an individual to succeed. We must not forget that, like Drake, many of the men of commerce, that driving force behind the nation's greatness, had risen from relatively humble beginnings. Drake is held up as an example to others. After the Spanish treachery at San Juan d'Ulua Drake was left penniless but undaunted:

> [He] retained at least his Courage and his Industry, that ardent spirit that prompted him to Adventures, and that indefatigable Patience that enabled him to surmount Difficulties. He did not sit down idly to lament Misfortunes which Heaven had put in his power to remedy, or to repine at Poverty while the Wealth of England was to be gained.[40]

Similarly, after the failure of the attempt to ambush the first mule train in 1572, Drake displays a gritty determination to make the voyage succeed. He 'turned his Thoughts to new Prospects, and without languishing in melancholy Reflections upon his part, employed himself in forming Schemes for repairing them'.[41] When Drake finally 'makes' the voyage, Johnson is pleased that 'the part [of the treasure] that was allotted to *Drake* was not sufficient to lull him to Effeminacy'.[42] By dwelling on Drake's virtues, Johnson attempts to highlight the degeneracy of the present age. The idea of a degenerate present is also explored in his satirical work 'London: A Poem'[43] (1738). Here Johnson's attack is aimed particularly at the Francophilia rampant among the country's elite. This was manifest in the very clothes that men (and women) wore. Colley makes the point that 'Up to the American Revolution and even beyond, elite male costume for attendance at court was the *habit a la francaise*.'[44] This was a very obvious signifier of wealth and leisure, at odds with the industry celebrated by the cult of commerce. Johnson contrasts an idealized Elizabethan past with a foppish present.

> *In pleasing Dreams the blissful Age renew,*
> *And call Britannia's Glories back to view;*
> *Behold her Cross triumphant on the Main,*
> *The guard of Commerce, and the Dread of Spain,*
> . . . .
> *But lost in thoughtless Ease, and Empty Show,*
> *Behold the Warrior dwindled to a Beau;*
> *Sense, Freedom, Piety refin'd away,*
> *Of France the mimic, and of Spain the prey.* (25–8, 103–6)

What 'London' shows is that Drake is not solely an example of determination to inspire the budding men of commerce, but a moral figure to be contrasted with the present, thus highlighting its failings. Indeed, Johnson's construction of Drake may be read in the light of the eighteenth-century debate between the Ancients and Moderns. This can be summarized as follows: 'Were the Greeks and Romans superior in all ways of life and thought to everything that followed after? Or had the moderns in one field or another succeeded in equalling or surpassing them?'[45] The argument raged amid a flurry of pamphlets but, in the end, neither side could have claimed to have won outright. Johnson did not align himself with either faction. He was not opposed to the dissemination of new knowledge and claimed 'I am always angry when I hear ancient times praised at the expense of modern times. There is now a great deal more learning in the world than there was formerly; for it is universally diffused.'[46] Yet in matters of morality Johnson is avowedly Ancient. Drake, of course, was not an ancient yet in Johnson's hands he becomes the very essence of pre-modern morality.

Johnson's 'Life of Admiral Drake' is, perhaps, the first work to develop this new thread in the Drake mythology. Certainly Drake had been revived as an exemplum before – both by Michael Drayton and John Sadler – but Johnson is the first to concentrate on Sir Francis as a specifically moral figure. Indeed, Johnson presents us with a fascinating interconnection of the separate elements of the Drake mythology. Drake as a military hero and opponent of Spain is the perfect figure to be recalled at a time of war. The emphasis on Drake as the self-made man is certainly an endorsement of commerce. But on another level the moral qualities that can bring about commercial success are used to emphasize the failings and degeneracy of the present. It is quite obvious that reviving Sir Francis Drake has become a far more complex process than simply presenting an idealized construction of an Elizabethan seafarer to encourage military or nautical endeavours.

Strangely, the ensuing wars of the eighteenth century did not produce the same amount of Drake material. Not even the naval victories of the Seven Years' War[47] – Boscawen's routing of the French off Lagos and Hawke's remarkable victory at Quiberon Bay (both 1759) – could elicit a celebration of Drake as the forerunner of those admirals. True, the standard work on Drake, Burton's *The English Hero*, reappeared with editions in 1750, 1756 and 1769, but there was no surge of interest as there had been in the 1740s and no new work appeared. This lacuna in the production of Drake material deserves careful consideration. The threat of a French invasion in 1759 saw the publication of a pamphlet titled *The History of the Spanish Armada*. The introduction claimed:

> A serious attention to the present critical state of Affairs, wherein France
> so loudly proclaims her preparations for a descent upon Great Britain or
> Ireland, or perhaps, both, will, 'tis presumed, furnish an Apology for this
> Retrospective to the state of England in that memorable year 1588, when
> it was threatened by total destruction by the Spanish Armada.[48]

Kennedy makes the point that after 1758 British naval superiority was such that a French invasion was never a serious possibility. At the time, of course, there was no such certainty. Only after Hawke's victory did the fear of a French invasion recede. Tobias Smollett reflects on the significance of the battle: 'It not only defeated the projected invasion, which had hung menacing so long over the apprehensions of Great Britain; but it gave the finishing blow to the naval power of France, which was totally disabled from undertaking any thing of consequence in the sequel.'[49] And it was the emergence of British naval ascendancy that was initially responsible for the break in the production of Drake material. The tradition of Sir Francis Drake as naval hero was most potent when the nation presented itself as standing alone, besieged by Catholic hordes. The problem for Drake was that the remaining years of the Seven Years' War were far too successful. Victories in the colonies and the massive territorial gains that followed had made Drake's familiar role as the champion of oppressed Protestantism redundant. The new anxiety was what to do with the unprecedented success.

It is curious that although Drake was often appropriated by the cult of commerce and credited with establishing British trade in the East, one of the major works on British commerce from the eighteenth century, Adam Anderson's *An Historical and Chronological Deduction of the Origin of Commerce*[50] (1764), gives the seafarer only a cursory mention. It is even more curious when we learn that '95 per cent of the increase in Britain's commodity exports that occurred in the six decades after the Act of Union was sold to captive and colonial markets outside Europe'.[51] Given that the colonial markets – which Drake had helped to establish – were becoming increasingly important, why is Drake neglected by Anderson? The answer can be found if we shift the emphasis away from Drake's treaty with the Sultan of Ternate and place it firmly on his privateering activities. It is important to remember that during the eighteenth century a distinction began to be drawn between pirates and privateers (licensed pirates who were particularly useful for distressing enemy shipping in times of war). British merchant shipping in the eighteenth century was frequently under threat from pirates, and many of Sir Francis Drake's exploits were piratical – no matter how frequently the notion of lawful reprisal was invoked to justify them. Moreover, the celebration of a commerce raider, particularly after the Seven Years' War when Britain suddenly found itself a major colonial power with many new trade routes to protect, may have seemed rather inappropriate. Let us not forget that Drake's early slaving voyages with Hawkins were breaking a Spanish monopoly; they were diverting the flow of treasure destined for Spain. While it was acceptable for British merchants to continue this practice in the 1740s, by the 1760s roles had been reversed. Britain was now attempting to protect its newly acquired territories, to protect its favourable balance of trade. Drake was continuing to prove a problematic character.

It is notable that the bicentenaries of both the Spanish Armada and Drake's circumnavigation went unmarked. There is no reference to any event in either the *Annual Register* or the *Gentleman's Magazine* in 1777, 1780 or 1788. Of course, we should be careful not to project the present-day preoccupation with historical anniversaries back in time. However, another significant date in the Protestant calendar, the Glorious Revolution of 1688, was celebrated. This suggests that the lack of Drake commemorations – or events in which Drake could be expected to play a major part – was not the result of an eighteenth-century disinclination to mark anniversaries. Nor can it be explained by an apathy towards the events of the Elizabethan era. Linda Colley has drawn attention to the way in which eighteenth-century almanacs recorded important Protestant dates, including Elizabeth's accession and the destruction of the Armada.[52] It is striking that the Glorious Revolution of 1688 took place one hundred years after the Spanish Armada. This perhaps meant that the 1788 celebrations of the Protestant succession were also a tacit commemoration of the earlier victory over Catholicism. David Cressy has suggested another reason for the lack of explicit Armada commemorations: 'it was not institutionalized, there being no "Armada Day", but the horror of the invasion attempt and the miracle of God's judgement were too remarkable to be forgotten'.[53] The continuing fear of invasion (or the outbreak of any war with Spain) had kept the narrative alive. The lack of circumnavigation celebrations is more difficult to account for, but we should remember that the anniversary occurred during the course of the American War of Independence. Drake may have laid claim to Nova Albion but it was hardly appropriate to celebrate the bicentennial of this achievement when Britain was rapidly losing control of North America.

The only condemnation of Drake to be found in eighteenth-century sources appears in George Anderson's *A New Authentic, and Complete Collection of Voyages Round the World* (1784),[54] a work primarily concerned with Captain Cook's voyages to the Pacific. The collection also contains accounts of circumnavigations and voyages of discovery by Anson, Byron, Wallis, Cartaret and, of course, Francis Drake. Anderson's purpose is to expose the 'real' Drake. 'If we have withdrawn the veil, which has hitherto covered his infirmities, it has been in the pursuit of truth: not with a design to detract from his true merit, but to shew his character in the true light.'[55] Anderson draws heavily on the sources used by Hakluyt and particularly the manuscript by Drake's detractor, John Cooke. Unlike Hakluyt, Anderson dwells on the episodes that damage Drake's reputation. For example, in the Spice Islands, 'They also took a young negroe girl, whom Drake or some of his companions having got with child, they afterwards inhumanely set her on shore on an island in their way home, just as she was ready to lie in.'[56] But it is the Doughty incident which provokes Anderson into a wholehearted condemnation:

> The ground of the malevolence with which Drake pursued Doughty under the colour of justice, has hitherto lain concealed from the public eye, but we shall now trace it, step by step, til the fatal period when the unhappy victim was brought to the block, and when Drake by suffering vengeance to triumph over virtue, left an indelible blot upon his character which no panegyric can wipe away.[57]

Anderson moves on to consider the two elements that made up Drake's career: privateer and Royal Naval Commander. He praises Cadiz but not the taking of the

San Felipe: 'The accident which afterwards threw the rich India ship in his way on the return home, did him no honour as a commander.'[58] Although little is known of Anderson, the text suggests that he was a dedicated proponent of the Cult of Commerce. His emphasis is firmly on Drake as a pirate. For Anderson, Drake's piratical activities could not be condoned or glorified when merchant shipping in his own day was open to attack from pirates. Of the Armada Anderson writes: 'Nor did his behaviour in the Channel when, instead of maintaining his post, he pursued the Hans merchant ships, add at all to his reputation as a Vice Admiral.'[59] Here we see Drake vilified because his actions refuse to conform to eighteenth-century notions of naval leadership. Piracy and murder also fitted uncomfortably with the positive or even glamorous new image the navy was beginning to acquire and which formed a central component of imperial ideology. Certainly no one in the sixteenth century commented when the San Felipe was taken, and Howard made no official complaint about Drake's capture of the *Rosario* or even his desertion of his post. Anderson's rhetorical meditation on Drake's career as a privateer is perceptive and worth quoting at length.

> In the current of success, even crimes of the deepest dye are sometimes patronized even by the public. The actions which gave rise to Drake's popularity, are as a courageous leader, with an hundred armed followers, might in these peaceable times easily perform, by entering the cities or towns on the coast of Britain, in the dead of night, cutting the throats of the watch and all who happen to be awake in the streets, breaking open and plundering houses and churches, seizing everything valuable that should fall into their hands, and, before the people could recover their consternation, making their escape with the booty. Were such a company masters of an armed vessel, if there were no ship of force to oppose them, what should hinder their sailing from place to place and … pursuing the like exploits in every town they come to? Would there be anything truly great in this? Or would the man who should undertake and execute an enterprise of such a horrid nature be justly entitled to the name of Hero? If not what shall we say of Drake's nocturnal enterprises on Nombre de Dios?[60]

Here are explicit charges of piracy, unheard since Drake's contemporary enemies condemned him on his return from the circumnavigation. But Anderson goes much further than anyone we have come across so far – Drake is accused of mass murder, looting and general freebooting. By adopting a perspective that runs against what the evidence suggests was the standard view of Drake in the eighteenth century, Anderson is able to strip away the exotic, adventurous aspect of Drake's South American privateering. Anderson's was a lone voice in the eighteenth century, and he did not succeed in promulgating a new version of Drake, in large part because events ensured that Sir Francis's construction was manoeuvred in a new direction. Those events were the wars with Revolutionary and Napoleonic France.

Notes

[1] Thomas Lediard, *The Naval History of England, In all its Branches from the Norman Conquest in the Year 1066 to the Conclusion of 1734* (London, 1735), preliminary leaf.

[2] The Nine Years' War (or War of the League of Augsburg) was the result of Louis XIV's invasion of the Rhineland in 1688. The underlying motivation was the struggle between the rival Habsburg and Bourbon dynasties over the balance of power in Europe. By appropriating the Rhineland, Louis was strengthening his claim to the Spanish throne in anticipation of the death of the Habsburg ruler, Charles II of Spain. It was partly Louis XIV's aggression that prompted William of Orange to sail for England. Austria, Bavaria, Saxony and, of course, England, rapidly formed the Grand Alliance with the aim of limiting Bourbon power.

[3] Linda Colley, *Britons: Forging the Nation 1707–1837* (1992; London, 1996), 24.

[4] John Sadler, 'Loyalty, Attended with Great News from Drake's and Raleigh's Ghosts', in *The Harleian Miscellany*, 12 vols (London, 1810), vol. 11, 32–9.

[5] Sadler, 32.

[6] Andrew Marvell, 'Bermudas', in Alexander Grosart, ed., *The Complete Works of Andrew Marvell*, 4 vols (1872; New York, 1966), vol. 1, 82–3.

[7] Colley, 83.

[8] Colley, 83.

[9] An accompanying note in the *Harleian Miscellany* explains (erroneously) that James I was poisoned by the Duke of Buckingham.

[10] Daniel Defoe, *A New Voyage Around the World, by a Course Never Sailed Before*, 1725, in *The Novels and Miscellaneous Works of Daniel Defoe*, 7 vols. (London, 1910–3), vol. 6, 191–459.

[11] Defoe, 193.

[12] Defoe, 204.

[13] Anna Eliza Bray, *The Borders of the Tamar and Tavy*, 2 vols (London, 1874), vol. 2, 30. Reprint of *A Description of the Part of Devonshire Bordering on the Tamar and Tavy*, 1836.

[14] The Seven Years' War (1756–63) was one episode in the eighteenth-century struggle between Britain and France. It was fought, on Britain's part, largely in order to win control of North America and India.

[15] See Adam Smith, *An Inquiry into the Nature and Causes of the Wealth of Nations*, 1776, ed. R. H. Campbell, A. S. Skinner and W. B. Todd, 2 vols (Oxford, 1979).

[16] Colley, 61.

[17] Quoted in Colley, 70. Lediard uses a slightly varied version of the speech in the opening pages of *The Naval History of England*.

[18] John Sinclair, *Thoughts on the Naval Strength of the British Empire* (London, 1782), 24.

[19] William Monson, *Naval Tracts*, in Awnsham Churchill, *A Collection of Voyages and Travels*, 8 vols (London, 1704), vol. 3, 154–560.

[20] Monson, 169.

[21] Monson, 174.

[22] John Campbell, *The Lives of the British Admirals, Containing a New and Accurate Naval History From the Earliest Periods*, 4 vols (1742; London, 1779).

[23] Campbell, vol. 1, 428.

[24] Campbell, vol. 1, 352.

[25] 'The Life of Admiral Blake', *Gentleman's Magazine*, vol. 10 (1740), 307.

[26] Gerald Jordan and Nicholas Rogers, 'Admirals as Heroes: Patriotism and Liberty in Hanoverian England', *Journal of British Studies*, vol. 28 (1989), 205.

[27] Dictionary of National Biography.

[28] 'On Admiral Vernon's Success in America', *Gentleman's* Magazine, vol. 11 (1741), 274.

[29] Thomas Birch, *The Heads and Characters of Illustrious Persons of Great Britain, with the Portraits Engraved by Mr. Houbraken and Mr. Vertue*, 2 vols (London, 1743).

[30] The image appears in vol. 2, facing page 176.

[31] For a detailed analysis of Gothic history, see Chris Brooks, *The Gothic Revival* (London, 1999), 38–8.

[32] James Thomson, *The Seasons: A Poem*, in J. Logie Robertson, ed., *The Complete Poetical Works of James Thomson* (London, 1963), 52.

[33] James Thomson, *Britannia: A Poem*, in Robertson, ed., 471–80.

[34] George Clarke, 'Grecian Taste and Gothic Virtue: Lord Cobham's Gardening Programme and its Iconography', *Apollo*, vol. 97 (1973), 568.

[35] William Gilpin, *A Dialogue upon the Gardens of the Right Honourable the Lord Viscount Cobham at Stowe*, 1748, in John Dixon Hunt, ed., *The Gardens at Stowe* (London, 1982), 28–9.

[36] Clarke, 570.

[37] Samuel Johnson, 'The Life of Admiral Drake', *Gentleman's Magazine*, vol. 10 (1740), 352, 389–96, 443–7, 509–15, 600–3; vol. 11 (1741), 38–44.

[38] Johnson, 'Admiral Drake', 352.

[39] Johnson, 'Admiral Drake', 352.

[40] Johnson, 'Admiral Drake', 389.

[41] Johnson, 'Admiral Drake', 444.

[42] Johnson, 'Admiral Drake', 447.

[43] Samuel Johnson, 'London: A Poem', in J. Fleeman, ed., *Samuel Johnson: The Complete English Poems* (London, 1971), 61–8.

[44] Colley, 177.

[45] Joseph M. Levine, *The Battle of the Books: History and Literature in the Augustan Age* (Ithaca, NY, 1991), 1.

[46] Quoted in Thomas Woodman, *A Preface to Samuel Johnson* (London, 1993), 52.

[47] In 1759 Admiral Hawke had pursued the French fleet into Quiberon Bay and inflicted severe damage; the victory was all the more stunning because it was achieved during a gale. In the same year Boscawen had routed a French fleet off Lagos, Portugal.

[48] Anon., *The History of the Spanish Armada* (London, 1759), unpaginated.

[49] Tobias Smollett, *The History of England*, 5 vols (1757; London, 1827), vol. 3, 445.

[50] Adam Anderson, *An Historical and Chronological Deduction of the Origin of Commerce*, 4 vols (London, 1787), vol. 2, 149–50.

[51] Colley, 74.

[52] Colley, 22.

[53] David Cressy, *Bonfires and Bells: National Memory and the Protestant Calendar in Elizabethan and Stuart England* (London, 1989), 120.

[54] George Anderson, *A New Authentic, and Complete Collection of Voyages Round the World* (London, 1784). Anderson is generally accepted as the author of the work, but as Gregory Robinson has noted, the title page makes reference to 'The editors'. See Gregory Robinson, 'A Forgotten Life of Sir Francis Drake', *Mariner's Mirror*, vol. 7, no. 1 (1921), 10–18.

[55] Anderson, *Collection of Voyages*, 397.

[56] Anderson, *Collection of Voyages*, 389.

[57] Anderson, *Collection of Voyages*, 380.

[58] Anderson, *Collection of Voyages*, 398.

[59] Anderson, *Collection of Voyages*, 398.

[60] Anderson, *Collection of Voyages*, 397.

CHAPTER FOUR

'Homage to Britannia'

Here are preserved a number of family portraits,
and the sword and buckler of Sir Francis Drake; in the other
apartments are the drum used by that commander in his warlike
expeditions and the folio black-letter bible which had been his
companion in the voyage round the world.
(Samuel Rowe, *The Panorama of Plymouth*, 1824)[1]

T he wars with Revolutionary and Napoleonic France are a crucial period
when charting the construction of Sir Francis Drake. Between the years
1793 and 1815 (and in the following decade) very little material appeared
that was concerned directly with Drake. This does not mean that Sir Francis was
on the verge of disappearing into obscurity – enough evidence exists to prove that
knowledge of his exploits was still in circulation – but reproduction of the Drake
narratives in printed form certainly seems to have slowed. In the previous chapter
I suggested that the tradition of Drake as a naval hero was at its most potent when
the nation regarded itself as standing alone against the foreign – and usually
Catholic –aggressor. Surely, then, Sir Francis was the ideal figure to stir patriotic
feelings during the protracted wars with France. How are we to account for the
scarcity of material recalling his deeds? Firstly, there was the matter of the maritime
present. As the war with France progressed the list of British naval victories began
to lengthen. Among them were Howe's 'Glorious 1st of June' (1794), when seven
French ships escorting a grain convoy were captured or destroyed, Duncan's capture
of eleven Dutch ships at the Battle of Camperdown and Jervis's engagement and
capture of enemy vessels off Cape St Vincent (both 1797). This series of victories
was unparalleled in British naval history but it did not lead to unqualified
celebration. The victories posed ideological problems that were not resolved until
Napoleon's overthrow of the Directory in 1799.[2] Before this point they could be
portrayed as attacks on new found French liberty by reformers or those with
Republican sympathies. 'But as Napoleon's territorial ambitions became clearer,
and as many radicals and reformers became increasingly disillusioned with the
course of the Revolution, naval victories became less politically contentious.'[3]
Nevertheless, the sea-battles of the 1790s diverted attention from the naval past and
focused it very firmly on the present.

A new commander had also emerged who would rapidly become one of the most celebrated naval figures of all time. Horatio Nelson's victories at the Battle of the Nile (1798), Copenhagen (1801) and Trafalgar (1805) were remarkable for their daring and, more importantly, they were immediate.[4] A glance at the *Gentleman's Magazine* in the months following each of these engagements reveals pages of poems celebrating the new hero. Here was a modern admiral whose actions eclipsed even Drake's. No one could doubt Drake's determination or his navigational skill, but his record as a Royal Navy commander was far from flawless. At the time, the West Indian raids were viewed as a failure – the anticipated treasure was not captured – Cadiz was a success, but deserting his post to intercept the *Rosario* during the Armada conflict and his failure to meet Norris at Lisbon during the Portugal expedition were hardly moments of great naval endeavour. Nelson, in contrast, seemed incapable of anything but success. Moreover, he secured heroic status by dying at the very moment of his greatest glory – something that Drake had failed to achieve. Dying of dysentery on an unsuccessful treasure-raiding voyage was hardly comparable. Nelson as a naval hero was less problematic than Drake in other ways. There were no Thomas Doughtys in his cupboard to blight his reputation. If occasionally his actions bordered on the insubordinate – and if his private life was frequently tainted by scandal – Admiral Nelson did not need defending from charges of piracy like his Elizabethan counterpart.[5] Significantly, there were no attempts to construct the new hero as a successor to Drake as there had been when Vernon was at the height of his popularity in the 1740s. (As we will see, the construction of Nelson as a reincarnation of Drake did not appear until late in the nineteenth century.)

The immediacy of Nelson's victories (and those of the other commanders) clearly drew attention from the naval conflicts of the past. But there is a further and very significant reason for the neglect of Drake. This can be found by looking at the military conflicts during which Drake as an individual inspirational figure was 'revived'. It soon becomes apparent that (with, perhaps, the exception of the Nine Years' War) these conflicts are united by a common factor: the absence of any real invasion threat. That is not to say that Britain did not portray itself as fighting for its very survival – we have seen how the War of Jenkins's Ear was presented as a further episode in the continuing struggle against Spain and Roman domination. Ideologically motivated interpretations of conflicts helped secure popular support for what were usually trade wars. Drake, then, was primarily revived when Britain was aggressively seeking out or attempting to secure commercial opportunities. In these conflicts military action usually took place well away from British shores (the Anglo-Dutch wars of the 1650s are the major exception but in this instance neither side contemplated invasion).

However, when the spectre of invasion loomed – as was the case in 1759 during the Seven Years' War – inspiration was found not in Drake himself but in the story of the Spanish Armada. Although a significant combatant in the Armada conflicts, Drake, at this date, was still only one element of the larger Armada narrative. This narrative performed a dual function during the wars with France. On one level it provided a historical precedent at a time when invasion fears were intense: what had been done before could be done again, and foreign aggressors could be sent packing. On another, it was a means of countering the allure of Revolutionary doctrine. We should be aware that mass loyalty – particularly during the war with revolutionary France – could not be taken for granted. Roger Wells has drawn attention to the extent of popular protests during this period. 'Which historian', he questions, 'dares to assume that the bulk of the masses would have rallied to the government, or obeyed the dictates of the local representatives of the establishment?'[6] Food riots were widespread and, in 1797, the navy was faced with mutinies at Portsmouth, Yarmouth and the Nore. The governing elite came under attack from radical reformers such as Thomas Paine and William Godwin. Paine's famous *Rights of Man* (1791) championed the political doctrine of the French Revolutionaries. These ideas were widely disseminated among the working classes, particularly the literate upper artisanate. Paine's attack on the character of the aristocracy in France (and in general) was very powerful.

> The more aristocracy appeared, the more it was despised; there was a
> visible imbecility and want of intelligence in the majority, a sort of je ne
> sais quoi, that while affected to be more than citizen, was less than man. It
> lost ground from contempt more than hatred; and was rather jeered as an
> ass, than dreaded as a lion.[7]

Portraying the landed interest as largely stupid and wholly useless was devastatingly effective. Many other works followed the same model. 'Such analyses were damaging not because they were correct in detail (they were not) but because they treated the landed interest as a separate class parasitic on the nation, rather than part of the nation and its natural leaders.'[8] Given the potential for even greater insurrection or even full scale revolution, recalling the Spanish Armada – harnessing the potent fear of invasion – was one means of attempting to secure loyalty.

Sir Francis Drake, of course, played an important part in the Channel engagements but the cultural products from this time do not generally elevate him above the other English commanders. However, divine intervention in England's fate – the reassurance of having a benign deity on one's side – continued to be a familiar motif when recalling the Armada. A copy of a sermon preached at St Stephen's, Walbrook, on 19 October 1803, the day appointed for a national fast which aimed at stirring English patriotism and resolve, was bound along with an account of the Armada.[9] When Benjamin West exhibited an Armada subject at the Royal Academy in 1794, the year following the commencement of hostilities, it depicted *Queen Elizabeth Going in Procession to St. Paul's After the Destruction of the Spanish Armada*. Of course, in 1794 the threat was not a Catholic one as it had been in 1588; the French Revolutionaries presented an even more alarming prospect: an atheist enemy. English anti-revolutionary invective was keen to dwell on this theme. In 1790 Burke condemned the 'spirit of atheistical fanaticism' that he believed was stalking the streets of Paris.[10]

Although no special role was assigned to Drake by 'high' culture, it is extremely likely that the tradition of Drake as Armada victor continued in popular culture.

Evidence for this assertion can be located in the sea-songs of the 'Ocean Bard', Charles Dibdin. Perhaps this is not altogether surprising when we recall that evidence for Drake's enhanced role in the defeat of the Armada first appears in popular ballads of the sixteenth century. The eighteenth-century songs may be seen as perpetuating a long tradition. Dibdin's ballads reflect contemporary pride in the Royal Navy and present an idealized and alluring version of life aboard the eighteenth-century men o'war. Indeed, it was often claimed that Dibdin had recruited more men into the Royal Navy than all the press gangs combined. When we consider that the navy expanded from 16,000 men in 1789 to 140,000 by 1812 we realize the importance of Dibdin's brand of patriotic propaganda.[11] A ballad called 'Naval Victories'[12] from the one-man entertainment *Tom Wilkins*, first performed in 1799, celebrates British naval victories through the ages culminating in the Battle of the Nile. The spirited first stanza conjoins Drake's famous metaphor for the destruction of Philip's invasion fleet at Cadiz in 1587 ('singeing the king of Spain's beard') with defeat of the Armada.

> *Queen Elizabeth, bless the old girl, was plac'd ready,*
> *If they landed, to shew 'em some true English sport;*
> *But their whiskers were sing'd by bold Drake, brave and steady,*
> *Just to save them a licking at Tilbury-fort.* (5–8)

Dibdin's son, John, had also ridiculed the threat of invasion in song. One song, 'This Snug Little Island',[13] from his musical farce *The British Raft* (1797) soon became particularly popular. In it John Dibdin uses a modified version of Gothic history to engage in the process known as Denying the Conquest. In its strictest sense this means denying that the Norman Conquest put an end to Anglo-Saxon polity. In this instance, however, Dibdin denies the act of *military* conquest. 'But party-deceit help'd the Normans to beat;/ Of traitors they managed to buy land' (25–6). The reference to 'party-deceit' is very telling in the context of the 1790s. During this period – when radical parliamentarians, notably Charles Fox, were sympathetic to France – party (or factional) politics were frequently perceived as subsuming national interests beneath party advancement. Of course, it is ridiculous to project party politics back to 1066, but Dibdin is not concerned with historical accuracy. The Norman Conquest becomes the terrible result of putting party before country. In contrast, the Spanish Armada gives Dibdin the opportunity to sing of an unsuccessful invasion attempt. He merrily puns:

> *These proud puff'd-up cakes thought to make ducks and drakes*
> *Of our wealth; but they hardly could spy land,*
> *When our Drake had the luck to make their pride duck*
> *And stoop to the lads of the island.* (41–4)

In dealing with past conflicts and naval actions the two ballads mentioned above are very much the exception – most songs by both Dibdins are concerned with the navy of the late eighteenth century. This is quite understandable given the dominance of the Royal Navy around which a whole mythology of invincibility developed. This was the age of Britain's wooden walls, the men o'war manned by Jolly Jack Tars – honest seamen who formed the subject of many of the Dibdins' songs. Although as I suggested above, the naval present was seen as surpassing Britain's maritime past, former successes had not been forgotten entirely. As the ballad 'Naval Victories' demonstrates, current naval successes and attendant pride in the Royal Navy engendered an interest in past victories. It was not long before plans for a monument to British naval exploits were mooted. The intended monument, a pillar or obelisk, was to be funded by public subscription, but although the project was discussed for over a decade, no commemorative piece was ever built.

Nevertheless, such a memorial can also be viewed as a product of what Linda Colley has called the 'cult of heroism'[14] that developed particularly after the War of American Independence. As we have seen, during the final quarter of the eighteenth century and the first quarter of the nineteenth, the ruling elite found themselves under enormous pressures. Colley argues that if proof was needed that landed interests had failed in their role as leaders, it was provided by the war in North America. The defeated British forces had been led predominantly by patrician commanders: Gage, Cornwallis and Burgoyne. Following the war, the elite were compelled to 'convince themselves as well as others that they had indeed done their duty to Great Britain, and done it well'.[15] The result was the cult of heroism or the desire to undertake military service for the nation's benefit coupled with the conspicuous display of signs of having performed that duty.

The naval monument was an obvious way of drawing attention to the victories achieved by the Royal Navy under the command of admirals who, for the most part, were from major landowning families. This signifier of national service was a means of countering the attacks of Thomas Paine, which portrayed the landed classes as a parasitic group. Rather ironically, the most famous and most successful commanders – Nelson and Drake – were not from the landed classes. This seemed to support Paine's contention but could be manoeuvred to reinforce the elite position by suggesting that there was no bar to reaching the upper echelons of society. However, as we know, Drake had detractors at Court who resented his sudden rise from obscurity. Admiral Nelson, a rector's son, was from a rather more conventional background for a naval officer – although it was less usual for someone from his social rank to rise to the highest levels – but his relations with the establishment were not always easy. He resented the baronetcy (the lowest rank of nobility) he received after the Battle of the Nile, believing that his services had warranted much more.

The Cornish portrait painter John Opie provided by far the grandest design for a monument. In a letter subsequently published in a volume titled *Lectures on Painting Delivered at the Royal Academy of Arts*,[16] Opie sets out his vision for a 'public memorial of the naval glory of Great Britain'.[17] Opie's proposal was not for a pillar or tower but for a building based on the Pantheon at Rome, which would be erected in London. Instead of being dedicated to all the gods Opie's temple is dedicated to naval figures who were being elevated to a god-like eminence. An internal circle would be divided into sections depicting dramatic scenes from the nation's naval history. Between each scene would be a space for a life-size statue of the seafaring heroes whose actions had been illustrated. Beneath the principal paintings would be other images connected to the role of the navy in commerce, colonization and discovery. The centre-piece of the building is very revealing in terms of how the Royal Navy was perceived at this time.

> In the centre of the building, under the dome, there be placed a colossal group in marble, representing Neptune doing homage to Britannia; and at the head of the room a statue of his present majesty, George III, in whose reign the British naval power has reached a point of exaltation, which seems to preclude the possibility of it being carried much higher by our successors.[18]

That the sea-god should stoop to Britannia is certainly a measure of the pride and complacency surrounding the navy – perhaps with good reason. British naval ascendancy after Trafalgar meant that a French invasion was never a serious possibility. Villeneuve could not provide the naval cover necessary for the transportation of an army. But what of Drake? Opie meditates on the pleasures that the 'Pantheon' will provide.

> How flattering to the imagination to anticipate the pleasure of walking round such an edifice, and surveying the different subjects depicted on its walls! Then to turn behold the statues and portraits to the enterprising commanders and leaders in the actions and expeditions recorded, and compare their different countenances; here a Drake and an Anson! There a Blake, a Hawke, a Boscawen and a Cook.[19]

It would obviously be an oversimplification (and grossly inaccurate) to claim that the Anglo-French conflict was a war in defence of rank and property rather than a trade war and that this accounts for the lack of Drake material. It is true that up until 1803 there existed a very real invasion threat, which saw a recourse to Armada narratives. This circumvented the need for an ideologically constructed version of the conflict. But what began as a European war rapidly spread to the colonies, and the reasons for this are not hard to find. The primary motives were strategic. Half of France's overseas trade was with the West Indies. Capturing Caribbean territories would strangle French commerce and also provide a market for British exports. Economically, the Caribbean was very important to Britain. 'The West Indies, which provided four fifths of the income from Britain's overseas investments … were now the concern of Lancashire cotton manufacturers as well as sugar planters, shippers and financiers.'[20] These economic interests needed protection from foreign aggressions; it was important to secure foreign harbours to protect British trade routes and wipe out enemy commerce raiders. It was during the French wars that the foundations of the Second British Empire were laid. Gradually and without spectacular victories Britain accumulated an impressive list of overseas possessions. Further gains were made in the east: Ceylon (Sri Lanka) was taken from the Dutch and greater areas of India came under British rule. Britain became the dominant colonial power in the West Indies and pressed ahead with colonial enterprises in Australia.

In the later years of the war with Napoleonic France a certain amount of material concerned with Drake's voyages did appear. By this time the actual invasion threat had receded – the preconditions for the revival of Drake had been met. However, we do not find Drake constructed as the quintessential Protestant hero as he had been formerly; the cultural products are muted in tone and make their concern with colonization clear. Focus is laid on Drake's discoveries rather than his military endeavours. Between 1807 and 1814 John Pinkerton, a Scots historian, published the seventeen-volume *A General Collection of the Best and Most Interesting Voyages in all Parts of the World*.[21] This is certainly the product of a renewed interest in colonization. Indeed, Pinkerton writes, 'I hope that this example will fully shew the use and value of good collections of voyages, because it is impossible to foresee all the advantages that may arise from any discovery or settlement at once.'[22] Unsurprisingly, concentration is upon the circumnavigation. Pinkerton employs long quotations from Francis Fletcher's narrative but is very critical of his account of the voyage along the west coast of America in search of the North West Passage. This, according to Pinkerton, 'was certainly a wise and great undertaking, and a prodigious improvement upon the design of his voyage'.[23] The design was, of course, to raid Spanish treasure and shipping in the Pacific. Pinkerton's grievance is that Fletcher's narrative – which mentions that the passage probably does not exist – discourages all hope of finding the elusive seaway. His concern with the North West Passage is explained in relation to Nova Albion. Having advanced Britain's strong claims on the territory which was then in Spanish hands – it was voluntarily surrendered by natives – Pinkerton gets around to the reason for its importance.

> The country, too, if we may depend upon what Sir Francis Drake or his chaplain says, may appear worth the seeking and keeping, since they assert that the land is so rich in gold and silver that upon the slightest turning it up with a spade or pick-ax, those rich metals plainly appear mixed in the mould.[24]

The North West Passage, if it could be found, would facilitate a relatively quick voyage back to Britain for vessels laden with gold.

A substantial life of Drake can be found in a volume entitled *Portraits of Illustrious Personages of Great Britain, Engraved from Authentic Pictures in the Galleries of the Nobility, and the Public Collections of the Country*[25] published in 1821. The portraits were engraved by Henry Meyer and accompanied by 'Biographical Memoirs' by Edmund Lodge. The volume is an example of the way in which the interests of the elite could be manoeuvred to give the appearance of benefiting the whole nation. Not only does *Portraits of Illustrious Personages* hold up members of the aristocracy (or even royalty) as individuals who have performed great services for their country, it also implies that their portraits are a national asset. The vast majority of art at this time was held in private collections – plans for a national gallery were not submitted until 1824. But the act of engraving and publishing the portraits serves to transform the images – and the men they represent – into the property of the nation: they really are the illustrious personages of (or belonging to) Great Britain.

Paradoxically, the title foregrounds private ownership in an effort to illustrate the collectors' service to the nation by permitting 'access' to their treasures.

The image of Sir Francis Drake[26] was supposedly made from an original painting in the collection of the Marquis of Lothian at Newbattle Abbey. Meyer's work is the first recorded engraving of the painting and it is difficult to ascertain whether the portrait was done from life. John Sugden speculates, 'It may be an authentic likeness. Certainly it represents Drake, it is one of the few portraits to display the wart on the left side of the admiral's nose.'[27] However, the silk cummerbund that Drake wears and the lack of any coat of arms or personal emblem suggests that the portrait was produced posthumously in the seventeenth century.

Edmund Lodge's accompanying biography is marked by a desire to work from reliable sources. This reflects a very contemporary trend in the writing of history, an approach that was pioneered by the historian Henry Hallam. Writing during the first decades of the nineteenth century Hallam's technique was to construct major historical narratives through the careful study of original sources. This went far beyond mere antiquarianism. For Lodge only accuracy can generate a narrative of interest. He writes, 'The narrative of a life for which the materials of which no better source could exist than the journal and log-book of a naval commander, and in the absence too of those very authorities, may seem to promise very little of general interest.'[28] Yet Drake is an exception. Although there are no carefully kept log-books from which to work, this has not diminished Drake's allure. Lodge provides evidence for Drake's continuing popularity; this contradicts the assumption that the lack of printed material represents a decline in knowledge of Drake's exploits.

> So dear is that character to Englishmen that they will dwell with delight on the insulated detail of his expeditions, on discoveries insignificant in the sight of modern navigations, and on tactics which have become obsolete; on motives which have long ceased to actuate our national policy, and on the results of the benefit of which we are no longer sensible.[29]

The narrative informs us that after encompassing the globe, Drake wanted to perform further privateering services but 'the rank ... to which his fame and immense wealth had now raised him in society forbade the further prosecution of that order of enterprise from which he had derived them'.[30] This does not take account of the fact that the 'Descent on the Indies' and the final voyage of 1595/6 were treasure-raiding enterprises on a massive scale. Drake's activities are, of course, interpreted from a very contemporary position – it would not do for a modern knight to wage such a private war. Similarly Drake's capture of the richly laden carrack on his return from the Cadiz raid is condemned as an 'indiscretion'. Obviously the action is judged by the standards of the Royal Navy of the 1820s. The cult of heroism is also projected back in time. After the completion of the Nombre de Dios raid Drake 'now gave way to a laudable ambition to shine in public service ... and fitted, at his own expense three frigates with which he sailed to Ireland'.[31]

An earlier work that concerned itself with Drake's deeds was Andrew Kippis's *Biographia Britannica: or, The Lives of the Most Eminent Persons who have Flourished in Great Britain and Ireland*.[32] This was first published in 1745 under the supervision of John Campbell, author of *The Lives of the British Admirals*. Kippis was employed by the booksellers to complete the second edition, which was published in five volumes between 1778 and 1793. The final volume contains a life of Sir Francis Drake, which comprises Campbell's biography from *The Lives of the British Admirals* with additional material by Kippis. The narrative moves through the familiar elements that make up Drake's career, including the well-rehearsed arguments that support or condemn his privateering. With a statement that has an extra resonance when we consider the emergence of the cult of heroism, Kippis accounts for the lack of any Drake memorial. 'It was not the custom in those times to set up cenotaphs, at least for private persons, otherwise one might have expected some monument should have been erected to the memory of Sir Francis Drake.'[33] The *Golden Hinde*, the only memorial to Drake, had long since rotted away.

★

With travel in Europe restricted by the wars with France (France, of course, had been the cultural centre for the British elite – polite society mimicked French fashion), the respectable tourist turned his attention to the remoter parts of Britain, its scenery – both natural and industrial – its monuments and its stately homes. Devon was one county where tourism increased. It was during the late eighteenth century that the coastal villages of Teignmouth and Torquay became popular as fashionable resorts – with their mild climate they provided a domestic version of the French Riviera. But there were more ideologically motivated reasons for exploring the less well-known quarters of the nation. From the 1780s antiquarians began to look closely at Britain's Gothic architecture. Medieval buildings and remains across the country became the focus for serious attention. This was partly owing to the curtailment of the Classical Grand Tour but also the result of a patriotic desire to mobilize Britain's Gothic heritage against the tyranny of Napoleonic Europe. 'Generally and specifically, the components of gothic's semantic – Britishness, martial prowess, free institutions, constitutional monarch, national liberty – could all be wheeled out to do ideological battle with France.'[34] This interest was not confined to antiquarians. In 1797 the draughtsman John Carter, who was responsible for producing many images of Britain's Gothic architecture, wrote that he knew 'of no way that can so well aid the general cause, as to stimulate my countrymen to think well of their own national memorials'.[35]

With this knowledge we can begin to understand the full significance of a small section towards the end of Kippis's otherwise standard biography of Drake. This lists various Drake artefacts found at Buckland Abbey. Here we find evidence that the abbey – a converted medieval monastery – had been or could be visited. Its associations with the English hero could only add to Buckland's ideological armoury. Like the *Golden Hinde* many years before, relics of Sir Francis Drake – notably his drum – would come to play an important part in the cultural construction of Drake. This cult of secular relics reached its zenith during the late nineteenth century but Kippis's *Biographia Britannica* shows its earlier emergence. Here is further evidence of the secularization of Catholic practices that began with the Reformation and saw Drake, the Protestant hero, manoeuvred so as to fill the void left by the abolished saints. Kippis informs the reader that in 1750 Sir Francis Henry Drake (fifth baronet) claimed he possessed a bible that had accompanied Drake on the circumnavigation. Other material mentioned includes a staff from the *Golden Hinde* (probably the reference is to a cross-staff) and a collection of sixteenth-century coins, one depicting a Drake or dove. It had long been an accepted practice for the owners of country houses to admit genteel tourists to their homes as private guests. 'The aristocracy have always exercised a lure for the other members of society, and their wealth, taste and material possessions have aroused an interest which is by no-means confined to the mid-twentieth century.'[36] This genteel tourism allowed the nobility to show off their collections of art or other treasures. Indeed, owners often produced catalogues of their collections that were sold to visitors. Tourism also provided another opportunity for the dominant classes to demonstrate their social position.

> To appreciate 'the remotest parts of Britain', as the guidebooks called
> them, in the proper manner, as to appreciate Rome, or Florence, or Paris,
> one needed to have acquired a fashionable, aesthetic education: a
> knowledge of Edmund Burke's theory of the sublime, a properly
> developed understanding of the picturesque.[37]

But there were no great collections of art at Buckland and nothing to test one's knowledge of the sublime. Indeed, tourism to Buckland Abbey before the wars with France was rare. Visitors were drawn to nearby Cotehele in the Tamar valley – George III had visited in 1789 – and the fashionable Mount Edgcumbe, commandingly positioned above Plymouth Sound. We should also be aware that in 1732, Sir Francis Drake (fourth baronet) inherited Nutwell Court near Lympstone in East Devon. After his death in 1740 his son chose to spend his time at Nutwell rather than at Buckland, and the abbey was neglected until substantial alterations were made in the 1770s. Visitors hoping to enjoy the company of the baronet would have to travel to the east of the county. However, the abbey received one notable visitor earlier in the century. The early part of the eighteenth century had witnessed a surge of interest in antiquities fostered largely by the efforts of William Stukeley. It was Stukeley's companion Samuel Buck who engraved the abbey in 1734. The image was published in *Buck's Antiquities* along with 423 other abbeys, castles and monasteries. Ivied ruins continued to exert a powerful fascination throughout the century and the plots of countless gothic novels unravelled amid the decay of medieval buildings.

> Wandering amid the ruins, the melancholy man's reflections on life's
> brevity could encompass the universal transience that breathed in the
> crumbling walls of monastery or castle. A sentimental overview of

mortality, a pious sense of the vanity of human wishes, gave piquancy to the knowledge that one belonged to a class that owned, built or visited ruins and had the leisure necessary for their proper contemplation.[38]

However, such an evocative ruin was not to be found at Buckland Abbey. Henry Carrington records his disappointment with Buckland in *The Plymouth and Devonport Guide* published in 1828:

> Let not the lover of grey antiquity indulge in the idea of beholding a crumbling ruin, vast, desolate, deserted, such as his imagination, in its wayward moments, has been apt to shadow forth! He must not expect to find the tottering pomp of Gothic arches, – light airy pillars entwisted by the wanton woodbine and hallowed by the wild rose blossoms – long silent aisles, full of the beauty of the graceful ash ... he who anticipates this will be cruelly deceived, for Buckland Abbey has been sadly modernized, and is still inhabited.[39]

Almost enough to discourage the most determined traveller! But although the modernized and inhabited abbey was not an obviously Romantic pile, it is possible that the Drake artefacts housed there provided a form of imaginative compensation – Kippis certainly thought them worthy of note. These old objects and their associations with the great seafarer could stimulate the imagination and make the journey to Buckland worthwhile.

Following Kippis, the next mention of Drake artefacts at Buckland appears in George Lipscomb's *Journey into Cornwall, through the Counties of Southampton, Wiltshire, Dorset, Somerset and Devon* (1799). Lipscomb writes that 'The sword of this great man along with an Old Drum, which circuited the world with him, are still preserved in the house.'[40] This is the first record of a drum being kept at Buckland, and Lipscomb's account has been cited frequently by those searching for the origins of the drum myth following the publication of Henry Newbolt's poem 'Drake's Drum' in 1896.[41] We do not know for certain whether the drum was carried on the circumnavigation as Lipscomb asserts. The drum is certainly old enough, although the Drake arms painted on the side date from the seventeenth century.[42] Nor can we know the source of Lipscomb's information. However, it is worth considering that 'Most tourists agreed that servants [who often acted as guides] were both ignorant and insolent, and housekeepers proved ... full of pretentious and wholly unreliable information'.[43] According to Kippis, it was the black-letter Bible at Buckland that had accompanied Drake around the world; it is easy to see how other Drake artefacts could also be credited with the same achievement.

We find the same Drake artefacts listed in Carrington's *Plymouth and Devonport Guide* and Samuel Rowe's *The Panorama of Plymouth: or Tourist's Guide to the Principal Objects of Interest in the Towns and Vicinity of Plymouth, Dock, and Stonehouse*[44] (1821). Other guidebooks focused their attention on Plymouth. Edward Clarke's *A Tour through the South of England, Wales and Part of Ireland made during the Summer of 1791* concentrates on Drake's major non-nautical endeavour:

> This town, till the reign of Queen Elizabeth, suffered great inconvenience
> from the want of fresh water. It is now well supplied by a spring, which
> rises at the distance of seven miles, the water of which was brought here at
> the expense of Sir Francis Drake, who was a native of this place.[45]

None of the tourist guides so far have anything to say about Drake's sea-faring
exploits. The one exception is Rowe's *Panorama of Plymouth*, which introduces an
extremely important theme when considering the cultural construction of Sir
Francis Drake. He writes,

> The access from town will be improved … by a Street … from Royal
> Hotel to the Hoe. This we are assured will be speedily carried into effect,
> and the new street, named Armada Street, to perpetuate the circumstance
> of the Spanish fleet having been brought to Sir Francis Drake, while
> engaged in playing at bowls near this spot.[46]

Much work has been done to trace the origins of the game of bowls, undoubtedly
the best known and most durable Drake myth.[47] The first mention of the game
appears in a piece of English propaganda dating from 1624. The full title of this tract
is *Vox Populi, or Gondomar in the likeness of a Machiavel in a Spanish Parliament. Wherein
are discovered his treacherous and subtle practices to the ruin as well of England as the
Netherlands. Faithfully translated out of the Spanish by a well-wisher to England*. This was
an attempt to stir up anti-Spanish feeling at the time of the Spanish Match. Diego
Gondomar was Spanish ambassador and wielded considerable power in James I's
Court – an influence that generated considerable hostility. It was Gondomar who
had introduced James to the idea of the Match. The tract is purportedly spoken by
the Duke of Braganza in the Spanish Cortes (or legislative assembly).

> Did we not, in 88, carry our business for England so cunningly and
> secretly, as well in that well-dissembled treaty with the English near
> Ostend, as in bringing our navy to their shores while their commanders
> and captains were at Bowls upon the hoe of Plymouth; and had my Lord
> Alonso Guzman, the Duke of Medina Sidonia, had but the resolution
> (but, in truth, his commission was otherwise) he might have surprised
> them as they lay at anchor.[48]

Drake's involvement is not recorded until the eleventh edition of Walter Raleigh's
History of the World published in 1736. This contained a life of Raleigh by William
Oldys inserted as a preface. Oldys assures us

> The captains and commanders were then it seems at bowls upon the Hoe
> of Plymouth; and the tradition goes, that Drake would needs see the game
> up; but was soon prevailed upon to go and play out the rubbers with the
> Spaniards.[49]

Already we can see how interpretations of the game have undergone a subtle shift
of emphasis. For the seventeenth-century pamphlet the bowling is a sign of
weakness – Plymouth could be attacked (if Medina Sidonia had the courage) when

the English commanders were wholly unprepared. In Oldy's work, however, Drake's reluctance to quit the game of bowls is meant to be read as a sign of his supreme confidence – there is no rush, the game can be finished before the Spaniards are beaten. The game has become a signifier of strength. Oldys's reference to a 'tradition' suggests that Drake's game of bowls was already widely disseminated and had been for some time. The street-naming that Rowe reports is certainly evidence that the tradition was taken seriously in Plymouth. That the news of the sighting of the Armada was brought straight to Drake, as Rowe's guidebook suggests, rather than to Lord Howard is no doubt connected to the popular tradition of Drake as Armada victor. This is a further example of the popular elision of all participants except Sir Francis Drake.

The period immediately after the war with Napoleonic France provides the earliest written evidence of the folk-traditions concerning Sir Francis Drake. The product of the Romantic Movement's quest for material in areas usually ignored by 'high' culture, the scholarly interest in folk culture emerged as genuine oral culture was falling into decline. A summary of Drake folk-tales can be found in a review by Robert Southey of a book called *Some Account of the Lives and Writings of Lope Felix de Vega Carpio and Guillen de Castro* by Henry Richard, Lord Holland.[50] There is no record of where Southey heard or read these tales although at least one is mentioned in Southey's *Common Place Book*, a record of material extracted from his wide readings and intended for later use.[51] It is, however, possible that the tales were remembered from when Southey toured Devon with Samuel Taylor Coleridge in the summer of 1799. Coleridge was, of course, a Devonian and was also widely read in sixteenth-century sea stories. These provided some of the sources for the 'Rime of the Ancient Mariner'.[52] In the review Southey concentrates on de Vega's poem *La Dragontea* (1598), which depicts Drake as Draco, the Dragon, who is finally vanquished by imperial Spain. Lope de Vega had sailed with the Armada and his poem displays a fierce hatred of Drake (who, for the Spanish, performed a synecdochic function: Drake was the English fleet) along with a great exaltation at his demise. Southey speculates on the origins of a myth that de Vega incorporates into his poem. The myth contends that Drake had sold his soul to the devil and possessed a ring in which lived a familiar spirit. This myth 'he [may] have heard from some of his shipmates in the Armada, who had themselves heard it when they were prisoners in London'.[53] This, Southey reasons, is highly probable as Drake still had the reputation 'among the vulgar' of being an enchanter.

Southey continues with examples of Drake's supernatural powers. We are assured that 'a wild tradition concerning him is still current in Somerset'.[54] It appears that before departing on the circumnavigation, Drake told his wife that if he did not return within ten years she should assume he was dead and, if the opportunity arose, remarry. Ten years having elapsed with no sign of Drake, his wife accepted a marriage proposal. However, on the way to church a great stone fell from the sky landing on the train of the bride's dress. She claimed that it had been sent from Drake and turned back immediately. Shortly afterwards Drake appeared at her door disguised as a beggar but was soon recognized and the couple were reunited. The stone, Southey continues, was used for a weight on the farm harrow and if removed from the estate, would always mysteriously return.

It would be wrong to think of this story as originating in the activities of Drake. As Southey points out, the hero of a medieval romance called *Guy of Warwick* (which was still circulating in various versions in the eighteenth century) returns from a long absence abroad and, disguised as a beggar, asks alms of his wife. Indeed, the returning hero is a standard narrative pattern frequently found in but not confined to folk-tales[55] – Odysseus returns to find Penelope surrounded by suitors; he disguises himself as a beggar so that he can take his revenge. It is not, in fact, uncommon for historical characters to be absorbed into folk literature and take the place of former heroes who become dated or 'unfashionable'. However, the process by which characters are selected is far from random. Lord Raglan's study of myth, *The Hero*, identifies specific determinants that seem to govern the appropriation of historical figures.

> First the person with whom the myths are to be associated must not be too recent, or the true facts of his career will be remembered, not too remote, or he will have been superseded and forgotten. … Secondly, he must have been famous or notorious in certain definite connections, and his exploits must be such as to afford pegs upon which the myths can be hung.[56]

Clearly Drake's return from the circumnavigation provides the first 'peg' upon which the myth can be hung. But there are other similarities between the romance and the Drake story. Guy is rejected by Felice, his love, because of his social inferiority. He undertakes a number of gallant exploits to prove his worth. Therefore, '[the] immediate attraction of Guy is the foundation of his story in social distinction and the need to demonstrate that disadvantage of birth can be overcome by talent and merit'.[57] Drake, as we know, had risen from humble beginnings to become a prominent courtier and even married into the aristocratic Sydenham family. It is clear that there are sufficient parallels between the two narratives for Drake to replace the fictional Guy: freed from history, Sir Francis can inhabit the world of myth.

A second tradition seems to be contained within the narrative that Southey reproduces, that of stones moving without assistance. This is a relatively common tradition. For example, one stone at Gittisham in east Devon, reputedly an ancient sacrificial site, is said to roll to the local river to cleanse itself of blood. Just why Drake should be connected to such a tradition is unclear, although it is likely that his reputation as an enchanter would allow him to be linked with any phenomenon that was considered vaguely magical. A stone, or rather a cannonball, said to be the one that landed on his wife's wedding dress, is now displayed in Combe Sydenham House in west Somerset. This was the family home of Drake's second wife, Elizabeth Sydenham. It is important to remember that the circumnavigation had taken place during Drake's marriage to Mary Newman, his first wife. Tour guides at the house will still recount a slightly varied version of this tale. Of course, it is extremely unlikely that the cannonball had any connection with Drake at all. We cannot know when the ball came to be regarded as the very stone from the narrative, but the fact that it still is demonstrates the enduring nature of the tale – and Sir Francis Drake's reputation.

It is entirely possible that the tales of Drake as an enchanter had their origins in the circumnavigation. We saw in the previous chapter that Drake was believed to have 'shot the gulf' or crossed from one plane of the earth's surface to the other. It is certainly possible that at some stage after his death this mythical feat came to be regarded as an act of sorcery and Drake magicked into an enchanter. Similarly, Drake's uncanny ability to locate Spanish treasure ships on the open ocean (notably the *Cacafuego*, captured during the course of the voyage around the world) may have suggested, to the superstitious mind, the intervention of magical spirits. Certainly, the Protestant (or heretic) Drake's pact with the devil would seem plausible to his Catholic foes.

Southey then turns his attention to other Drake folk-tales. Instead of paying for Plymouth Leat out of his own fortune, as many historical narratives or tourist guides suggest, another tradition contends that the leat water magically followed his horse's heels as Drake rode into Plymouth. This folk-tale almost certainly originates in the pomp and ceremony that accompanied the opening of the new waterway. One of the earliest published accounts of this occasion appeared in the local journal the *South Devon Monthly Museum* in 1834.

> On the 24th April 1594, it seems the water was brought into town; on which occasion a good procession of the mayor and gownsmen, with music, went out to meet Sir Francis and the water, and ushered them into the town in state; whether the water was dammed back, to keep pace with their worships, or whether their worships galloped along in double quick time, to keep pace with the water, neither record nor tradition hands down to us.[58]

A modern Plymouth historian makes the point that when diverting water into an unlined channel the initial flow must be little more than a trickle to avoid damaging the banks.[59] This seems to undermine the notion that Drake raced into Plymouth at a breakneck speed in an effort to keep up with the rushing waters. Contemporary records show that a considerable sum was spent on this special occasion but, unfortunately, the accounts do not make clear exactly what happened.[60] But if the records do not provide a precise account of the day's events, the folk-tale certainly suggests that Drake accompanied the water on its way into the town. It is also worth noting that the miraculous ability to summon or lead water has long been attributed to saints – one need look no further than the holy wells of Devon and Cornwall to find evidence of this tradition.[61] That in folk culture Drake, too, should possess this power reinforces the notion of Sir Francis as a secular saint.

Southey's review also provides more evidence for the popular cultural construction of Drake as Armada victor.

> He is said to have delivered England from the Spanish Armada, not by his courage and seamanship, but by taking a piece of wood and cutting it in pieces over the side of his own vessel, when every chip became a man of war as it fell into the sea.[62]

Similar traditions are present in different cultures. A version exists in the Greek myth of Cadmus who was advised by the oracle at Delphi to found the city of Thebes. To bring water to the new city Cadmus had to slay a dragon; having done this he sowed the dragon's teeth in the ground, and from these sprang a race of earthborn warriors. The warriors fought among themselves until only five were left – from them the Theban aristocracy was descended. The planting of dragons' teeth is also incorporated into the myth of Jason who, like Drake, was an epic voyager.

The connection between Drake and Jason as seafarers is notable, but the Drake folk-tale probably has its origins in a Northern European version of the myth. The ability to multiply ships (rather than warriors) was also possessed by the Irish sea-god Manannan Mac Ler. This god inhabited the Isle of Man (hence the island's name) and protected it from invasion by 'causing mists to rise and conceal the island, making one man look like a hundred, and throwing small chips of wood into the sea to make them appear like warships'.[63] With the coming of Christianity this power was transferred to St Michael, the patron saint of seafarers.

The comparative absence of written material from the period 1793 to the late 1820s hardly supports Edmund Lodge's assertion that Drake was still a character dear to the English people. But I have tried to show that, far from falling into historical obscurity during these years, Sir Francis was actually undergoing a crucial repositioning. There is a notable shift from a military to a Romantic imperative: the result is a Drake far more populist and anecdotal in construction. Rather than being solely a naval figure, Drake is more broadly positioned across English culture, a process that made possible his emergence as a hero of imperialism in the middle years of the nineteenth century.

Notes

[1] Samuel Rowe, *The Panorama of Plymouth: or, Tourists Guide to the Principal Objects of Interest in the Towns and Vicinity of Plymouth, Dock, and Stonehouse* (Plymouth, 1821), 264.
[2] After the abortive Egyptian campaign of 1798 Napoleon returned to France and overthrew the Directory of Brumaire (the executive power in France between 1795 and 1799). This was replaced by the Consulate, a system of three supposedly equal consuls, which lasted until 1804. In practice, however, Napoleon as First Consul was able to overrule the other two members and act as a dictator.
[3] Gerald Jordan and Nicholas Rogers, 'Admirals as Heroes: Patriotism and Liberty in Hanoverian England', *Journal of British Studies*, vol. 28 (1989), 214.
[4] At the Battles of the Nile and Copenhagen some of Nelson's ships attacked the anchored enemy vessels on the landward side rather than the conventional seaward. From January to October 1805 he followed Villeneuve's fleet across the Atlantic and back before defeating it at Trafalgar. At Cape St Vincent Nelson broke away from the English line to intercept the regrouping enemy ships.
[5] Nelson's very public relationship with Lady Emma Hamilton (and the fact that he brought her and her husband, Sir William, to live with him) caused great scandal in polite circles. At the Battle of Copenhagen Nelson had ignored orders to disengage the Danish fleet, supposedly holding the telescope to his blind eye. At Cape St Vincent he did not wait for orders from Jervis (which may not have come) to attack the regrouping Spanish ships. Although successful on each occasion these were, in effect, acts of insubordination.

[6] Roger Wells, *Insurrection: The British Experience 1795–1803* (Gloucester, 1983), 258.

[7] Thomas Paine, *Rights of Man* (1791; London, 1985), 106.

[8] Linda Colley, *Britons: Forging the Nation 1707–1837* (1992; London, 1996), 162–3.

[9] Anon., *A sermon Preached on October 19th 1803, the day appointed for a National Fast. To which is added an account of the destruction of the Spanish Armada* (London, 1803).

[10] Edmund Burke, *Reflections on the Revolution in France*, 1790, ed. Conor Cruise O' Brien (London, 1976), 262.

[11] Statistics quoted in Colley, 301.

[12] Charles Dibdin, 'Naval Victories', in *The Professional Life of Mr. Dibdin, Written by Himself*, 4 vols (London, 1803), vol. 4, 197–8.

[13] John Dibdin, 'This Snug Little Island', in *Dibdin's Sea Songs* (London, 1841), 228–31.

[14] Colley, 192.

[15] Colley, 192.

[16] John Opie, *Lectures on Painting Delivered at the Royal Academy of Arts with a Letter on the Proposal for a Public Memorial to the Naval Glory of Great Britain* (London, 1809).

[17] Opie, title page.

[18] Opie, 175.

[19] Opie, 175.

[20] Paul M. Kennedy, *The Rise and Fall of British Naval Mastery* (London, 1983), 129.

[21] John Pinkerton, *A General Collection of the Best and Most Interesting Voyages and Travels in all Parts of the World*, 17 vols (London, 1812).

[22] Pinkerton, vol. 12, 173.

[23] Pinkerton, vol. 12, 169.

[24] Pinkerton, vol. 12, 173.

[25] Edmund Lodge, *Portraits of Illustrious Personages of Great Britain, Engraved from Authentic Portraits in the Galleries of the Nobility and the Public Collection of the Country*, 4 vols (London, 1821).

[26] Meyer's engraving faces page 233.

[27] John Sugden, 'Sir Francis Drake: A Note on his Portraiture', *Mariner's Mirror*, vol. 70 (1984), 305–6.

[28] Lodge, vol. 1, 233.

[29] Lodge, vol. 1, 233.

[30] Lodge, vol. 1, 235.

[31] Lodge, vol. 1, 234.

[32] Andrew Kippis, *Biographia Britannica: or, The Lives of the Most Eminent Persons who have Flourished in Great Britain and Ireland*, 5 vols (London, 1778–93), vol. 5, 353.

[33] Kippis, vol. 5, 353.

[34] Chris Brooks, *The Gothic Revival* (London, 1999), 130.

[35] Quoted in Brooks, 134.

[36] Esther Moir, *The Discovery of Britain 1540–1840* (London, 1964), 58.

[37] Colley, 186–7.

[38] Brooks, 111.

[39] Henry Carrington, *The Plymouth and Devonport Guide with Sketches of the Surrounding Scenery* (London, 1828), 133–4.

[40] George Lipscomb, *A Journey into Cornwall through the Counties of Southampton, Wiltshire, Dorset, Somerset and Devon* (Warwick, 1799), 313.

[41] See Particularly E. M. R. Ditmas, *The Legend of Drake's Drum* (Guernsey, 1973).

[42] The best source of information on the age of the drum is Cynthia Gaskell Brown, *The Battle's Sound: Drake's Drum and the Drake Flags* (Tiverton, 1996).

[43] Moir, 60.

[44] Samuel Rowe, *The Panorama of Plymouth: or, Tourists Guide to the Principal Objects of Interest in the Town and Vicinity of Plymouth, Dock and Stonehouse* (Plymouth, 1821), 244.

[45] Edward Clarke, *A Tour Through the South of England, Wales and Part of Ireland made during the Summer of 1791* (London, 1793), 59.

[46] Rowe, 74.

[47] See particularly Christopher Lloyd, 'Drake's Game of Bowls', *Mariner's Mirror*, vol. 39 (1953), 144–5.

[48] Reprinted in Lloyd, 145.

[49] William Oldys, Preface, *The History of the World in Five Books,* by Walter Raleigh (London, 1736), xliv.

[50] Robert Southey, 'Some Account of the Lives and Writings of Lope Felix de Vega Carpio, and Guillen de Castro, by Henry Richard, Lord Holland', *Quarterly Review*, vol. 18 (1817–18), 1–46.

[51] Robert Southey, *Common Place Book*, 4 vols (London, 1851) vol. 4, 424.

[52] For a detailed analysis of Coleridge's sources, see John Livingston Lowes, *The Road to Xanadu: A Study in the Ways of Imagination* (New York, 1927).

[53] Southey, 'Writings of Lope de Vega', 27.

[54] Southey, 'Writings of Lope de Vega', 27.

[55] Both the return of the hero and his disguise are identified as 'functions' of the folk-tale by Vladimir Propp. His structural analysis of the folk-tale identifies thirty-one functions from which all folk narratives are comprised. See Vladimir Propp, *Morphology of the Folktale*, 1928, trans. Laurence Scott (Austin, TX, 1998), 25–65.

[56] Fitzroy Richard Somerset, *The Hero: A Study in Tradition, Myth, and Drama* (1936; Westport, CN, 1975), 214.

[57] John Simons, ed., Introduction, *Guy of Warwick and Other Chapbook Romances. Six Tales from Pre-Industrial England* (Exeter, 1998), 21.

[58] 'Drake's Leat', *South Devon Monthly Museum*, vol. 4, no. 22 (1834), 159.

[59] Crispin Gill, *Plymouth: A New History* (Tiverton, 1993), 124.

[60] The expenses for the opening ceremony are recorded in the *Widey Court Book*, a volume of borough accounts. Extracts relating to the leat are reproduced in Richard Nicholls Worth, *Calendar of the Plymouth Municipal Records* (Plymouth, 1893), 131–2.

[61] See Sabine Baring-Gould, *The Lives of the Saints*, 16 vols (Edinburgh, 1914).

[62] Southey, 'Writings of Lope de Vega', 28.

[63] Angela Blaen, *The Mystery of Michael* (Guernsey, 1987), 19.

CHAPTER FIVE

'Who the New World Bade British Thunders Shake?'

The gallant conduct of Drake in this expedition is known
to every reader of history.
(Anna Eliza Bray, *The Borders of the Tamar and Tavy*, 1874)[1]

In the previous chapter it was suggested that knowledge of Sir Francis Drake
during the first decades of the nineteenth century was becoming increasingly
anecdotal. Versions of the famous mariner were disseminated from tourist
guide-books as much as from the pages of naval histories. In 1834, however, the first
full-length biography of Drake since the final edition of Robert Burton's *The
English Hero* (1777) was published. This appeared in Robert Southey's *The Lives of
the British Admirals*[2] (1833–7). Southey had been commissioned to write the series
of naval biographies for Dionysius Lardner who used the work as part of the
famous *Cabinet Cyclopaedia*, published in 133 volumes between 1830 and 1849.

Southey's life of Drake is marked by the author's usual scholarly attention to
detail and learned digressions, but this approach does not preclude an engagement
with folk culture. Southey elaborates on the folk-tales that he first approached in a
review of Lope de Vega's work several years before. The author accounts for the
transposition of the Spanish version of Drake – a sorcerer in league with the devil
– into English folk culture. According to Southey, the common people believed
'that there was a white as well as a black art magic and that Drake, like Shakespeare's
Prospero, and friars Bacon and Bungay, with whom they were better acquainted,
employed the spirits under his command only in good works'.[3] (Bacon and Bungay
were characters from an early prose romance that was widely known.) Many of the
tales are repeated from Southey's earlier review yet some contain slight variations,
an indication of the malleable nature of folk narratives – even in the hands of a
serious academic attempting to record examples of genuine lore. In this version of
the warships tale, for example, the magical ships are combined with the game of
bowls, as seen in the previous chapter. The game itself becomes kales (or skittles)
and Drake insists on seeing out play before chopping a piece of timber into pieces
and throwing the chips into the sea to become the warships that attack and destroy

the Armada. This certainly suggests that Drake's cool response to the news of the Armada's approach was well established in folk culture. The tale of the construction of Drake's Leat is also slightly modified: Drake now speaks a magic spell over the stream before leading the water into Plymouth.

The Drake/ Guy of Warwick narrative is present in the new work, but this time there are two versions. Southey differentiates between a Devonshire and Somerset version of the tale. In the Devon tale Drake hears of his wife's intentions through one of his spirits; to prevent the marriage he fires a cannonball through the Earth which emerges between the bride and groom in the church just as the wedding service is about to commence. "'It comes from Drake!'" cried the wife to the now unbrided bridegroom; "he is alive! And there must be neither troth nor ring between thee and me.""[4] The Somerset version is that which Southey recorded in his earlier work: a stone falls from the sky and lands on the bride's dress, later Drake appears dressed as a beggar. For Southey this 'shows how strongly the romantic character of Drake's exploits, and the extraordinary celebrity which he obtained, impressed the imagination of his countrymen'.[5] One intriguing tale had not been printed before, and this has Drake perpetrating a ruthless murder. We are told that Drake shot the gulf or crossed from one plane of the Earth's surface to the other.

> [H]e asked his men if any of them knew where they were, a boy made answer that they were then just under London Bridge: upon which, stung by jealousy, Drake exclaimed, 'Hast thou too a devil? If I let thee live there will then be one greater man than myself;' and with that he threw him overboard.[6]

It is just conceivable that the origins of this myth lie in the Doughty affair. After all, this episode sees the execution (or murder) of a potential rival on the far side of the world.

In his biography Southey seems intent on revising the significance of Drake's adventures in terms of imperial progress. Of Drake's exploits at Ternate, so important to the cult of commerce in the eighteenth century, he writes 'but the English did not yet extend their view of commerce so far, and Drake had not come there "to spy the land," even with mercantile intentions'.[7] Similarly, Southey seeks to overturn the familiar story of Drake's stay among the Coast Miwok Indians: 'That the natives meant to make a sacrifice of their country by these ceremonies is what none but men prepossessed with notions which were common to all Europeans in that age could have supposed.'[8] But it is the Doughty affair that most taxes Southey's resources. For Southey the fact that 'panegyrical biographers' have failed to engage with the affair has deepened the suspicion with which the incident is viewed. He mounts a spirited defence of Drake, claiming that Doughty was intent on making off with a ship and setting himself up as a rival to Drake. '[I]f this were proved, the sentence cannot be deemed unjust.'[9] He doubts the truth of Drake and Doughty sharing a last supper together, claiming that Drake's nephew (for whom *The World Encompassed* was published) must have concocted the story believing that readers would think 'a narrative so incredible never would have been invented'.[10]

It is notable, however, that although Southey complains of selective dissemination on the part of other biographers, he himself omits Drake's excommunication of Francis Fletcher, a further episode that suggests Drake's behaviour could be far from exemplary. The account concludes with a meditation on Sir Francis's achievements.

> The expeditions undertaken in Elizabeth's reign against the Spaniards are said to have produced no advantage to England in any degree commensurate with the cost of money and expense of life with which they were performed. … If the advantage were to be considered only in tangible gain, this would be undeniable: but the effects produced upon the navy and upon the national character must be taken into account.[11]

It was the nautical skills perfected on privateering voyages and the mood of national confidence that these expeditions produced that equipped England to deal with the mighty Armada sent by Spain.

Southey's work is closely linked with that of Anna Eliza Bray whose *A Description of the Part of Devonshire Bordering on the Tamar and Tavy*, first published in 1836, takes the form of a series of letters between herself and Southey. An accomplished novelist, Anna Bray was the wife of the clergyman-poet the Reverend Edward Bray, vicar of Tavistock. Her work is important because it gives us an idea of how Drake had come to be perceived by educated society in the town of his birth. She writes,

> I have not unfrequently been surprised to find that, even some who are considered reading persons in this neighbourhood, knew very little more of Drake than that he was born here, sailed around the world, and fought the Armada; whilst of his personal adventures, and the more minute circumstances of his history, replete as they are with wild and romantic interest, they knew nothing whatever, nor seemed to suspect that there was anything worth knowing about them.[12]

This seems rather strange in a town which, less than fifty years later, would feel sufficient pride in its most famous son to erect a fine statue of him. The lack of interest shown by the 'reading persons' of Tavistock was obviously not shared by Bray and her husband. Edward Bray composed poetic inscriptions that were carved on rocks in the vicarage garden; one couplet was addressed to Sir Francis Drake: 'By thee, bold chief! around th'astonished world,/ Britannia's sovereign flag was first unfurl'd.'[13] Sadly these garden commemorations no longer survive. Of greater significance, however, is the very modern desire Anna Bray reveals to preserve the tangible remains of Drake – the cottage at Crowndale where he was born.

> [A]nd here stood the old barn-looking cottage (for it was no better) in which he first drew breath, with its antique windows, and all its character of past times about it, till, alas for modern innovation! This poor building, which should have been held sacred as long as one stone would rest upon another, was pulled down to give place to an ox-stall, or some such common appendage to the farm-house hard by.[14]

A note records that the cottage was sketched by Edward Bray and that this drawing was inaccurately copied by Frederic Lewis in *The Scenery of the Rivers Tamar and Tavy*.[15] Clearly, Bray identifies Sir Francis Drake as a major historical figure, and her dismay at the destruction of his birth-place can be seen as an early manifestation of the imperative to preserve the tangible past. (Shakespeare's birthplace was not bought for the nation until 1847.) As David Lowenthal has written, 'Only with the nineteenth century did European nations closely identify themselves with their material heritage, and only in the twentieth have they launched major programmes to protect it.'[16]

Yet Bray's concentration on the cottage reflects much more than a simple desire to commemorate a local hero. She describes the cottage as 'a vestige so replete with interest to all who are not insensible to the power of local and historical associations'.[17] Bray herself was responsive to the power both of history and of locality, the latter a issue of increasing cultural significance in the early nineteenth century: it is no coincidence that many of her novels are historical fictions concerned with major West Country families. The power of 'historical associations' can only be released, however, when the present is felt to be utterly separate from the past: 'It is discontinuity not continuity that brings historical consciousness into being.'[18] We can see the destruction of the Drake cottage – and Bray's reaction to that destruction – as analogous to the vast process of disjunction which, during the first half of the nineteenth century, severed effectively the past from the present.

To understand just what lay behind this historical disjunction we need to look at the economic transformation that was changing the structure of British society. During the eighteenth century agrarian capitalism had emerged as the dominant mode of production. This dominance, however, was relatively short-lived; by the mid-nineteenth century industrial capitalism had taken its place as the primary mode of production. This economic upheaval had huge social consequences. The old rural economic order (which Sir Francis Drake would certainly have recognized) with its systems of deference and obligation was replaced by a class system. Farmers and agricultural entrepreneurs joined the expanding middle classes while farm labourers became a rural proletariat. A process of urbanization fuelled by rapid population increase and equally rapid industrial development, particularly in the north, saw the growth of large cities. Enclosures deprived many of those left in rural areas of common land. In a relatively short space of time the pre-capitalist social order disappeared. Chris Brooks has argued that the social unrest of the 1830s and 1840s 'can be seen as attempts, frequently desperate, to negotiate the disjunction between the past and the present that had been effected, or was being effected, by the triumph of capital'.[19] In other words, violent disturbances were attempts at recapturing the working conditions of a lost pre-industrial age or, at the very least, of finding a way of accommodating change. And it is here we can locate the beginnings of a new historical self-consciousness.

If machine-breaking and incendiarism were desperate working-class responses to a severance from the past, then Anna Bray's dismay at the demolition of the Drake cottage with its 'antique windows' and 'character of past times' is a rather less desperate but nonetheless genuine response from a middle-class intellectual. It is important to realize that the destruction of the cottage is itself a sign of continuity. In the pre-capitalist, pre-industrial age the present was generally regarded as a continuation of the past, and Drake's cottage held no special historical significance. However, by the 1830s an awareness of irretrievable change led to Bray's desire to fix things in time. This desire was, of course, not confined to Bray. David Lowenthal neatly summarizes early and mid-Victorian Britain's engagement with the past.

> No other society had so rapidly embraced innovation or seen its everyday landscapes so thoroughly altered. Yet no other society viewed its past with such self-congratulatory gravity or sought so earnestly to reanimate its features, Scott's historical novels, Gothic Revival architecture, neo-chivalric fashions of dress and conduct, classical standards of beauty, successive passions for all things Roman, Greek, Egyptian, Chinese, early English – all this betokened a people besotted with the past.[20]

But there was more behind this historical awareness than a nostalgic backward glance at a past that seemed infinitely more attractive than the present (although this is certainly what *A Description of the Part of Devonshire* is doing in its emphasis on the Drake cottage). For all social classes constructing the past played a vital role in explaining the disjunction that they experienced. Particularly important was the narrative of causation, historical accounts that elided the fact of disjunction and explained the present through a seamless sequence of historical cause and effect.[21] For all Anna Bray's efforts Sir Francis Drake was not the focus for great attention in the 1830s. By the middle of the century, however, he had become a very important figure when it came to constructing narratives of causation to explain the imperial present: but much more of this later.

Bray continues that had her husband not been in London, he would have warned the Duke of Bedford (the local landowner) of the impending destruction. Now that it was too late to save the cottage, Edward Bray suggested that the duke position a block of granite there to act 'like the Romanized-British stones'.[22] This proposed memorial (which was never put in place) reflects a contemporary antiquarian engagement with the ancient British past. Of particular interest to Edward Bray were the curiosities of Dartmoor. He (incorrectly) identified the small estate of Bairdown in the centre of the moor – where the Brays owned a property – as a site once sacred to druids or bards. The name Bairdown, he believed, meant Bard's Hill, and to reinforce this identity Bray composed many couplets that were inscribed on the granite boulders scattered there. Many of the couplets were addressed to 'illustrious characters who have been remarkable for their attachment to the country'.[23] These included Shakespeare, Francis Bacon and Sir Isaac Newton. He produced another couplet that could be inscribed on the stone that was to mark Drake's birthplace: 'Who the New World bade British thunders shake?/ Who marked out bounds to both? – Our native Drake.'[24] It is significant that both the couplet for the commemorative rock and for the vicarage garden celebrate Drake's exploits in terms of imperial progress. Following Waterloo British overseas territories had continued to grow. New markets were needed for the products of industry; British possessions provided new sources of raw materials and (as Richard Hakluyt had argued over two hundred years before) could provide an outlet for the growing population. A programme of annexation in northern India began in 1826 that received widespread patriotic support in Britain. It is notable that for the Drake memorial Bray chooses to appropriate evidence of Roman rule – the 'Romanized-British stones'. Of course, the couplet that was to be inscribed on the rock celebrates British achievements: Drake's role in the development of British expansionism. The implication of this appropriation is that Britain is creating an empire that is equal to, or even greater than that of Rome.

We find the same notion expressed in William Cowper's poem 'Boadicea'[25] (1782). Cowper's work was widely read by the Victorians and in this poem the ancient British Queen Boadicea, defeated in her revolt against Roman rule, receives a prophetic vision of a British empire that will outdo that of Rome.

> *'Then the progeny that springs*
> *From the forests of our land,*
> *Armed with thunder, clad with wings,*
> *Shall a wider world command.*
>
> *'Regions Caesar never knew*
> *Thy posterity shall sway;*
> *Where his eagles never flew,*
> *None invincible as they.'* (25–32)

A Description of the Part of Devonshire includes a life of Drake, but by Bray's own admission this is little more than a brief outline of the main elements of the admiral's career. Of more interest are the further examples given by Bray of folk-tales concerning Francis Drake. She meditates on the 'extravagant' stories that surround his deeds, particularly the popular construction of Drake as possessor of supernatural powers. She concludes,

> Nor can we feel surprised at this credulity when we recollect that even in these days, with the peasants of Devon, witchcraft is still believed to be practiced. ... Thus was our hero converted, by popular opinion, into a wizard; and as such the 'old warrior' (for so the lower classes here call Drake) is to the present time considered among them. [26]

The continuity between past and present cannot be made more explicit. Yet we should not overlook the fact that Bray was recording folk-tales at the very moment when genuine oral culture was falling into decline. Folk-tales require continuity for their transmission, but, as we have seen, during the first decades of the nineteenth century this unbroken link with the past was being destroyed. We should, perhaps, see Bray's work (and, of course, that of Southey) as a further manifestation of the desire to fix things in time. Although most of the tales that Bray records also appear in Southey's biography her comments upon them are of interest. For Bray the fireships tale contains elements of the sublime.

> Wild as this story is, there is something of grandeur in the idea of Drake
> standing on such a commanding elevation as the Hoe, with the sea, which
> spreads itself at the foot, before him, and that element together with the
> fireships obedient to the power of his genius, whose energies were thus
> marvellously exerted for the safety of his country.[27]

There are slight variations between other tales Bray mentions and those recorded
by Southey. For instance, the story of the unusually clever boy that Drake found
aboard his ship is revised. Bray suggests that the story 'represents him as acting from
motives of jealousy and cruelty in a way he was very little likely to do'.[28] When
Drake quizzes the boy about their location the boy replies 'Bath Place' (purportedly
the local name for Buckland Abbey), but the end result is the same. Further
narratives on which Bray dwells have Drake offering to make Tavistock a sea port
if he was granted the local estate of Milemead, and the devil helping Sir Francis
move a large stone when he was repairing Buckland Abbey. Perhaps the origins of
this tale can be traced to the topographical writing of Thomas Westcote who states
that Drake's leat was brought through a 'mighty rock generally supposed impossible
to be pierced'[29] (see the discussion of Drake's Leat later in this chapter).

The most ambitious work on Drake to emerge during the 1840s was
undoubtedly *The Life, Voyages, and Exploits of Admiral Sir Francis Drake, Knight*,[30] which
was first published in 1843. The author was John Barrow, the son of Sir John Barrow,
Secretary of the Admiralty, and himself a naval biographer. The account of Drake's life
is remarkable for its minute detail and for the number of original sources that the
author has consulted and reproduced. By this date the use of original documents was
well established as the starting point for the construction of historical narratives or, in
this case, for establishing the 'authentic' Drake. This followed the precedent set by
empirical science. According to James Anthony Froude – later, as we will see, to play
a major role in the construction of Drake – 'History itself depends on exact
knowledge, on the same minute, impartial, discriminating observation and analysis of
particulars which is equally the basis of science.'[31] But, for the historian, documents
replaced experimental data. Finding these original sources, however, was far from
easy; about halfway through the book Barrow bemoans the lack of a central
document repository. 'It is indeed much to be regretted, that a nation like England
should have no suitable building appropriated solely for the reception of her historical
and other valuable documents.'[32] Nevertheless, the account is crammed with letters
from Drake to the Queen, to Burghley, Seymour and numerous other statesmen and
commanders. These demonstrate Drake's disregard for coherent sentence structure
and, more importantly, his absolute faith in God and conviction about the rightness
of his actions. Drake's correspondence includes the usual religious references that we
may expect from the time but, when written by someone known to be guided by an
unshakable faith, these appear like genuine expressions of belief rather than mere
rhetorical devices.

The chapter on the Spanish Armada is revealing in terms of what Barrow chooses
to include and omit. Of the capture of the *Rosario* he states: 'Our chroniclers make

a great deal too much of this affair, and, no doubt, more than is strictly true.'[33] But anyone expecting a revised account of the incident will be disappointed. Barrow merely repeats the familiar story of de Valdez surrendering on hearing that his assailant is Drake. However, Drake's desertion of his post in order to intercept the Spanish *capitana* provokes little comment. We are merely told that Drake forgot the light when giving chase 'but no harm ensued'.[34] Barrow's biography provides an important element in the development of the bowls story. He quotes the story of the news of the Armada's arrival from Oldys's *Life of Raleigh*, adding (as if part of the quotation), 'Drake insisted on the match being played out, saying, that "There would be plenty of time to win the game, and beat the Spaniards too."'[35] Drake's words may well be an invention of Barrow's or they may have been circulating in an oral form of the narrative for some time. Whatever the origin, their appearance in a biography concerned with 'fact' provides a prime example of how historical narratives develop by accretion.

Although Barrow's quest for authenticity means that the work is largely concerned with documentary sources – letters and reports – he does not overlook the significance of literary products. For example, when dealing with the fate of the *Golden Hinde* after Drake's arrival in England, he is able to state that the ship 'would appear to have become a resort of holiday people, the cabin being converted into a sort of banqueting house'.[36] His evidence comes from Ben Jonson's drama *Eastward Ho!* (Barrow mistakenly calls it *England's Hoe*), and he quotes the lines spoken by Petronell Flash reproduced in Chapter Two above.[37] Barrow uses poetic material as evidence of Drake's popularity on his return from the circumnavigation and to demonstrate that his death was keenly felt. Among the fragments of poems he reproduces are the verse found in Camden that was pinned to the main mast of the *Hinde*; a section of Cowley's meditation on the chair made from the ship's timbers; several stanzas from Fitzgeffrey depicting Drake as the fearful dragon, and a form of epitaph from an unrevealed source.

> *Where Drake first found, there last he lost his name,*
> *And for a tomb left nothing but his fame.*
> *His body's buried under some great wave,*
> *The sea that was his glory is his grave.*
> *On whom an epitaph none can truly make,*
> *For who can say, 'Here lies Sir Francis Drake?'*[38]

The biography is also the first work to suggest that accounts of Drake's voyages may have inspired Shakespeare. The author suggests that as Shakespeare is known to have borrowed from Holinshed and other chroniclers this is quite possible. Barrow claims that Drake's time with the native American Indians, particularly their belief that the Englishmen were gods, 'cannot fail to remind one of parts of *The Tempest*'.[39] He quotes Caliban's lines,

> *These be fine things, and if they be not sprites.*
> *That's a brave god, and bears celestial liquor;*
> *I will kneel to him.*[40]

If the date of the play is somewhere around 1611, then we can guess that Shakespeare may have been familiar with the account of the famous voyage found in Hakluyt. Barrow is certainly the first of Drake's biographers to mention the only poem attributed to Sir Francis: 'Sir Fraunces Drake, Knight, in Commendation of this Treatise.' This was a commendatory verse appended to George Peckham's treatise on Humphrey Gilbert's discoveries titled *A True Report of the Late Discoveries, and Possession taken in the right of the Crowne of Englande, of the New Found Landes,* published in 1583. The sonnet commends the treatise for demonstrating the way to gain fame and wealth. It concludes 'So that for each degree, this Treatise dooth unfolde/ The path to fame, the proofe of zeal and way to purchase gold' (13–14).[41] There were few figures better qualified than Drake to comment on the way for the ambitious to 'purchase gold'. As with the folk-tales and tourist visits to Buckland Abbey discussed at the end of the last chapter, the effect of this concentration on literary products – particularly Barrow's mobilization of Shakespeare, such a potent signifier of Englishness – was to embed Drake even further into English culture.

We find a very modern interpretation of the Spanish Armada in Edward Creasy's *The Fifteen Decisive Battles of the World: From Marathon to Waterloo.* This book, first published in 1851, was extremely popular – a twelfth edition had appeared by 1862. Drake and the other commanders are gathered on the bowling green of Plymouth Hoe when the news of the sighting of the Armada arrives. This version of events, which did not appear in any account until 1735, is now an essential part of the narrative. Creasy describes the action following the announcement.

> [T]here was a shouting for the ships' boats; but Drake coolly checked his comrades, and insisted that the match should be played out. He said that there was plenty of time both to win the game and beat the Spaniards. The best and bravest match that ever was scored was resumed accordingly. Drake and his friends aimed their bowls with the same steady calculating coolness with which they were about to point their guns. The winning cast was made; and they went on board, and prepared for action, with their hearts as light and their nerves as firm as they had been on the Hoe Bowling Green.[42]

Even allowing for Drake's natural arrogance, this is hardly the reaction of a commander preparing for battle. Sir Francis is actually constructed according to the desirable virtues of the 1850s rather than the 1580s. He displays what was supposedly a typical English coolness in the face of danger. Drake and the other commanders treat the impending battle in the same light-hearted fashion as the game of bowls. What we are faced with is the appropriation of Drake as a vehicle for imperial ideology: he embodies a particular version of Englishness. We need to realize that British expansionism could be justified, in part, by the supposed superiority of the English character. Unflappable, loyal and patriotic, the Englishman had a duty to bring order and good government to those less fortunate than himself – whether the 'help' was wanted or not. An important element of this Englishness was the ability to treat war as a game – an ethic that had been inculcated in the public schools for over half a century and that found its most succinct expression in the remark attributed to the Duke of Wellington, 'The field of Waterloo was won on the playing fields of Eton.' Sir Francis Drake, in Creasy's hands, is able to treat the Armada as if it was an extension of the game he was already playing.

The great narrative histories of the first half of the nineteenth century dedicate far more space to the Spanish Armada than to the circumnavigation. This is slightly surprising given the emphasis that was placed on Drake as a founder of English commercial expansionism in the eighteenth century. John Lingard's *A History of England from the First Invasion by the Romans*[43] allows the famous voyage just two pages. Lingard was a Roman Catholic and may have taken a dim view of Drake's personal war against his faith. The same cannot be said for James Mackintosh whose *History of England*,[44] deals with the circumnavigation in a similar amount of space. Perhaps the concentration on the Spanish Armada by these works is not entirely surprising, the repulse of an invading force is bound to have a significant impact on a nation's consciousness. Moreover, the fear of invasion was felt very keenly during the mid-century. In 1852, following a successful *coup d'état* the previous year, Louis Napoleon was crowned emperor of France. This led to widespread rumours in England that the new emperor would begin a war with Britain in an attempt to secure popularity by restoring the national esteem that had been lost on the battlefield of Waterloo. The very name 'Napoleon' was synonymous with French military ambition, and this fuelled speculation that an invasion was imminent. We should also be aware that the Royal Navy's mastery of the Channel waters meant that this was little more than scaremongering. But the hysteria the 'threat' produced certainly suggested that it was very effective. Some years earlier, Louis Philippe's admiral, the Prince de Joinville, had been responsible for a minor invasion scare. Realizing the relative weakness of the French navy in the mid-1840s, he argued for the acquisition of steamships – the prince's rather bellicose remarks were interpreted as evidence for French territorial ambitions.

But these invasion scares do not account fully for the increasing emphasis on the Spanish Armada at the cost of the circumnavigation. What appears to be happening is a repositioning of emphasis when constructing the past. And, of course, how the past was represented was conditioned by the present: Britain had an ever-increasing number of overseas possessions to enlarge and defend. As we have seen, the Armada provided an inspiration for Britons on the defensive. This patriotism could also be mobilized in the colonial theatre. The intended Spanish invasion came to perform an important ideological function – particularly during the rapid expansion of the formal empire in the 1880s. It provided the potent image of England as a small peaceful country going about its business but besieged by aggressors on all sides. Mythologizing of this type helped to obscure the fact that Britain had aggressively appropriated vast areas of the Earth's surface. Of course, the greatest irony was that colonies – or, perhaps, British interests – often needed 'defending' from their native inhabitants. This change of emphasis is particularly important when we realize the appeal of history writing during this period. 'These were the years of history as best-selling literature … and the middle classes of

Victorian England devoured history with the same hunger as they had for the historical novel.'[45] Again this interest in the past was an attempt at negotiating the historical disjunction that had sundered effectively the past from the present – although it was the middle classes who largely benefited from the changes. Although Drake is not credited with the dominant role in the defeat of the Spanish fleet by the histories mentioned above, we can detect a subtle move toward the representation of the Armada as his finest hour. And this representation was consumed by a very large audience.

But if narrative histories were not greatly concerned with the famous voyage, the same could not be said for the visual arts. In 1846 John Hollins (whose history paintings remain largely unexplored) exhibited a work at the Royal Academy entitled *The Circumnavigator Drake Receiving the Honour of Knighthood from Queen Elizabeth on board his Ship the Golden Hinde, at Deptford, 1581*. The location of this is now unknown. As Roy Strong has observed, the middle decades of the nineteenth century were the great age of history painting. Here we find 'the generation [of artists] for whom the past was a major ingredient in their intellectual background and in that of their public'.[46] Yet scenes from history were not painted for their own sake. The past provided valuable precedents for contemporary events – and a major determinant in the way history was represented was the rise and enfranchisement of the middle classes. In the first half of the nineteenth century the nation's economic well-being fell increasingly into the hands of industrialists and merchants who gained a certain amount of political representation under the 1832 Reform Bill. Crucially, it was possible for new wealth to be assimilated into the landed gentry (usually through marriage). This assimilation was mutually beneficial: the landed interest had an obvious financial interest while the upper-middle classes could adopt the culture and enjoy the social prestige of the gentry. What better historical figure to demonstrate the rise of an individual through his own exertions and his assimilation into the upper reaches of society than Sir Francis Drake? As Strong argues, 'The events of the British past as reflected in the art of the age were conditioned by a middle-class gloss.'[47] On 30 March 1861 the *Illustrated London News*, which was read by a large middle-class audience, incorporated a detailed engraving of Drake receiving his knighthood. It is notable that all visual representations of Drake receiving his knighthood show the Queen bestowing the honour. In fact she actually passed the sword to Monsieur de Marchaumont, the French ambassador, who was supposed to be negotiating the marriage between Elizabeth and the Duc d'Alencon, the brother of the French king.

The knighting of Sir Francis Drake is also depicted in the Palace of Westminster. A bronze bas-relief by the sculptor William Theed forms part of the decorative scheme of the Prince's Chamber (PLATE 6). The design for the bronze was first exhibited at the Royal Academy in 1858, although it was not installed for several years. The Prince's Chamber functions as an ante-room to the House of Lords and is the penultimate apartment through which the royal party processes at the opening of parliament. The old Palace of Westminster was destroyed by fire in 1834. The new palace, the work of Charles Barry and Augustus Welby Pugin, was created

QUEEN ELIZABETH KNIGHTING DRAKE

PLATE 6. William Theed, Elizabeth Knighting Drake, bas-relief, Prince's Chamber, House of Lords. An example of upward social mobility at the heart of an increasingly representative legislative assembly.

between 1835 and 1868. Responsibility for the works of art that were to decorate the new building fell to the Royal Commission under the chairmanship of Prince Albert with Charles Eastlake, later president of the Royal Academy, as its secretary. It was decided that the Prince's Chamber should be decorated so as to reflect the great events of the Tudor period, a period that had revived the country's fortunes following the Wars of the Roses. Full-length portraits of Tudor monarchs, nobles and their wives, taken from original sources, would fill the middle panels of the room. Theed, who was much favoured by the Prince Consort, was awarded the commission for the series of twelve bas-reliefs depicting scenes from sixteenth-century history that are positioned below the portraits. Drake kneeling before Elizabeth takes his place among bronzes of Raleigh spreading his cloak before the Queen, the death of Sir Philip Sidney and the murder of David Rizzio, to name but three. As we have seen, Drake's knighthood provided a perfect example of the possibility of social mobility and here it was, placed at the very heart of the increasingly representative British legislative assembly. Projecting the existence of such assimilation back in time gave the middle classes an historical precedent that seemed to justify their rise.

The mid-century thirst for historical knowledge was responsible for a proliferation of learned societies with an interest in publishing previously unknown narratives. Formed in 1846, the Hakluyt Society regarded itself as completing the work of the famous geographer. In 1854 the Society published *The World Encompassed by Sir Francis Drake*,[48] a new edition of the work that originally appeared in 1628. This narrative is accompanied by Hakluyt's 'The Famous Voyage of Sir Francis Drake' and several other extracts from the *Principal Navigations* that are connected with Drake's circumnavigation. Extracts from the narrative by Francis Fletcher are printed alongside the text of *The World Encompassed* where there is any noticeable variance between the texts. Four short appendices contain transcriptions of documents relating to the voyage and to the trial of Thomas Doughty. These include a list of unlikely claims supposedly made by Doughty during the voyage (including the admission that he was a conjuror), and the narrative of Drake's detractor, John Cooke, simply titled 'For Francis Drake'. Far from shedding new light on the strange trial of Doughty, the material merely obfuscates the matter further. The introductory essay by William Vaux is forced to conclude, 'If they who knew him best were content to believe … that no charge of blood guiltiness could be brought against Sir Francis Drake in the matter of Mr. Doughty, we are content.'[49] The weight of evidence tends to exonerate Drake who emerges from the pages of *The World Encompassed* with his reputation intact. This still leaves the problem of the narrative of John Cooke; all the editor can do is dismiss this as a possible fraud or a 'gross exaggeration'.[50]

But it was not just material relating to Drake's sea-faring exploits that was published. In 1845 *A View of Devonshire in MDCXXX* by Thomas Westcote, the topographer, was published for the first time (the work had existed as a manuscript only since 1630). Of Plymouth Westcote wrote 'The streets are fairly paved and kept clean and sweet, much refreshed by the fresh stream running through it plenteously to their [the inhabitants'] great ease, pleasure and profit.'[51] It was Westcote who first compared the construction of the leat with Hannibal making his way through the Alps, an analogy later copied by John Prince. During the mid-century a certain amount of attention appears to have been directed towards Drake's Leat. An oil painting titled *Bringing in the Water by Burrator Falls* (PLATE 7)

PLATE 7. Attributed to Samuel Cook, *Bringing in the Water by Burrator Falls*, c.1840. Drake's greatest non-military feat. A product of bourgeois pride in urban improvement in the mid-nineteenth century.

attributed, perhaps strangely, to the water-colourist Samuel Cook was produced probably in the late 1830s or 1840s. The image depicts the leat under construction near its source on Dartmoor. This was, in fact, one of the most problematic sections of the new waterway to construct. The difficulties arose from the steep sides and clitters of Burrator Gorge, which meant that in several places the water had to be carried through long wooden conduits. Contrary to the assertion of Thomas Westcote,[52] there was no huge rock through which a channel was cut. The misunderstanding in the early topographical account appears to have arisen from the wording given on Spry's Plot, an attractive map of the Plymouth area by Robert Spry that depicted the course of the intended waterway. (A copy was submitted to the Privy Council with the Water Bill in 1584.) This reads, 'Here the river is taken out of the old river [the Meavy] and carried 448 paces through mightie rockes which was thought unpossible to carrie water through.' Probably Westcote misread or misremembered this wording.

In the painting Sir Francis Drake and two members of the Plymouth Corporation –dressed in the red gowns adopted during Drake's mayoralty – inspect the work in progress. Cook was a local man (he was born at Camelford, north Cornwall, and worked in Plymouth) and so would have knowledge of the corporation gowns and Drake's part in their introduction. Although the painting is primarily a landscape, the representation of Drake's face shows the artist's attention to contemporary portraiture. This reflects the preoccupation of Victorian history painting with accuracy of detail. Edmund Lodge's *Portraits of Illustrious Personages of Great Britain* became an invaluable source of reference when researching portraiture. Cook, however, had a rather more immediate image to observe: the copy of the three-quarter-length painting attributed to Abraham Janssen that was hung in Plymouth Guildhall. In the Cook image Drake's head is turned slightly to the right but he wears the same ruff and gloves and is wearing the hat that he carries in the older image. But Cook's attention to detail seems to end with the correct representation of the face. Drake is the tallest figure in the painting – despite contemporary accounts that describes him as 'short of stature' – so that the group of workmen bending to their task must look up at Sir Francis as he speaks. The attitude is almost one of deference. This notion of deference to the great seafarer and benefactor of Plymouth is made clear by a further figure on the left of the group who bends on one knee to look at a map that is unfurled at Drake's feet. The depiction of this section of the leat allows Cook to introduce elements of the sublime into the image. These include Claig Tor, the huge granite rock that looms over the figures; Burrator Waterfall on the far left, and the distant (rather exaggerated) tors rising above the tower of Meavy church.

Interest in the leat was not confined to Samuel Cook, however. In 1856 the *Illustrated London News* reported on a ceremony connected with Drake's Leat. This was the annual Fishing Feast. The ceremony was described thus.

> The source of this leat is at the Head Weir, in a Romantic valley
> surrounded by Tors on the confines of Dartmoor. At this spot the Mayor

and Town Council of Plymouth assemble once a year to inspect the leat, when the following ceremony is observed. The party being assembled, one of the goblets belonging to the Corporation is filled with water by the Town Surveyor, and is handed by him to the chairman of the Water Committee of the Council, who presents it to the Mayor, requesting him to drink 'to the pious memory of Sir Francis Drake.' The goblet is then passed to the Aldermen and other members of the town council, who drink to the same toast. Another goblet being then filled with wine is presented to the Mayor who drinks to the toast 'May the descendents of him who brought us water never want wine.' This toast is also drunk by all assembled. Meanwhile the water is turned out of the leat into the river, and a number of trout are caught in the leat by the conservator, who goes into the stream with a small net.[53]

The article was accompanied by an engraving of the event. The silver goblet is passed from the chairman of the Water Committee to the Mayor prior to the toast to the memory of Sir Francis Drake. The figure third from the left is the conservator who is represented with a net used for catching the trout that would form the basis of the feast. Following the inspection, the party retired to a local inn where the trout were prepared and a great feast followed. The article continues that an unusual number of the Town Council and visitors had attended the feast that year. This was 'owing to the great popularity of the Mayor, Mr. John Kelly, who on that morning had the honour of waiting on her Majesty on her departure from Plymouth'.[54] The piece concludes with a further example of a notion that we have encountered many times: that the construction of the leat was an act of great benevolence on Drake's part. 'Drake generously spent a considerable portion of his prize money in the water supply of Plymouth ... would that the fruits of conquest were always so well applied.'[55]

The origins of the Fishing Feast are not altogether clear. The earliest record in the Plymouth City archives is dated 1731.[56] The eminent local historian Richard Nicholls Worth suggested that the first feast was held during the Recordership of Sir Francis Drake (third baronet) who frequently used his ancestor's illustrious name to further his political aspirations.[57] (This was the same Sir Francis who is believed to have commissioned the snuff-boxes from John Obrisset.) If this is correct, then the first Fishing Feast took place sometime between 1697 and 1717. It is important to remember that Drake's Leat was Plymouth's main water supply for three hundred years. Even during the later decades of the nineteenth century, when most of the city was supplied with piped water from service reservoirs, the basic water supply from Dartmoor still came via the leat. Not until 1898 when the new reservoir at Burrator was completed – which completely submerged the old Head Weir – did the leat fall into disuse.[58] Although the Fishing Feast was probably inaugurated by the third Sir Francis Drake a hundred years after the death of his famous ancestor, it is a mark of the gratitude the city felt towards Drake that this custom continued to be enacted.

Some years earlier the removal of a Drake 'relic' connected with the leat caused some comment. In Plymouth the water from the leat was fed to a series of conduit houses. Improvements carried out in 1827 meant that these houses were no longer required, and the last one was demolished in 1834. In the same year the *South Devon Monthly Museum* received a letter from George Wightwick[59] who, it appears, was involved with the removal of the conduit house. He writes:

> The destruction of the conduit, at the head of Old Town Street, has been lamented. … The front of the building has been identically re-erected in the wall on the east side of the road to North Hill, with the addition of two or three hitherto neglected and valuable fragments of the Drake period, and a tablet in compliment to the present mayor. If, as an instrument in this work I lose any portion of any good mans esteem, let me endeavour in a measure to reinstate myself by graphically restoring the revered building, precisely as it originally stood. Peace to the remains of Francis Drake.[60]

The letter was accompanied by a drawing of the conduit house.[61] The Drake arms are clearly seen to the right of the plaque to the mayor. Breaking this link with the past, destroying the tangible remains of Sir Francis's service to the town – albeit outdated for the needs of Plymouth in the 1830s – seems to have engendered a certain nostalgia and even dismay. This parallels Anna Bray's reaction to the destruction of the Drake cottage. Yet the conduit was destroyed as part of a programme of urban improvement – that major nineteenth-century expression of newly found civic pride. In this instance active steps were taken to memorialize the past – through both the preservation of the conduit's façade and through Wightwick's drawing.

What broad conclusions can we draw about the representation of Sir Francis Drake in the early middle part of the century? It is notable that the defeat of the Armada began to emerge as a more important event than the circumnavigation. This is, perhaps, the result of the switch from the creation of an empire to the defence of imperial possessions. Not every work that dealt with the Armada saw Drake as the single-handed victor, yet the tradition of Sir Francis as the bowls-playing principal combatant was embraced by historical accounts intended for a popular audience. The game was becoming an integral part of the Drake – if not the Armada – narrative. But while the bowling on Plymouth Hoe acted as a vehicle for imperial ideology, Drake was not yet fully established as one of the founding fathers of English expansionism. For this construction we must turn to the work of James Anthony Froude.

Notes

[1] Anna Eliza Bray, *The Borders of the Tamar and Tavy*, 2 vols (London, 1874), vol. 2, 99. Reprint of *A Description of the Part of Devonshire Bordering on the Tamar and Tavy*, 1836.

[2] Robert Southey, 'Sir Francis Drake', *The Lives of the British Admirals,* 5 vols (London, 1833–7), vol. 3, 99–242.

[3] Southey, *British Admirals,* vol. 3, 239.

[4] Southey, *British Admirals,* vol. 3, 240.

[5] Southey, *British Admirals,* vol. 3, 241.

[6] Southey, *British Admirals,* vol. 3, 240.

[7] Southey, *British Admirals,* vol. 3, 167.

[8] Southey, *British Admirals,* vol. 3, 160.

[9] Southey, *British Admirals,* vol. 3, 131.

[10] Southey, *British Admirals,* vol. 3, 132.

[11] Southey, *British Admirals,* vol. 3, 242.

[12] Bray, *Tamar and Tavy,* vol. 2, 37.

[13] Bray, *Tamar and Tavy,* vol. 2, 14.

[14] Bray, *Tamar and Tavy,* vol. 2, 28.

[15] Frederic Lewis, *The Scenery of the Rivers Tamar and Tavy* (London, 1823). The image appears on page 15.

[16] David Lowenthal, *The Past is a Foreign Country* (1985; Cambridge, 1997), 385.

[17] Bray, *Tamar and Tavy,* vol. 2, 28.

[18] Chris Brooks, 'Historicism and the Nineteenth Century', in Vanessa Brand, ed., *The Study of the Past in the Victorian Age* (Oxford, 1998), 3.

[19] Brooks, 'Historicism and the Nineteenth Century', 5.

[20] Lowenthal, 97.

[21] Brooks, 'Historicism and the Nineteenth Century', 6–8.

[22] Bray, *Tamar and Tavy,* vol. 2, 28.

[23] Anna Eliza Bray, ed., *Poetical Remains, Social, Sacred, and Miscellaneous of the Late Edward Atkyns Bray,* 2 vols (London, 1859), vol. 2, 281.

[24] Bray, *Tamar and Tavy,* vol. 2, 28.

[25] William Cowper, 'Boadicea', in Robert Aris Willmott, ed., *The Poetical Works of William Cowper* (London, 1895), 180.

[26] Bray, *Tamar and Tavy,* vol. 2, 45.

[27] Bray, *Tamar and Tavy,* vol. 2, 30.

[28] Bray, *Tamar and Tavy,* vol. 2, 32.

[29] Thomas Westcote, *A View of Devonshire in MDCXXX* (Exeter, 1845), 378.

[30] John Barrow, *The Life, Voyages, and Exploits of Admiral Sir Francis Drake, Knight* (London, 1843).

[31] James Anthony Froude, 'Scientific Method Applied to History', *Short Studies on Great Subjects,* 4 vols (London, 1894), vol. 2, 566.

[32] Barrow, 255.

[33] Barrow, 291.

[34] Barrow, 293.

[35] Barrow, 286.

[36] Barrow, 171.

[37] The lines are quoted in Barrow, 59. From Ben Jonson, *Eastward Ho!,* Act 3, Scene 3.

[38] Quoted in Barrow, 403.

[39] Barrow, 143.

[40] Quoted in Barrow, 143. From *The Tempest,* Act 2, Scene 2.

[41] 'Sir Fraunces Drake, Knight, in Commendation of this Treatise', reproduced in Barrow, 409.

[42] Edward Creasy, *The Fifteen Decisive Battles of the World: From Marathon to Waterloo* (1851; London, 1862), 346.

[43] John Lingard, *A History of England from the First Invasion by the Romans,* 14 vols (Paris, 1826), vol. 8, 258–60.

[44] James Mackintosh, *The History of England,* 10 vols (London, 1831), vol. 3, 182–4.

[45] Roy Strong, *And When Did You Last See Your Father? The Victorian Painter and British History* (London, 1978), 32.

[46] Strong, 42.

[47] Strong, 45.

[48] William Vaux, ed., *The World Encompassed by Sir Francis Drake* (London, 1854).

[49] Vaux, ed., Introduction, *The World Encompassed,* xxxix.

[50] Vaux, ed., Introduction, *The World Encompassed,* xl.

[51] Westcote, *A View of Devonshire*, 378.

[52] See Westcote, 378.

[53] 'Fishing Feast of the Plymouth Town Council', *Illustrated London News*, 30 August 1856, 219.

[54] 'Fishing Feast', *Illustrated London News*, 30 August 1856, 219.

[55] 'Fishing Feast', *Illustrated London News*, 30 August 1856, 219.

[56] See Edwin Welch, 'The Origins of the Plymouth Fishing Feast', *Devon and Cornwall Notes and Queries*, vol. 30 (1965–7), 155.

[57] Richard Nicholls Worth, *The History of Plymouth From the Earliest Period to the Present Time* (Plymouth, 1890), 456.

[58] For a detailed account of the history of Drake's Leat, see David J. Hawkins, *Water From the Moor: An Illustrated History of the Plymouth, Stonehouse and Devonport Leats* (Newton Abbot, 1987).

[59] George Wightwick (1802–72) was an important regional architect. He had moved to Plymouth as John Foulston's partner in 1829. Among other buildings, Wightwick was responsible for Plymouth Town Hall (1839–40) and the Cottonian Library (1850).

[60] George Wightwick, 'The Old Town Conduit, Plymouth', *South Devon Monthly Museum*, vol. 15, no. 4 (1834), 89.

[61] The image is found on page 88.

CHAPTER SIX

'The Prose Epic of England'

And the first thunder birth of these enormous forces and the flash
of the earliest achievements of the new era roll and glitter through the
forty years of the reign of Elizabeth with a grandeur which, when once
its history is written, will be seen to be among the most sublime
phenomena which the earth as yet has witnessed.

(James Anthony Froude, 1852)[1]

Reference has already been made to the nineteenth-century preoccupation with narratives of causation, with stories that sought to connect past and present through uninterrupted sequences of cause and effect eliding moments of historical disjunction. Charles Knight's *Old England* is clearly engaged in this process. For Knight the naval supremacy and empire that was enjoyed by Victorian Britain could be attributed to the activities of the Elizabethan sea-dogs – particularly Drake – who had wrested control of the high seas from Spain. But one historian did more than any other to shape the way in which the Elizabethan maritime past was perceived: James Anthony Froude. It was Froude who was principally responsible for popularizing the notion that the origins of the nation's naval power were located in the energies of the late sixteenth century. With its central theme that the Reformation brought about the freedom that allowed England to expand its commerce and colonies, his work changed the popular perception of sixteenth-century history. Put simply, Froude was concerned with mythologizing the imperial past – and Sir Francis Drake played a major part in this project.

Before looking at Froude's treatment of Drake, however, we must turn our attention to the two main determinants that shaped his writing of English history. The first significant influence on Froude was the religious thought of his elder brother, Richard Hurrell Froude and that of his fellow Oxford student, John Henry Newman. Hurrell Froude and Newman were principal members of the Oxford Movement, a body of churchmen and academics which aimed at reasserting the Catholicity of the Church of England. Together with John Keble and Edward Bouverie Pusey, the other leading figures in the Movement, they argued that the Church of England remained part of the holy Catholic Church (of which the Roman Catholic and Greek Orthodox Churches were also branches). For the members of the Movement, apostolic succession had not been broken by the Reformation and the Anglican Church remained a sacramental and priestly Church. Reasserting Catholicity meant a renewed emphasis upon the mystical dimensions of the Church such as the Eucharist and, crucially, the role of the clergy. The Movement rested their faith upon a dual revelation:

> upon the Bible, as the Church and the Councils of the Church alone knew how to interpret it, but still more certainly upon the existence and authority of the Church itself. They held the prestige, the independence, the supremacy, of the Church to be more important than anything else in the world.[2]

The origins of the Oxford Movement can be traced to John Keble's sermon 'On the National Apostasy' (1833). This aimed at rousing the Anglican clergy against outright control by the state – the immediate motivation for the sermon was a statute abolishing ten bishoprics in Ireland. Between 1833 and 1841 the religious views of the Movement were set out in a series of 90 pamphlets titled *Tracts for the Times* (from which the term 'Tractarianism', sometimes applied to the views of the Oxford Movement, was derived).

Closely involved with the movement, James Anthony Froude was elected a fellow of Exeter College, Oxford, in 1842 and became a deacon in holy orders belonging to the High Church party in 1845. However, increasing religious scepticism – deepened by Newman's conversion to Roman Catholicism – saw him resign both posts in 1849. Unprepared to follow Newman to Rome and with his faith in the Oxford Movement shaken, Froude steadily abandoned the High Church metanarrative. This crisis in faith was explored in his controversial third novel *The Nemesis of Faith* (1849), which, although not autobiographical, is concerned with the religious doubts of a young clergyman who eventually resigns the ministry. Of course, the rejection of something that had been so central in Froude's life inevitably left a huge void. English history served to fill this vacuum. In place of the religious metanarrative Froude manoeuvred a secular grand narrative, that of Britain's rise to greatness and empire. The belief in the independence of Church from state that had been so central to Tractarian thought was replaced by a mythology of the state itself. The central theme of Froude's historical writing, the victory of the Reformation – and with it the subordination of the Church to secular powers – may be seen as his revenge on Newman for his abandonment of Froude and the Oxford Movement.

It was, perhaps, fortunate for Froude that his break with the Oxford Movement coincided with a shift in the perception of the nation's overseas possessions. The military campaigns of the 1840s had generated a great deal of popular support that led, in turn, to a growing self-awareness of Britain as an imperial power. Froude's work dealt with the origins of this imperial status. His major contribution to the shaping of imperial discourse was the work *History of England from the Fall of Wolsey to the Defeat of the Spanish Armada*[3] published in twelve volumes between 1856 and 1870. Again Froude's timing was impeccable – the first volume appeared a year before the Indian Mutiny, an event that would have a great impact on the public's engagement with empire. What the British termed the Indian Mutiny, a rebellion by native troops under British command at Meerut, led rapidly to further uprisings across the north of the subcontinent. The mutiny became a widespread struggle for independence. Brutal suppression by the British – of which Froude approved – led to further, violent reprisals on the part of the Indians. At home the effect of this shockingly violent and entirely unexpected event was to focus attention even more closely on the empire. In 1858 the East India Company was abolished – it had taken most of the blame for allowing the mutiny to take place – and India became the greatest possession of what became known as the formal Empire or those possessions ruled directly by the Crown. When the partially autonomous colonies of white settlement were added to the list of British territories, the full extent of the nation's imperial status became clear. It was up to the myth-makers like Froude to explain why and how this had happened.

The second major determinant that shaped Froude's view of history was the work of the historian and social commentator Thomas Carlyle. The two men first met in 1849 and, although they later argued, Carlyle's thought continued to influence Froude's work. (Carlyle annotated the first drafts of the early volumes of Froude's *History of England*.) An important development in Carlyle's work – and a major influence on Froude's construction of Sir Francis Drake – was the notion of the hero. Carlyle's position is made plain by the much-quoted lines from *On Heroes, Hero-Worship and the Heroic in History* (1841), 'Universal History, the history of what man has accomplished in this world, is at bottom the History of the Great Men who have worked here.'[4] In Carlyle's later works the hero is foremost a man of action, a great military leader who rebuilt or saved his country from 'chaos', the most wretched of states. This was their 'work'. These heroic figures are never despotic but respond to the needs of their society by using strength or might to establish right. The hero is unequivocally a power for the good; he acts 'with his force direct out of God's own hand'.[5] Oliver Cromwell, with his fervent Christian convictions and desire to reconstruct a degenerate nation, was the perfect embodiment of Carlyle's notion of the heroic. He first addressed Cromwell in *On Heroes and Hero-Worship* but dealt with his subject in greater detail in *Oliver Cromwell's Letters and Speeches, with Elucidations*[6] published four years later. A work appeared in the late 1850s that reinforced Carlyle's hero theory: the six-volume *History of Frederick II of Prussia, Called Frederick the Great*[7] (1858–65). Here was a military leader who had greatly enlarged Prussian territory and made the nation a significant power in European affairs – although Carlyle was taxed to justify some of Frederick's actions.

In his earlier works, however, Carlyle's version of the hero was less rigid. Abbot Samson, a medieval cleric, is elevated to heroic status in *Past and Present*[8] (1843). Carlyle's method in this work is to compare the condition of Britain in the nineteenth century – concentrating on the condition of the working classes – with that of a twelfth-century monastic community at St Edmundsbury. The feudal past emerges as an attractive alternative to modern capitalism. Abbot Samson, although not a man of action in the same sense as Cromwell, is nevertheless 'an eminently practical man'.[9] He provides clear and strong leadership at a time of insecurity. The active leadership of the abbot is compared with the attempts of the Oxford Movement 'to save themselves and a ruined world by noisy, theoretic demonstrations'.[10] In *On Heroes and Hero-Worship* the idea of the hero is rather more fluid. Carlyle identifies six types of hero: the Hero as Divinity, as Prophet, Poet, Priest, Man of Letters, and King. He discusses examples of each type; these include Luther as priest, Dante as poet and Oliver Cromwell as king (or as a figure functioning as king). What unites these disparate figures is the ability to appreciate the 'reality' of things, an unrealized truth (or what Carlyle, borrowing a term from Transcendentalist theory, terms the 'Divine Idea') that is unobtainable by the ordinary man. A staunch believer in authoritarianism and a fierce opponent of any form of democracy, Carlyle saw the need for a hero to rebuild the Britain of the 1840s. He saw very clearly and condemned the poverty forced upon the working classes (this is made clear by the initial pages of *Chartism*,[11] which appeared in 1840), but believed that this situation could not be rectified by democratic means. He was fiercely opposed to both Utilitarianism and Chartism. His approach has been neatly summarized,

> The masses of the people can never be safely trusted to solve for themselves the intricate problems of their own welfare. They need to be guided, disciplined, at times even driven, by those great leaders of men.[12]

J. A. Froude first approached the heroic themes that were to engage so much of his energy in an article published in the *Westminster and Foreign Quarterly Review* in 1852. Revealingly titled 'England's Forgotten Worthies',[13] this was intended as a corrective or as a means of reversing (what Froude perceived as) the lack of interest shown in the seafarers of Elizabeth's reign. Sir Francis Drake, as we have seen, was far from being forgotten (although the great narrative histories of Lingard and Mackintosh pay him little attention). Yet, for Froude, Drake's reputation – and that of Hawkins, Raleigh, Gilbert and their fellow voyagers – required reassessment. Just why Froude regarded the Elizabethan seamen as so hugely important is soon made clear. Referring to an edition of Hakluyt that had appeared early in the century, Froude states, 'The five-volume quarto edition, published in 1811, so little people then cared for the exploits of their ancestors, consisted but of 270 copies.' He then comes to the crucial point. 'And yet those five volumes may be called the prose epic of the modern English nation.'[14] For Froude these nautical tales deserve to be regarded as an epic because they tell the story of the nation's rise to greatness and are comparable to – or even surpass – the epics of the ancient world.

> They contain the heroic tales of the exploits of the great men in whom the new era was inaugurated; not mythic, like the Iliads and the Eddas, but plain broad narratives of substantial facts, which rival legend in interest and grandeur.[15]

The fact that the narratives are 'plain' and unembellished with fantastic and obviously invented incidents heightens their appeal. As suggested in Chapter Four, during the early decades of the nineteenth century an historical methodology emerged based upon original documentation and 'fact'. (By the mid–century a similar development was taking place in literature as realism emerged as a dominant creative mode in European culture.) Hakluyt's collection of narratives, some of which were written by barely literate participants in the voyages they describe, was, it seems, ideal material. In Froude's words, 'We can conceive nothing, not the songs of Homer himself, which would be read among us with more enthusiastic interest than these plain massive tales.'[16]

Froude identifies another significant difference between Hakluyt's narratives and the old epics. The 'prose epic' of England does not concern itself with kings and princes but with common seamen. Froude employs a telling analogy:

> But, as it was in the days of the Apostles, when a few poor fishermen from an obscure lake in Palestine assumed, under the Divine mission, spiritual authority over mankind, so, in the days of our own Elizabeth, the seamen from the banks of the Thames and the Avon, the Plym and the Dart, self-taught and self-directed, with no impulse but what was beating in their own royal hearts, went out across the unknown seas fighting, discovering, colonizing, and graved out the channels … through which the commerce and enterprise of England has flowed out over all the world.[17]

Aligning English mariners with the Disciples of Christ is a bold move and one that hints very clearly at divine sanction for English maritime expansion. (Of course, regarding themselves as divinely favoured is not an uncommon practice among peoples at the height of their hegemony.) It also suggests the way in which, for Froude, the grand narrative of imperial development had replaced that of religion. The foregrounding of the 'poor' and 'self-taught' serves to strengthen the idea central to Froude's version of English history: that the Reformation was responsible for England's rise to greatness. This break with the old order provided the liberty necessary for common men like Francis Drake to play an important part in English history. But here we are confronted with a grand paradox: the fact that Froude's heroes of the Reformation are 'common' men suggests a democratizing impulse in his work. Yet Froude heartily embraced Carlyle's authoritarian stance. The notion of the hero was born from Carlyle's perception of the chaos or anarchy that would result from the movement towards democracy. Froude's adherence to this brand of authoritarianism is revealed when he wrote 'I regarded the Reformation as the grandest achievement in English history, yet it was equally obvious that it could never have been brought about constitutionally.'[18] The Reformation, for Froude, was the work of two figures: Henry VIII, founder of the Royal Navy, and Elizabeth. To unravel the paradox we need to understand just what Froude means when he writes of the liberty occasioned by the Reformation. Clearly, he is not referring to a system where 'the wise and foolish, the worthless and the worthy alike [are] free to do as they please and have an equal voice in the Commonwealth'.[19] This is, in Froude's own word, 'delusory'. The freedom to which he refers is that which allows the heroism, the qualities of leadership, in the common man to come to the fore. The break with Rome provided that freedom:

> The Catholic faith was no longer able to furnish standing ground on which the English or any other nation could live a manly or godly life … Thenceforward, not the Catholic Church, but any man to whom God had given a heart to feel and a voice to speak, was to be the teacher to whom men were to listen; and great actions were not to remain the privilege of the families of the Norman nobles, but were laid within the reach of the poorest plebeian who had the stuff in them to perform them.[20]

The common mariners of the nation's sea towns, guided by 'their own royal hearts', had, it seems, this 'stuff' in abundance.

Of course, Sir Francis Drake did not rebuild England in the same way as Oliver Cromwell, the greatest of Carlyle's heroes. For Drake to be fitted neatly into the role of Carlylean saviour-hero a certain amount of manoeuvring was required. There is no doubt that the Reformation reshaped England and, in Froude's mind, the break with Rome was finally secured by the defeat of the Spanish Armada. Drake had certainly contributed to this victory, but his heroism was derived primarily from his privateering activities. These had played a major part in bringing about the war with Spain that led to the failed invasion attempt. The war was, it seems, a necessary evil. Moreover, the victory over the Armada was made possible largely by the superior sea-faring skills of the English mariners. These skills had been developed on the privateering voyages to the Spanish Caribbean, and it was Drake who led the way. Therefore, although Sir Francis Drake was not responsible for the Reformation in England, Froude sees his buccaneering activities as central to its survival. Drake's credentials as a Carlylean saviour-hero are developed in Froude's major contribution to the Victorian version of sixteenth-century history, the *History of England from the Fall of Wolsey to the Defeat of the Spanish Armada*. Froude believed the period encompassed by the work (1529 to 1588) witnessed the final emphatic victory of Protestantism. (Concluding with the defeat of the Armada also meant that Froude did not have to engage with Drake's failed expeditions.) This, of course, demonstrated a complete lack of regard for the events that took place in the century after his closing date, events that suggested the Reformation was far from secure. Particularly important were the increasing identification of Charles I with Catholicism and James II's attempts at turning the country into a Catholic absolutism. This is exactly the type of discontinuity that the narrative of causation sought to elide.

Froude devotes a lengthy chapter to Drake's circumnavigation and its political ramifications. He begins by setting out what he considered to be the two objectives of the voyage from the queen's perspective: to seize a great amount of treasure for future use, and to show Philip that the Spanish colonies, the source of his wealth, were not secure and so frighten him into peace. This is followed by Elizabeth's famous statement on the lawful freedom of English mariners to navigate the South Seas. This allows the author to draw a contrast between the political manoeuvrings of the Court and the admirably simple way in which Drake saw his mission:

> To Drake himself, all that he might do appeared more than justified. He
> was the avenger of the English seamen who had perished in Mexican
> dungeons, on the Cadiz galleys, or had been burnt to death at Seville. ...
> This was sufficient motive for Drake, and was a better excuse for
> retaliation than ambiguous theories of property in the Indian seas.[21]

Here we can detect the unmistakable influence of Carlylean thought. Like the
heroes in Carlyle's later works, Drake is essentially a man of action. He is not
motivated by abstract notions, the 'ambiguous theories of property', but by the very
real suffering of his fellow sailors. Moreover, his response is eminently practical – to
deprive Philip of his wealth through the interception of Spanish shipping. This was
God's will and Drake clearly saw it. The emphasis on Drake's action, his 'work', is
contrasted to political impotence, the ultimate futility of attempting to negotiate
with Spain. Like Cromwell in particular, he combines strength (energy and naval
brilliance) with a conviction that he acted with God's approval. 'Along with Drake's
genius there was in him the Puritan conviction that he was fighting on God's side,
which created success by the very confidence with which success was anticipated.'[22]
He becomes a Christian soldier, or more correctly, a Protestant soldier fighting the
never-ending struggle against the evil of Rome. This anticipates the construction
of the Elizabethan seafarers that we will come across in the work of Charles
Kingsley – a construction shaped by the ethical ideal of Christian manliness.

   In Sir Francis Drake's case the term that Froude employs in his journal article,
'England's Forgotten Worthies', is slightly misleading. Froude's aim in the article and
in the History of England is not to revive but to reconstruct Sir Francis. Froude shifts
the emphasis away from Drake as a highly successful (and usually gentlemanly)
pirate and places it very firmly on Sir Francis as a patriotic naval commander.
Rather surprisingly, in the 'Forgotten Worthies' he chooses to illustrate this deft
piece of manoeuvring by dwelling on the Doughty incident. His treatment of this,
the most controversial episode of Drake's career, reveals a certain manipulation of
sources. (Froude was, in fact, frequently attacked for his historical inaccuracies).[23]
We are told that Drake's affection for his old friend prevented him from leaving any
record of Doughty's offences. There is no evidence whatsoever that Drake felt any
loyalty towards Doughty. Indeed, after the execution he lectured his crews on the
inevitable fate of traitors. This is followed by a long quotation from Hakluyt dealing
with Doughty's trial and execution. Froude concludes that for the crew of a
'common ship' to conduct such an orderly proceeding at a location as wild as Port
St Julian 'is not to be reconciled with the pirate theory'.[24] He does, however,
concede that Drake captured a huge amount of treasure from Spanish ports and
shipping while England and Spain were not officially at war. As we have seen, this
undoubted piracy held no problems for Froude who takes the opportunity to
reiterate Drake's motives. There is no attempt to follow the routes taken by Drake's
apologists – that of excusing his buccaneering on the grounds that notions of right
and wrong were indistinct in the sixteenth century or that as common sailor, he
knew no better. The treasure is taken because of the treatment of English seamen

at the hands of the Inquisition. Far from simply seeking recompense for his losses sustained at San Juan d'Ulua, Drake has become a dispenser of justice.

But if Froude's construction of Drake's motivation is to be really effective it is necessary for the Spanish to become the Others who define the supposed moral superiority of Drake (and, of course, the English in general). This is achieved by representing the Spanish as especially cruel. Indeed, Froude seems to take delight in setting before the reader the atrocities committed by the Inquisition. The emphasis on Spanish brutality serves to highlight the humanity of Sir Francis. 'There was no gratuitous cruelty in Drake; he was come for the treasure of Peru, and beyond seizing his plunder he did not care to injure the people.'[25] There is nothing new in emphasizing Drake's good treatment of natives and prisoners. The accounts of his voyages that appeared in the early seventeenth century continually foreground his humanity. What had changed by the time Froude was writing, however, was Britain's status in the world. This construction of Drake must be read in terms of British imperialism in the nineteenth century. In the 1630s England was making its first successful attempts at colonial expansion. By the 1870s, Britain was attempting to justify possession of its vast and steadily growing empire. Projecting the supposedly inherent English moral superiority that Drake exemplifies back in time – to a point when England was a secondary power – performs an ideological function: it serves to make the superiority seem natural. In this way the myth-makers could present Britain as more deserving of empire than its Iberian predecessor.

In Froude's *History of England* it is Sir Francis Drake's privateering that ultimately persuades the queen to commence the war that would settle the Reformation in England. This is a further example of the manoeuvring that allows Drake to be constructed as a hero responsible for saving his country from 'chaos'. Drake's relationship with Elizabeth is presented as one of mutual understanding. 'Intellectually vacillating, yet delighting in enterprise and energy, she had found in Drake a man after her own heart, whom she could disown without fear that he would resent her affected displeasure.'[26] When writing of his project to produce a history of the English Reformation, Froude admitted that Elizabeth intrigued him.

> It was Elizabeth, however, who chiefly interested me. The figure of this
> solitary woman braving and ruling the tempest surrounded by
> conspiracies, the special object of hate of the catholic world ... made
> intelligible to me the enthusiasm with which she was worshipped by the
> noblest of her subjects.[27]

Yet this fascination was to lead to disappointment. As his work progressed Froude was forced to modify some of his previously formed opinions. 'A qualified defence of Henry VIII was forced upon me by the facts of the case. With equal reluctance I had to acknowledge that the wisdom of Elizabeth was the wisdom of her ministers.'[28] For Froude, Elizabeth was essentially a weak ruler. Walsingham and Burghley spent their time guiding the queen's policy in the right direction. It was Walsingham (and, of course, Drake) who realized that war with Spain was the only course of action, yet he had to convince the queen of this. His major obstacle was finance. Elizabeth has, perhaps unfairly, gained notoriety for her reluctance to part with money. Froude dwells on this when dealing with the defeat of the Spanish Armada: she even berates Drake for wasting money on target practice. But it is her financial interests that eventually determine the right course of action. 'She shrunk from war, because war was costly, but he [Walsingham] taught her to see by Drake's exploit that war might give her the wealth of the Indies.'[29]

There is little doubting Froude's ability to write compelling prose, which surely contributed to the popularity of his work. Among nineteenth-century historians only Creasy rivals him for his tight control of the dramatic elements of his narrative. For Froude, history seems to have revealed itself as a drama. Of the Reformation he wrote, 'The coming of the Armada was the last act of a drama of which the divorce of Queen Catherine was the first.'[30] There is something theatrical about the way Drake is introduced to us.

> His dress as he appears in his portraits, is a loose dark seaman's shirt, belted at the waist. About his neck is a plaited cord with a ring attached to it, in which, as if the attitude was familiar, one of his fingers is slung, displaying a small, delicate, but long and sinewy hand.

Displaying a flair for the dramatic, Froude quickly shifts from the image to the man. 'Such was Francis Drake when he stood on the deck of the Pelican in Plymouth harbour, in November, 1577.'[31] In this case, however, Froude's carefully crafted narrative is deflated somewhat when we realize that the portrait he has been describing is almost certainly that of Sir John Hawkins now held at the National Maritime Museum, Greenwich.. The section on the circumnavigation concentrates on the voyage along the Pacific coast of South America omitting most of the crossing of the Atlantic. Hugely partial, Froude's treatment of Drake's raids on the Spanish ports is not without humour. Of the treasure taken at Valparaiso he writes,

> Mr Fletcher's provision for the sacrament was enriched by a chalice, two cruets, and an altar cloth. A few pipes of wine, some logs of cedar, and a Greek pilot who knew the way to Lima, completed the booty.[32]

Froude also does much to reinforce the idea of the Elizabethan mariners as hearty sea-dogs. Indeed, the term 'sea-dogs' seems to have become popular around the mid-nineteenth century and has, in one commentator's words, 'the virtue of reluctant admiration attached to it'.[33] The admiration was reluctant because of the problematic nature of Drake and the other Elizabethan voyagers. No matter what attempts were made at justification, their activities were essentially piratical. And yet, when constructing a narrative of causation that explained Britain's lofty position in the world, most Victorian myth-makers agreed that the nation's rise began with the expansionism of the sixteenth century – with the privateers. The name 'dog', usually a derogatory term, implies a lowly coarseness but also a capacity for great loyalty. According to the Victorian myth-makers, the Elizabethan sea-dogs were marked by their excellent seamanship, courage, loyalty, sense of fair play and physicality. This construction is part of the larger English tradition of physical manliness. The link between sporting and military manliness (and Froude's obvious approval) is made plain when the English board a moored Spanish vessel. 'Thomas Moore, a lad from Plymouth, began the play with knocking down the first man that he met, saluting him in Spanish as he fell and crying out "Abajo, perro" – "Down, dog, to –."'[34]

The 'Descent on the Indies' is not dealt with in the same detail as the circumnavigation. This is largely because, in financial terms, the voyage was not viewed as a great success. Anxious that the hero, Drake, should not be associated with failure, Froude writes that the expedition 'did more to shake the Spaniards' confidence in themselves, and the world's belief in their invincibility, than the accidental capture of dozens of gold fleets'.[35] Obviously Froude enjoys describing the anxiety caused by the news that Drake was anchored off the Spanish coast. 'All Spain was in agitation at the news that the world-famed corsair was on the coast. The council of State sat for three days discussing it.'[36] He juxtaposes events in Europe with those in the New World. Elizabeth negotiates with Parma for permission for Drake to return unpunished while on the other side of the Atlantic Froude merely states, 'St. George's cross was floating over St. Iago, and the plunder of the town was secured in the holds of his cruisers.'[37] Given that the heroic is inextricably bound with action in Froude's work, there is no doubt as to what he sees as the correct course of action. But although this was a treasure-raiding voyage on a massive scale we are assured that 'Drake was no destroying vandal'.[38] Froude provides little evidence to back up this assertion – indeed, some of his material implies quite the reverse. Drake's company are certainly happy to desecrate the sacred objects they find at Vigo. Here they take 'liberties with the saints, to provoke them to show they were alive'[39] and treat the Madonna with 'some indignity'. Obviously, for Froude, vandalism is acceptable when the end result is the destruction of 'idols'. Of course, it is unlikely that Drake, himself, took part in these activities. He was concerned with destruction on a much wider scale. Froude assures us that 'He was unwilling to sack St. Domingo if the inhabitants were prepared to redeem its safety.'[40] But when the ransom money was slow in coming, Drake became rather more willing to use coercive methods. He ordered two hundred sailors to raze the town street by street. Froude's celebratory version of Drake's privateering is a far cry from Robert Southey's meditation on Drake's activities written twenty years earlier. He suggested that much civilization had been destroyed for the loss of many English lives. Both, however, agree that the effect of these voyages upon the skill of English seamen was marked.

The raid on Cadiz provides Froude with a much more successful action with which to work. Perhaps with an eye on Nelson's highly successful acts of insubordination, Froude has Drake slipping away from Plymouth just before a message arrives instructing him to abandon the expedition. Such an audacious raid as Cadiz could only have been undertaken by Sir Francis Drake, and Froude is keen to contrast the admirable English daring of Drake with the cowardice of William Borough, the expedition's vice-admiral. Borough argued against Drake's plan of entering the heavily guarded harbour. 'Admiral Burroughs', as Froude spells his name, 'was loud in opposition. He refused to be responsible for the danger to her majesty's fleet, with the other formulas generally used in such cases by incompetent officers.'[41] This is undoubtedly unfair on Borough, a rather more conventional captain, who had gained renown, primarily, for charting the White Sea and for work on navigational techniques. But he lacked the reckless bravery that the Victorian reader wanted in his sixteenth-century heroes. For Froude, this made him a coward: 'A single shot hit the Lion, and Burroughs, seeing nothing before him but destruction, dropped his anchors, [and] warped his vessel out of range.'[42] Similarly, the conservative Borough was not in favour of storming the forts that guarded the anchorage at Faro. Drake ignored him and captured the batteries. He then turned his attention to his problematic vice-admiral. Froude seems to enjoy Borough's downfall. 'The axe and block at Patagonia had shown what Drake was capable of doing to his second in command. This time milder methods sufficed.'[43] Borough was relieved of all responsibility and confined in his cabin. According to Froude, he 'slipped away and went home'.[44] Actually a mutiny occurred aboard the *Golden Lion* occasioned by poor provisions. Borough's part in this is unclear but the ship returned to England and Borough escaped punishment. Drake, on the other hand, displays English manly courage. He even baits Santa Cruz, the Spanish admiral whose fleet was anchored at Lisbon, knowing full well that the Spanish strength was formidable.

> He sent in a challenge to Santa Cruz to come out and fight him; and having thus, with but four small ships of war and a handful of London privateers, defied at their own doors the united navies of Spain and Portugal, he sailed to Coruna.[45]

Froude's early engagement with the seafarers of the sixteenth century, 'England's Forgotten Worthies', was read with great interest by Devon-born clergyman-novelist (and later Froude's brother-in-law), Charles Kingsley. Having spent his boyhood in Devon, Kingsley was well aware of the reputations of Drake, Hawkins, Raleigh and the other West Country sea-dogs. But Froude's 'Forgotten Worthies' served to renew his interest in the maritime affairs of the late sixteenth century – an interest that resulted in the hugely popular and intensely patriotic novel of Elizabethan privateering, *Westward Ho!*[46] (1855). Reflecting on the 'Forgotten Worthies' some years after its publication, Froude wrote 'besides the further notice of myself which it had the fortune to call out, it suggested to Kingsley his brilliant novel'.[47] Although Froude may, probably justly, claim some credit for inspiring *Westward Ho!*, Kingsley's reading on the subject was much wider and included Prince, Raleigh and particularly Hakluyt from whom he gathered much material.

Westward Ho! is a rollicking tale of nautical adventure that follows the exploits of Amyas Leigh, a fictional Elizabethan seafarer. His story is woven into the very real events of the late sixteenth century culminating in the defeat of the Spanish Armada and Sir Francis Drake plays a major part in the narrative. Before looking at the way in which Kingsley constructs Drake, however, it is important that we establish the political and religious imperatives that produced *Westward Ho!* Clearly the novel provides a vehicle for an extended attack on the Catholic Church. This was partly the result of Kingsley's personal opposition to Rome, which will be discussed later. But we must also realize that *Westward Ho!* was riding a wave of renewed anti-Catholic fervour. This was occasioned by the so-called 'Papal Aggression' of 1850 – the name given to the restoration of a Catholic hierarchy in Britain as part of which the pope appointed Cardinal Wiseman achbishop of Westminster. The press represented this as unacceptable interference in national affairs and a considerable amount of public and political indignation was raised. However, we should be aware that the Roman Catholic population of Britain, particularly in the large cities, was growing rapidly. This arose partly from an influx of immigrants from Ireland, the result of the catastrophic potato famine of 1845/6. From this perspective the restoration of the Catholic hierarchy was not 'Papal Aggression' but merely an attempt to meet the needs of the nation's Catholic population. But this was not the sole reason for the anti-Catholic feeling. As mentioned in the previous chapter, Louis Napoleon's elevation to emperor of France in 1852 sparked a short but intense invasion scare. To make matters worse, France was believed to be acting with the full support of the pope. In 1850 Louis Napoleon had intervened to restore Pope Pius IX who had fled Rome two years earlier following the establishment of the Roman Republic during the Year of Revolutions. The prospect of a foreign aggressor acting in concert with the pope inevitably revived memories of another invasion attempt with papal blessing that had taken place in Elizabeth's reign – the Spanish Armada. The conditions were perfect for a patriotic novel dealing with the repulse of a Catholic invader.

However, the fear of a French invasion quickly receded when Britain became engaged in another armed struggle, this time in the Crimea. 'The French aggressor of 1853 had become Britain's ally in the Crimean war by 1854. But one patriotic cause could be very much like another ... Anti-French feeling was overlaid with anti-Russian feeling.'[48] As far as Britain was concerned the war was fought for strategic reasons. Russian control of the Straits connecting the Black Sea with the Mediterranean may have affected national interests in the East. *Westward Ho!* appeared during the middle of the Crimean War (1854–6) and is certainly a product of the popular patriotism with which the conflict was greeted. Of course, Russia was not a Roman Catholic country but Kingsley's personal antipathy towards everything Catholic was reinforced when John Newman spoke out against the war. For Kingsley, his unpatriotic rhetoric at such a sensitive time was analogous to the popish conspiracies of Elizabeth's Court. It was clear that Catholic priests could not be trusted. (Kingsley, as we will see later, initiated a great controversy over the issue of Roman Catholicism and 'the truth'.) This belief found expression in *Westward Ho!* where two unfortunate priests are heard to claim '"Yea, what is a country? An arbitrary division of territory by the princes of this world, who are naught, and come to naught."'[49] At this point we must turn our attention to Kingsley's construction of the events of the late sixteenth century.

Westward Ho! introduces us to a wide and very lively selection of characters from Elizabeth's reign. Early in the novel Kingsley acknowledges his debt to Froude. Not only does he make reference to Froude's 'Forgotten Worthies' but he also shares the belief that the Reformation was secured by the defeat of the Armada. The anti-Catholic invective sets the tone for what is to come.

> It was the men of Devon, the Drakes and Hawkinses, Gilberts and
> Raleighs, Grenvilles and Oxenhams, and a host more of 'forgotten
> worthies,' whom we shall learn one day to honour as they deserve, to
> whom she owes her commerce, her colonies, her very existence. For had
> they not first crippled, by their West Indian raids, the ill-gotten resources of
> the Spaniard, and then crushed his last huge effort in Britain's Salamis, the
> glorious fight of 1588, what had we been by now, but a Popish appanage of
> a world-tyranny as cruel as heathen Rome itself, and far more devilish?[50]

Kingsley and Froude, both Devon men, engaged in the construction of a cult of the
West that celebrated the West Country as the cradle of the nation's maritime
prowess. (The West Saxon King Alfred rather than Henry VIII was often credited
with establishing the Royal Navy.) Given that *Westward Ho!* is a tale of adventure
on the high seas it is hardly surprising that the Devon worthies Kingsley selects are
all men of action. Yet there is more behind the emphasis on action than simply the
desire to produce a ripping yarn. To fully comprehend Kingsley's treatment of
Drake and the other sea-dogs we need to explore the ethical ideal of Christian
manliness that runs through his work.

Charles Kingsley was a fierce opponent of Roman Catholicism and the Oxford
Movement. In a review of Froude's *History of England* – or rather those volumes
dealing with the popish conspiracies of Elizabeth's court – he notoriously attacked
the Roman Catholic clergy. 'Truth for its own sake', he wrote, 'had never been a
virtue of the Roman clergy. Father Newman informs us that it need not, and on
the whole ought not to be.'[51] For Kingsley, Newman's writings as both a High
Churchman and as a Roman Catholic were marked by their tricky equivocation;
Newman was not being honest about his intentions. Tractarianism, Kingsley
believed, sought to subvert the Church of England. Newman responded powerfully
to Kingsley's personal attack with the autobiographical *Apologia pro Vita Sua*. But
this controversy was about much more than Newman's honesty. We need to realize
that Kingsley's liberal theological position was at odds with the core belief of both
the Tractarians and Evangelicals. Although promoting hugely different means by
which grace could be achieved, both the High Church Tractarians and Low
Church Evangelicals agreed that 'the physical world [was] of no consequence in
comparison with the heavenly world which forms the goal of Christian
aspiration'.[52] Kingsley had been influenced by the thought of his friend Frederick
Maurice (who had himself been influenced by Coleridge's Incarnational theology),
who insisted 'on the present world as the arena of divine activity'.[53] His rejection
of the dichotomy between sacred and secular or world and spirit led Maurice to
found the Christian Socialist movement of which Kingsley was a great supporter.
For the supporters of Christian Socialism active reform took precedence over the
concentration upon the individual soul and personal salvation. Kingsley had no
time for Catholic or High Church spirituality. Believing that man was made in the
image of God and, therefore, that 'Physical strength, courage and health are
attractive, valuable and useful in themselves and in the eyes of God',[54] he devoted

himself to the service of the Almighty through action in the physical world. His position is spelt out early in *Westward Ho!* In a church service held to mark the safe return of the heroes from the circumnavigation, the preacher thanks God for his assistance in guiding Drake through the Strait of Magellan and for sparing the *Golden Hinde* when she was grounded upon a reef. Kingsley writes,

> Smile, if you will: but those were days (and there were never less superstitious ones) in which Englishmen believed in the living God, and were not ashamed to acknowledge, as a matter of course, His help and providence, and calling, in the matters of daily life, which we now in our covert Atheism term 'secular and carnal'.[55]

And this is where we return to the ideal of Christian manliness. In Froude's *History of England* we saw a celebration of the physical and courageous aspect of manliness. The aim of Christian manliness was to conjoin this physical manliness – and the other secular qualities that could be termed manly, particularly courage and chivalry – with a Christian moral purpose. *Westward Ho!* is dedicated to two exemplars of Christian manliness, the white Rajah Sir James Brooke and George Selwyn, bishop of New Zealand. Brooke developed a scheme to plant a settlement on Sulawesi (now Borneo). His motives – which echo those of Sir Francis Drake – have been described as 'partly love of adventure, and largely the desire to introduce commerce as well as British ascendancy into Borneo'.[56] The combination of independent enterprise, sea-faring adventure and the desire to extend British possessions make Brooke a very Drakean figure. The scheme was put into practice in 1841. After helping quell a local rebellion, Brooke was awarded the governorship of Sarawak (a province of northern Borneo) along with the title Rajah. He initiated free trade, suppressed piracy and introduced a new code of law. Later he was accused of cruel and illegal conduct in his suppression of piracy but was acquitted of all charges. The energetic George Selwyn travelled extensively among the Pacific islands spreading his Christian message and developed a scheme for the self-government of his diocese. Kingsley wrote, 'That type of English virtue, at once manful and godly, practical and self-sacrificing, which he has tried to depict in these pages, they have exhibited in a form even purer and more heroic.'[57] The Elizabethan characters of *Westward Ho!* provide a purportedly early illustration of this combination of physical manliness with a Christian mission.

But how is Sir Francis Drake constructed by a work so thoroughly shaped by the ideal of Christian manliness? Although Drake does not appear in the novel until near the end, his presence permeates *Westward Ho!* Obviously, many of the historical characters that appear in the novel had very real connections with Drake: Oxenham took part in the raid on Nombre de Dios, Winter returned from the circumnavigation having lost contact with Drake, Philip Sidney was prevented from sailing on the 1585 West Indian raids and Grenville – in some ways Drake's rival – sold Buckland Abbey to the newly wealthy Sir Francis. The fictional characters, too, have close associations with the greatest Elizabethan mariner. Amyas Leigh, the principal character of the novel, sails on the circumnavigation, and the faithful

Salvation Yeo accompanied Drake to Panama. Indeed, it is possible to argue that, although absent, Sir Francis is the main character in the novel. His exploits facilitate the action – and these deeds were impelled by his religious convictions. As we will see, Drake is Kingsley's ultimate practitioner of Christian manliness.

The name 'Drake' is continually linked with naval success. The voyages with which he is not connected often end in disaster or defeat. And it is the moral imperative driving Drake's exploits that seems to guarantee his success. (Like Froude, Kingsley does not focus on the events that occurred after 1588 – these would demonstrate that Drake was far from invincible.) Drake's privateering actually serves God. Of his piratical activities Richard Grenville states

> I have always held … that Mr Drake's booty, as well as my good friend
> Captain Hawkins's, is lawful prize, as being taken from the Spaniard, who is
> not only *hostis humanii generis*, but has no right to the same, having robbed
> it violently, by torture and extreme iniquity from the poor Indian.[58]

Drake is merely carrying out God's will by removing the treasure from undeserving Spanish hands and using it to strengthen the Reformed Church. '[I]f it be not the cause of God, I, for one, know not what God's cause is!'[59] The same cannot be said of John Oxenham. His ill-fated return expedition to Panama is undertaken without Drake who, we are informed, was serving his country by fighting in Ireland. The enterprise ends with Oxenham and most of his crew dead. For Kingsley, this is the result of a voyage undertaken solely for personal gain. Lust for gold cannot be said to lie behind Humphrey Gilbert's attempt to colonize Newfoundland. But this, too, resulted in the death of the adventurer. Christian manliness is also able to account for this failure. Kingsley writes 'He got his scheme perfect upon paper; well for him, and for his company, if he had asked Francis Drake to translate it for him into fact.'[60] Kingsley's concentration upon physical manliness led to his ethical ideals being conveniently grouped under the rather trivializing term 'muscular Christianity'. In the case of *Westward Ho!*, however, muscular Christianity seems an apposite phrase. Action is continually elevated above the academic as a manly activity. Nowhere is this clearer than in Drake's prophetic words to Amyas the night before Gilbert sails for Newfoundland.

> For learning and manners, Amyas, there's not his [Gilbert's] equal; and the
> Queen may well love him, and Devon be proud of him: but book-
> learning is not business; book-learning didn't get me round the world;
> book-learning didn't make Captain Hawkins, nor his father neither, the
> best shipbuilders from Hull to Cadiz; and book-learning, I very much fear,
> won't plant Newfoundland.[61]

Sir Francis Drake is largely responsible for shaping the conduct of Kingsley's young protagonist, Amyas Leigh. The qualities he instils are those valued as manly Christian. We have already seen how Drake warns Amyas of the perils of book-learning. But Christian manliness is reflected in numerous other ways, particularly in his initiation into sea-faring life. 'Drake had trained him, as he trained many another excellent officer, to be as stout in discipline, and as dogged of purpose as he himself was: but he had trained him also to feel with and for his men.'[62] (Here, undoubtedly, are echoes of Froude's assertion that English naval supremacy originated in the circumnavigation.) Kingsley is keen to dwell on the physical or sporting pursuits that formed a major portion of the education of the Renaissance Englishman. 'The English officers ... brought up to the same athletic sports, the same martial exercises, as their men, were not ashamed to care for them.'[63] This was the key to the nation's maritime success. Unlike the Spanish who ordered military life along strictly hierarchical principles, English officers led by example.

> Drake touched the true mainspring of English success, when he once (in his voyage round the world) indignantly rebuked some coxcomb gentlemen-adventurers with, 'I should like to see the gentleman that will refuse to set his hand to a rope. I must have the gentlemen to hale and draw with the mariners.'[64]

The words spoken by Drake (which Kingsley misquotes) must be read in their true context. The speech, made shortly after the execution of Doughty, aimed at curbing the simmering animosity between the gentlemen-adventurers and seamen. In the normal course of events, it is unlikely that gentlemen would take part in the day-to-day sailing of the ships. Nevertheless, Kingsley clearly appreciated the link between military heroism and sport. Later Amyas receives a letter from Drake inviting him to take part in the raid on Cadiz (an active strike-first policy found favour with Kingsley). Unable to join the expedition, Leigh takes the news of Drake's success with discontent: 'he merely observed, grumbling, that Drake had gone and spoiled everybody else's sport'.[65]

   The plot of *Westward Ho!* moves inexorably toward the climactic Armada battles. And it is Kingsley's treatment of the Spanish Armada that reveals his close attention to the narratives of the conflict. The description of the English commanders ('England's forgotten worthies' – the phrase is used again) gathered at the bowling green on Plymouth Hoe is undoubtedly adapted from Creasy's *Fifteen Decisive Battles*. Creasy's prose certainly comes closest to the reverential tone with which Kingsley introduces us to Raleigh, Howard, Grenville, John Hawkins and a host of lesser-known Elizabethan mariners. Finally, Sir Francis Drake appears in the narrative that his exploits have made possible – but his appearance is not what we might expect.

> [B]ut who is that short, sturdy, plainly-dressed man, who stands with legs a little apart, and hands behind his back, looking up, with keen, grey eyes, into the face of each speaker? His cap is in his hands, so you can see the bullet head of crisp brown hair, and the wrinkled forehead, as well as the high cheek bones, the short, square face, the broad temples, the thick lips, which are yet firm as granite. A coarse plebeian stamp of a man: yet the whole figure and attitude are that of boundless determination, self-possession, energy; and when he at last speaks a few blunt words, all eyes are turned respectfully upon him – for his name is Francis Drake.[66]

Energy and boundless determination, yes. But a coarse, plebeian stamp of a man? A few blunt words? We know that Drake never refrained from ostentatious show – aboard ship he dined from a silver plate to the accompaniment of music. Several commentators, notably Monson, have felt the need to defend Drake's bombast. But this version of Drake has little to do with the Elizabethan admiral. Drake's integration into courtly life and his cultivation of aristocratic manners do not concern Kingsley. He is keen to construct Drake as a common man – a man ready for work. The defeat of the Spanish Armada in *Westward Ho!* is actually the victory of the Devon worthies, the minor gentry originally from local yeomen stock: the Grenvilles, Hawkinses and the fictional Leighs. Although landowners, none of these families are of the same social standing as aristocrats like the Lord High Admiral, Charles Howard. Indeed, Kingsley concentrates on the local heroes' lack of sophistication. Amyas speaks 'like Raleigh, Grenvile, and other low persons, with a broad Devonshire accent'.[67] Sir John Hawkins is 'A burly, grizzled elder, in greasy sea-stained garments';[68] he, too, speaks with a 'broad Devon twang'.[69] Yet Drake is distanced from even these figures. Of course, Drake received a knighthood and he was certainly an important figure in the Plymouth area, but he could not claim the same pedigree as many of the other seafarers from small landowning families. Kingsley's revelation is that the driving force behind the defeat of the Spanish Armada, the figure that connects the numerous characters and enables the whole narrative is, in fact, a coarse plebeian: Francis Drake.

Kingsley's celebration of the Devon yeomen was, perhaps, motivated by his concerns for the suffering of the labouring poor. Although this interpretation is largely speculative, we should note that Kingsley had already demonstrated his readiness to approach the subject in his early fictional work. His novel *Yeast* (1850), is concerned, in part, with the plight of agricultural workers on a poorly managed estate. As a curate in rural Dorset during the Hungry 'Forties Kingsley was sympathetically aware of the distress caused by the establishment of agrarian capitalism as the dominant mode of production. He had also shown considerable sympathy with Chartism at the time of the 1848 agitation. But in what way is Kingsley's construction of the sixteenth-century seafarers a response to the upheaval brought about by economic revolution? The so-called forgotten worthies who defeat the Armada represent the vanished pre-capitalist rural social structure. Based upon custom and tradition, this structure linked all levels of society through a paternalistic system of obligation and deference. In return for the deference of the labourer, it was the responsibility of the landowner to look after those beneath him. But this traditional order could not survive the switch of economic systems. Agrarian capitalism brought with it a new social structuring: that of class. The vertical ties of responsibility that had previously connected the lord of the manor with the lowliest agricultural labourer were replaced by horizontal class divisions. The labourers found themselves severed from their traditional way of life: they became a rural proletariat, alienated from the landowning classes. Kingsley's response was to revert to an imagined – and, indeed, idealized – social order that, crucially, was pre-capitalist. This was a familiar strategy of conservative thinking in the 1840s and 1850s and was by no means confined to Kingsley. Thomas Carlyle, a great influence on Charles Kingsley, repines for the feudal aristocracy as a remedy for contemporary problems in *Past and Present* (1843). But unlike Carlyle, Kingsley goes to a pre-capitalist social order and finds not aristocratic but plebeian leadership.

The workmanlike sea-dogs provide a contrast to the aristocracy. The aristocratic Lord Howard turns to Drake for advice that is not forthcoming. '"They'll come soon enough for us to show them sport, and yet slow enough for us to be ready."'[70] With this, Drake and Hawkins resume their game of bowls (and, for some reason, it is Hawkins who decides to see the game out). These two captains exemplify typical English coolness in the face of danger. Moreover, their experience tells them that it is pointless to warp the ships out of the harbour prematurely, 'to knock about on a lee-shore all the afternoon'.[71] Howard has to content himself with the knowledge that 'when the self-taught hero did bestir himself, he would do more work in an hour than any one else in a day'.[72] The use of the term 'work' hints at the influence of Carlyle, and the idea of Drake as a Carlylean hero finds rather more explicit expression when Sir Francis asks why Amyas isn't hurrying to his ship. Leigh simply replies that he follows his leader. Later we are told that Amyas 'worshipped' Drake. Instead of dwelling on the magnitude of the forthcoming battles – on the fact that the future of England is at stake – Drake and John Hawkins turn their minds to the prizes that await them. Their plan is to follow the Armada along the Channel. '"Let them go by, and go by, and stick to them well to windward, and pick up stragglers, and picking, too, Jack – the prizes, Jack!"'[73] Drake's interest in treasure at such a crucial moment is hardly heroic conduct. But because Kingsley has gone to great lengths to construct him as God's agent in the grand scheme of things, he can allow him to be unheroic in terms of personal advantage. And self-betterment was, after all, part of Protestant individualism. Kingsley finds Drake's desertion of his post in an effort to capture the *Rosario* entirely unproblematic. Sir Francis writes to Amyas Leigh telling him of his pursuit of the 'galleons' that proved to be German merchant ships and of Pedro de Valdez's bravado and false sincerity. '[K]issing my fist, with Spanish lies of holding himself fortunate that he had fallen into the hands of fortunate Drake.'[74] The response of Will Cary, Leigh's second in command, is indulgent. 'That cunning old Drake! how he has contrived to line his own pockets, even though he had to keep the whole fleet waiting for him.'[75] We can only imagine what Kingsley would have made of this lust for gold if a Catholic character had displayed it. But although Drake is interested in profit, Kingsley assures us that 'when the battle needs it none can fight more fiercely among the foremost'.[76] He takes his place in the thick of the action during the battle off Gravelines.

The popularity of *Westward Ho!* certainly ensured that James Anthony Froude's 'forgotten worthies' did not fade into obscurity. Kingsley's vivid and energetic prose revived the Elizabethan sea-dogs for a popular audience. The fact that both Kingsley and Froude produced narratives of causation that explained the origins of Britain's dominant position in the world did much to focus attention on the Elizabethan past. But to what extent did their versions of the sea-faring past inform the Drake material produced in the later years of the century? And how was Sir Francis Drake used to explain and justify the possession of empire in the 1880s and 1890s? The following chapter will explore the cult of Drake that flourished during the height of British hegemony.

Notes

[1] James Anthony Froude, 'England's Forgotten Worthies', *Westminster and Foreign Quarterly Review*, new series, vol. 2 (1852), 39.

[2] Geoffrey Faber, *Oxford Apostles: A Character Study of the Oxford Movement* (London, 1933), 72.

[3] James Anthony Froude, *History of England from the Fall of Wolsey to the Defeat of the Spanish Armada*, 12 vols (London, 1856–70).

[4] Thomas Carlyle, *On Heroes, Hero-Worship and the Heroic in History* (1841; London, 1928), 1.

[5] Carlyle, *Heroes and Hero Worship*, 13.

[6] Thomas Carlyle, *Oliver Cromwell's Letters and Speeches, with Elucidations*, 2 vols (London, 1845).

[7] Thomas Carlyle, *History of Frederick II of Prussia, Called Frederick the Great*, 6 vols (London, 1858–65).

[8] Thomas Carlyle, *Past and Present* (1843; London, 1928).

[9] Carlyle, *Past and Present*, 108.

[10] Carlyle, *Past and Present*, 113–14.

[11] Thomas Carlyle, *Chartism* (London, 1840).

[12] William Henry Hudson, Introduction, *Sartor Resartus and On Heroes, Hero-Worship and the Heroic in History*, by Thomas Carlyle (1841; London, 1916), xvi.

[13] Froude, 'Forgotten Worthies', 32–67.

[14] Froude, 'Forgotten Worthies', 34.

[15] Froude, 'Forgotten Worthies', 34.

[16] Froude, 'Forgotten Worthies', 34.

[17] Froude, 'Forgotten Worthies', 34.

[18] Quoted in Waldo Hilary Dunn, *James Anthony Froude: A Biography*, 2 vols (Oxford, 1961), vol. 2, 202.

[19] Quoted in Dunn, vol. 2, 203.

[20] Froude, 'Forgotten Worthies', 39.

[21] Froude, *History of England*, vol. 11, 120.

[22] Froude, *History of England*, vol. 12, 295–6.

[23] For contemporary criticism of Froude's historical inaccuracies, see particularly: 'Froude's History of England', *Edinburgh Review*, vol. 119, pt 1 (1864), 243–79. 'Froude's History of Queen Elizabeth', *Edinburgh Review*, vol. 131, pt 1 (1870), 1–39. 'Froude's *Queen Elizabeth*', *Quarterly Review*, vol. 128 (1870), 506–44.

[24] Froude, 'Forgotten Worthies', 52.

[25] Froude, *History of England*, vol. 11, 131.

[26] Froude, *History of England*, vol. 11, 119.

[27] Quoted in Dunn, vol. 1, 172.

[28] Quoted in Dunn, vol. 2, 313.

[29] Froude, *History of England*, vol. 11, 156.

[30] Quoted in Dunn, vol. 2, 313.

[31] Froude, *History of England*, vol. 11, 122.

[32] Froude, *History of England*, vol. 11, 130.

[33] Cynthia Fansler Behrman, *Victorian Myths of the Sea* (Athens, OH, 1977), 85.

[34] Froude, *History of England*, vol. 11, 130.

[35] Froude, *History of England*, vol. 12, 37.
[36] Froude, *History of England*, vol. 12, 34.
[37] Froude, *History of England*, vol. 12, 35.
[38] Froude, *History of England*, vol. 12, 36.
[39] Froude, *History of England*, vol. 12, 33.
[40] Froude, *History of England*, vol. 12, 36.
[41] Froude, *History of England*, vol. 12, 292.
[42] Froude, *History of England*, vol. 12, 292.
[43] Froude, *History of England*, vol. 12, 294.
[44] Froude, *History of England*, vol. 12, 295.
[45] Froude, *History of England*, vol. 12, 296.
[46] Charles Kingsley, *Westward Ho!* (1855; London, n.d.).
[47] Quoted in Dunn, vol.1, 172.
[48] Norman Vance, *The Sinews of the Spirit: The Ideal of Christian Manliness in Victorian Literature and Religious Thought* (Cambridge, 1985), 88.
[49] Kingsley, 78; ch. 4.
[50] Kingsley, 8; ch. 1.
[51] Charles Kingsley, 'Froude's History of England: Volumes VII and VIII', *Macmillan's Magazine*, vol. 9 (1863–4), 217.
[52] Vance, 31–2.
[53] Vance, 55.
[54] Vance, 105.
[55] Kingsley, 40; ch. 2.
[56] Dictionary of National Biography.
[57] Kingsley, unnumbered preliminary leaf.
[58] Kingsley, 19-20; ch. 1.
[59] Kingsley, 20; ch. 1.
[60] Kingsley, 255–6; ch. 11.
[61] Kingsley, 254; ch. 11.
[62] Kingsley, 405; ch. 21.
[63] Kingsley, 390; ch. 21.
[64] Kingsley, 390; ch. 21.
[65] Kingsley, 565; ch. 30.
[66] Kingsley, 582; ch. 30.
[67] Kingsley, 15; ch. 1.
[68] Kingsley, 582; ch. 30.
[69] Kingsley, 582; ch. 30.
[70] Kingsley, 594; ch. 30.
[71] Kingsley, 594; ch. 30.
[72] Kingsley, 594; ch. 30.
[73] Kingsley, 594; ch. 30.
[74] Kingsley, 598; ch. 31.
[75] Kingsley, 599; ch. 31.
[76] Kingsley, 606; ch. 31.

CHAPTER SEVEN

'Mould him in bronze'

Nearly all are thus men of the West Country, whose names
are familiar to us as household words.
(*Smith's Plymouth Almanac*, 1876/7)[1]

During the final quarter of the nineteenth century the work of Charles
Kingsley and James Anthony Froude continued to exert a powerful
influence over the way in which the Elizabethan past was constructed. The
bowls myth in particular seems to have caught the popular imagination. Although
this had become an integral part of the Drake narrative by the 1840s, it was
Westward Ho! that was chiefly responsible for the wide dissemination of the
tradition in printed form. Kingsley was, in fact, becoming popularly identified as
the source of the story. An article on the origins of the mythical game published in
the *Western Antiquary* felt it necessary to clarify his relation to the narrative. 'Many
people have imagined that the story originated with Charles Kingsley, who has
woven it, with great tact, into his inimitable story. ... But it is not an invention of
this patriotic Devonian.'[2] The article went on to identify the tract *Vox Populi* as the
earliest printed reference to the game. That the story was frequently attributed to
Kingsley may seem to undermine the argument that I have put forward: if Drake
as the bowls-playing Armada victor was a popular cultural tradition, then 'many
people' would have recognized it as such. But, with print culture replacing oral
culture, by the mid-century – and certainly by the 1880s – the novel-reading public
would have had little access to the oral tradition.

It was to *Westward Ho!* that the stained-glass makers Heaton, Butler and Bayne[3]
turned when commissioned to produce a window commemorating the defeat of
the Spanish Armada. The Armada Window, designed by the little-known artist J.
Milner Allen, was one of a series of fourteen 'historical' windows that were to
decorate the great hall of Plymouth's new guildhall, a building that claimed to be
the finest public room in the west of England. This was created between 1870 and
1876. Like the removal of the last remaining conduit house in Plymouth, the new
guildhall was erected as part of a scheme of urban improvement. It replaced a
Jacobean building that did not provide an adequate expression of flourishing
bourgeois pride. The windows were to depict the great moments from the history

of Plymouth, civil as well as military. The scenes rendered in stained glass included the sacking of the town by Bretons in 1403, the arrest of Sir Walter Raleigh following his unsuccessful voyage to find the golden city of Manoa, the sailing of the Pilgrim Fathers, the building of the first naval dock by William III, and the establishment of William Cookworthy's Plymouth pottery. The Armada window, a gift from alderman William Foster Moore, who was mayor of Plymouth from 1874 to 1877, was the first to be set in place and occupied the central position on the south wall. Regrettably the guildhall was gutted by bombing in 1941 and the windows destroyed. No complete plans or sketches of the stained glass survive.[4] However, an article titled 'The Historical Windows in the New Guildhall',[5] published in *Smith's Plymouth Almanac*, provides a detailed description of the windows. From this we learn that John Drake was depicted in the act of bowling while Sir Francis waited his turn on the green. Sir John Hawkins drew attention to the arrival of Fleming, while looking on were the other 'forgotten worthies': Raleigh, Howard, Grenville and Frobisher. Martin Frobisher was portrayed enjoying a pipe of tobacco, exactly as Kingsley chose to represent him in his novel. In the background the English fleet rode at anchor in the Cattewater.

Drake's game of bowls, scarcely represented before the middle decades of the century, was now a source of great civic pride and was portrayed at the very heart of local government. But we cannot be insensible to the great irony involved here. Kingsley's Drake is an anti-bourgeois hero: he represents the lost pre-capitalist social order. Yet the famous bowling scene from *Westward Ho!* was represented in a building that expressed the newly acquired power of the bourgeoisie, the outright victors of capitalism. Kingsley's construction of Drake had been reversed by the very success of *Westward Ho!* and its dissemination of the bowls tradition. In fact the whole sequence of stained-glass windows lighting the great hall demonstrates the way in which the past could be appropriated by bourgeois ideology. The events from Plymouth's past become narrative episodes from which all signifiers of revolution and disjunction are elided. The Siege Window, for example, neutralizes the political struggles that led to the Civil War, during which Plymouth actively opposed the Crown. This revolutionary episode in the history of Plymouth is just one more historical scene in the sequence. The late Victorian present – the triumph of bourgeois, mercantile Plymouth – becomes the inevitable outcome of the narrative episodes, the point to which the past has been building. The guildhall was both the end product and the validation of the narrative that the windows told. Put simply, the story must be true or there could be no guildhall.

But the Armada Window was not the only image of Drake to be found in the new guildhall: there was also the Drake Window. This was a representation of Sir Francis's great non-military achievement: the bringing of fresh water to Plymouth. Not only was Drake the founder of naval and colonial expansion, he could also be presented as the predecessor of the good burghers of Plymouth who had done so much to improve the urban environment – including its water supply. Created by Fouracre and Watson[6] of the Plymouth-based West of England Stained Glass Works, the window was donated by Charles Whiteford, another mayor of Plymouth. The first light depicted Drake standing on the steps of a newly opened conduit pointing at the stream of water released for the first time. Above Sir Francis were several workmen opening a water hatch while in the distance was the waterwheel of a mill erected on the leat and leased by Drake. In this way the window combined the bourgeois values of enterprise and public spiritedness. Represented in the second light were the mayor in his robes, the town clerk and other cheering townsfolk along with trumpeters and standard bearers. The window's third light represented a young girl 'looking complacently at the flowing stream, and feeling glad, no doubt, that her task of fetching water will be made now comparatively easy'.[7]

The northern portion of the guildhall was occupied by the Council Chamber. This also contained windows by Heaton, Butler and Bayne. In the heads of the four main windows were medallion portraits of Queen Elizabeth, Queen Victoria, Drake and Raleigh. More important, perhaps, was a statue of Francis Drake positioned on the outside of the building that watched over the activities on the Hoe. *Smith's Plymouth Almanac* described the statue thus,

> Drake the great Elizabethan hero of Plymouth is represented in a life-size statue, occupying the gable-end of the Council Chamber. The famous circumnavigator and admiral stands bare-headed, overlooking the sea, whereon he lived and won his fame, on which he died, and in which he found a grave.[8]

There is no record of the statue's appearance or its maker. It was, however, the first statue of Sir Francis Drake to be raised in Britain (this, of course, excludes the bust of Drake found in the Temple of British Worthies at Stowe). As we will see, others were soon to follow.

Returning to the game of bowls, perhaps the most famous visual representation of the tradition is John Seymour Lucas's canvas *The Armada in Sight* (1880), which was engraved by Paul Girardet in 1882 (PLATE 8). The painting was exhibited at the Royal Academy together with an account of the game of bowls.

> It was on the 19th July that Fleming sailed into Plymouth and announced that he had seen the Spanish fleet off the Lizard. This intelligence was communicated to Drake when he and some of his officers were amusing themselves with bowls on the Hoe. It caused a lively sensation and a great manifestation of alacrity to put to sea, which Drake laughingly checked by declaring that the match should be played out, as there was plenty of time to win the game and beat the Spaniards too.

Like the Armada window in Plymouth guildhall, the painting was almost certainly inspired by Kingsley's novel. The image depicts the scene moments after the news of the sighting of the Armada has been delivered. In the right background the first of the chain of warning beacons that stretched along the south coast of England flares into life. On the left of the canvas Richard Grenville points excitedly towards the smoking brazier. The group of English commanders – whose faces are all taken from contemporary engravings – seem to await orders. But the man in charge, Lord

PLATE 8. Paul Giradet after John Seymour Lucas, *The Armada in Sight*, 1882. A visual representation of Charles Kingsley's version of events on Plymouth Hoe.

Howard, anxiously approaches his second-in-command. With great self-assurance Drake holds a restraining arm towards Howard and bends to deliver his next wood. The game can be finished before the other game – that of thrashing the Spaniards – begins. The relegation of Howard to a peripheral role reflects, perhaps, the shift in economic power from the great landowning families to the industrially based middle classes. Drake represents the archetypal self-made man, and, of course, the man on whom the nation's well-being depends: he is a very bourgeois hero. We have already encountered the irony involved in the bourgeois appropriation of Kingsley's version of Drake. Nowhere does the construction of the anti-bourgeois, pre-capitalist Drake seem to be more dramatically reversed than in this painting. Attempts were made to bring the work to Plymouth but it eventually left the country when sold to Sir William Clarke, a Melbourne collector.

The Armada in Sight is just one product of a cult of Drake that emerged during the 1880s, and which was particularly vociferous in Drake's native West Country. Of course, the tercentenaries of most of Drake's exploits occurred during the last twenty years of the nineteenth century, but this does not provide an adequate explanation for the huge amount of attention that the Elizabethan admiral came to receive. To fully understand the enthusiasm for Sir Francis Drake in the 1880s we need to return once more to the British Empire and its rapid expansion. The final decades of the century witnessed a dramatic acceleration in colonial annexation. This was primarily caused by a deep anxiety about Britain's economic dominance. With other capitalist economies – particularly those of Germany and the United States – threatening the nation's industrial hegemony, the competition for overseas markets became intense. Other European nations were also beginning to show an interest in Africa, a continent that Britain had for many years regarded as her own. This potential threat to existing British interests, particularly those on the eastern coast trading with India, caused considerable alarm. As far as Britain was concerned, the series of annexations that took place in Africa were necessary to secure trading interests – many of which had been established independently of the government – from the territorial ambitions of rival nations.

The first phase of what became known as the Scramble for Africa began in the mid-1870s and continued well into the 1880s. During this period Cape Colony was greatly extended but not without resistance from the native Zulus and the Dutch settlers of the Transvaal and Orange Free State. The Zulu War of 1878–9 – during which an entire regiment of 1600 men was lost at Isandhlwana – and the Anglo-Boer War of 1881 demonstrate that the division of Africa was a far from smooth process. Nevertheless, British East Africa (later Kenya) was established and, in 1876, Britain gained control of the Suez Canal when Disraeli unexpectedly bought the Khedive's 44 per cent share in the Suez Canal Company – this was particularly important in terms of providing a fast route to India. British expansionism was not confined to Africa, however. In 1876 Victoria was created Empress of India and in the years that followed British possessions radiated outward from the subcontinent: Malaya was made a protectorate later in the late 1870s and Burma annexed in 1885–6.

The colonial gains made in the final decades of the century were accompanied by a new self-awareness of Britain as an imperial power. As the list of overseas possessions grew, so did the mythology of empire. Explaining and justifying Britain's position as the world's foremost colonial power became a major cultural project. A familiar strategy was to construct the imperial past so as to make the colonial present seem inevitable – the natural culmination of a process set in motion centuries before. The high seas of the sixteenth century were as rich in material for the imperial myth-makers as they had been in gold for Drake. In the third quarter of the nineteenth century Froude and Kingsley had, of course, popularized the notion of the Elizabethan privateers as directly responsible for Britain's contemporary hegemony. As we have seen, Drake was identified as the most significant of these pioneering figures. He had, in Froude's words, 'laid the foundation of the naval empire of England'. The defeat of the Armada, with which Drake was intimately connected, had cleared the way for Britain's naval dominance. By the 1880s many other historical works were promoting similar ideas.[9]

But while celebrating the events of the imperial past was frequently a self-congratulatory business, this was not the entire story. As suggested above, Britain's colonial expansion – particularly in Africa – was prompted by deep fears about her economic well-being. Of course, the threats to British hegemony were not confined to rebellious natives and Boers in southern Africa. Russia was expanding into the area north of Afghanistan, and this was felt to pose a significant threat to Britain's greatest possession, India. Russian designs on the Ottoman empire could also result in Britain being denied access to India through the Suez Canal – and 80 per cent of the traffic using the Canal was British, a measure of the waterway's economic importance. Adding to Britain's troubles was the fact that Germany was expanding its colonial possessions and, even more worryingly, its navy. In the face of these threats, the empire, at times, seemed impossible to defend. The undoubted triumphalism of the cult of Drake helped obscure Britain's anxieties but also, paradoxically, implicitly acknowledged them. In the 1880s and later, the narrative of Drake and the Spanish Armada performed a dual function. It was, of course, a source of great pride and identified the point from which Britain's rise to greatness could be charted. But, as this research has attempted to demonstrate, it also provided reassurance at times of threat, whether the threat was to the mother country or to her colonial interests. The defeat of the Spanish Armada was as potent a symbol at the height of British hegemony as it had been eighty years earlier, when Napoleon seemed set to invade the mother country herself.

Nowhere was interest in Drake greater than in his native West Country. The Plymouth-based *Western Antiquary* clearly demonstrates that Sir Francis Drake was engaging the attention of the middle classes as never before. The journal began circulation in March 1881 and was edited by the borough librarian, W. H. K. Wright. The journal sought to publish articles and letters on legends, traditions, anecdotes, heraldic and genealogical matters, and curious scraps of quotations. The amount of material concerning Drake that appeared over a ten-year period is huge. It is difficult to turn a page in any volume without finding a reference to Sir Francis. The very first article in the first issue dealt with Drake's coat of arms. This number also contained material on the earliest recorded mention of the game of bowls; Drake's house in London (obviously taken from Barrow's biography); the Drake portraits and their authenticity; the first reference to Drake as a pirate; and a Drake bibliography. Many items are poorly researched while other material is undoubtedly pedantic: one letter complains that the statue of Drake erected in Tavistock had got Sir Francis's face wrong. Nevertheless the diverse range and sheer amount of material demonstrates a very great and enduring enthusiasm for Drake throughout the 1880s.

Perhaps of greater interest than the squabbles over whether Sir Francis was entitled to quarter his arms with the wyvern of the Drake's of Ashe were the poetic outpourings that were frequently published in the journal. These provide further evidence for the existence of a hero-worshipping cult of Drake. His immortality is touched upon by an intriguing sonnet by the Reverend Hardwicke Drummond Rawnsley, one of the founding members of the National Trust. 'Sir Francis Drake, The Hoe'[10] was taken from a volume titled *Sonnets Round the Coast* published in 1888:

> *Mould him in bronze, or hew him out of stone,*
> *His name shall live beyond what hands can make,*
> *Who with his fifty fighting men durst rake*
> *That sea, which heaving cloth of gold, had shone*
> *Since first those long grey eyes had looked thereon,*
> *And he had felt the South Pacific wake*
> *Unconquerable daring – gallant Drake.*
> *Prince, soldier, sailor, buccaneer in one,*
> *He sailed his Hind, the sea-scourge of the world,*

> *Then, round the Horn, as full as hull could hold*
> *Of Devon's courage and Spain's dubloons*
> *Steered home, but England has never since furled*
> *Her sails of enterprise in lust for gold.*

The poem begins with a reference to the statue of Drake erected on Plymouth Hoe in 1884 and then moves on to celebrate his 'gallant' buccaneering exploits undertaken during the course of the circumnavigation. The Pacific Ocean was first seen by 'those long grey eyes' (the description is taken from Froude) when Drake climbed a tree in Panama in 1572. Clearly Rawnsley accepts the tradition of Drake as a heroic pioneer of English expansionism and as a key figure in the development of the nation's naval power, yet the poem concludes rather unexpectedly. For Rawnsley, English enterprise appears as an unceasing quest for gold. The activity to which he refers is not simply maritime endeavour – expansionism was, of course, driven by the need to create new markets for domestic products – but the whole sphere of economic enterprise. The poem implies that the pursuit of gold has negative consequences. This must be read in relation to Rawnsley's concern for the preservation of the nation's heritage. The National Trust came into being as a result of anxieties about spreading urbanization and the exploitation and spoliation of areas of outstanding natural beauty. Rawnsley's personal interest was in saving the Lake District from increasing tourism and development. The final lines of his sonnet are a wry expression of his awareness of the damaging consequences of the 'lust for gold'.

The tercentennial celebrations of Drake's exploits were also largely confined to the West Country. The first occasion to be marked in Plymouth, albeit in a rather muted way, was that of Francis Drake's mayoralty. On 17 September 1881, three hundred years after Drake took office, the municipal flag was proudly flown from the guildhall. With commensurate pride – and not a little exaggeration – the *Western Daily Mercury* drew attention to the anniversary and suggested that

> During the Mayoral year 1581–82 there can be no doubt Plymouth held up its head municipally with the biggest borough in the country. … For had the burgesses not, as their chief magistrate, the foremost man of his day in the whole country.[11]

Restrained as this flag-flying commemoration was, the anniversary of Drake's mayoralty received rather more attention than the tercentenary of his departure for or his return from the circumnavigation of the globe. These dates passed without significant celebration. This may seem to undermine the assertion that the 1880s saw the emergence of a cult of Drake. The apparent neglect seems all the more strange when we consider that Drake's popularity was the result of an intensifying consciousness of empire and that the circumnavigation was often portrayed as an expansionist undertaking. Yet we should not lose sight of the fact that by the 1880s the basis of Drake's fame had shifted from sailing around the world to the defeat of the Spanish Armada. Furthermore, Drake's exploits were so well known and, as the *Western Antiquary* demonstrates, so frequently discussed, that to set aside a special day to remember him may have seemed unnecessary.

Yet one West Country figure was to change all that. This was a Newlyn-based clergyman, the Reverend W. S. Lach-Szyrma. He initiated a campaign for a Drake memorial, a campaign that rapidly gained momentum. Lach-Szyrma had been greatly impressed by the events organized in Penzance in 1878 to commemorate the centenary of the birth of Humphry Davy and clearly thought that Plymouth should honour Drake in a similar fashion. In a letter to the *Western Antiquary* some years later he outlined his role in the scheme:

> As the period when the tercentenary anniversary of the return of Drake from his great voyage of circumnavigation approached, the thought struck me that Plymouth ought to keep up the great event. … Not perceiving any sign of action, I wrote to the Plymouth papers, suggesting a tercentenary observance of the event. The matter was taken up by some leading men, but it was said that there was scarcely time to get up a fitting commemoration.[12]

This was not strictly true; the idea actually gained considerable local support and a committee was formed with the task of planning and raising funds for a Drake memorial. The mayor, William Derry, led the way by making the first donation of £50. For the Memorial Committee, Drake's importance in shaping English history meant that the memorial should represent the entire nation's debt to the local hero. The Prince of Wales was even enlisted as the scheme's patron. Yet the rest of the country did not respond with the anticipated enthusiasm – or cash. Drake remained predominantly a West Country hero. After overcoming initial disagreements about what form the memorial should take (the committee eventually voted for a statue), finance remained a problem. A vocal champion of the scheme, the *Western Daily Mercury* noted:

> The attempts made to give a national character to the scheme failed. In spite of the cordial help rendered by the Press at home, on the continent, and in our colonies – in spite also of the Mansion House meeting and the patronage of the Prince of Wales and many influential noblemen – the thing seemed to hang fire.[13]

This seems to indicate a discrepancy between the official and semi-official cultural and colonial discourse – represented in this instance by the newspapers and Prince of Wales – and the actual perception of the British people. Writing about English responses to the process of decolonization, Bernard Porter makes a telling point: 'the mass of people, as they had all along, cared very little'.[14] The lack of support for the Drake memorial seems to bear out the observation that, for the populace, the empire was not a matter for great concern. The cultural reality fell rather short of the imperial rhetoric.

Although the tercentenary of the circumnavigation passed with no sign of a statue, the scheme to provide Drake with a suitable memorial was not abandoned. In January 1882 a deputation of dignitaries from Plymouth travelled to Tavistock, Drake's home town, in an effort to secure subscriptions for their memorial. This was not an entirely uncontroversial undertaking: after all, why should Tavistock contribute towards another town's statue of *her* most famous son? At the meeting Plymouth's mayor, Charles Burnard, attempted to quell any feelings of animosity. 'He felt sure that if they had gone to any other town and opened the campaign, Tavistock would have been justly displeased.'[15] He also pointed out (rather ironically given the fund-raising problems) that the movement was national rather than local and that Drake's great importance should override local rivalries. The case for locating a statue at Plymouth, it was argued, was very strong: it was an extremely important naval town and was also the port from which Drake had sailed on his expeditions. These assertions were politely but coolly received.

Burnard's rhetoric did not persuade the inhabitants of Tavistock to support the scheme. Inevitably the plan to locate the statue in Plymouth gathered opponents. Edward Spencer, headmaster of the local grammar school, argued that if a statue was to be raised, it should be in Tavistock. Things had certainly changed in the fifty years since Anna Eliza Bray observed the apathy of the town's educated society when it came to Drake. A meeting of prominent local figures was held, and it was resolved that a bronze statue of Sir Francis Drake should be erected in Tavistock. Fears about the cost were allayed when the ninth Duke of Bedford offered to pay the considerable sum of £4000 for the work. By the end of the nineteenth century the Bedfords had been associated with Tavistock for well over three hundred years. They had, in fact, effectively controlled the town since the surrender of the abbey in 1539. Far more even than the Drakes, the Russells had profited from the Reformation. John Russell, the first earl, had assisted in the Dissolution of the Monasteries and had been rewarded with forfeited lands as well as the family seat of Woburn and former monastic holdings in Covent Garden and Bloomsbury. In Devon, Cornwall and Somerset he received thirty manors that had formerly belonged to the abbey. Importantly, Francis Russell, the second earl, is believed to have been Sir Francis Drake's godfather and patron; Drake himself was responsible for the dissemination of this story.

The Austrian-born sculptor Joseph Edgar Boehm, Sculptor-in-ordinary to the Queen, was commissioned to create the statue. He visited Tavistock and helped select the site where the statue would stand: the junction of the Plymouth and Callington Roads, close to Crowndale where Drake was born. Work took just over a year to complete and on 27 September the following year John Jarrett Daw, the Portreeve, unveiled the first public memorial to Sir Francis Drake (PLATE 9). The occasion was cause for great celebrations. A procession led by the band of the local volunteers assembled in the guildhall. The party made its way to the statue through streets decked with flags and bunting and, after a prayer, *Sir Francis Drake* was unveiled to the tumultuous cheers of a large crowd; the band played and maroons were fired. In the evening it was planned to illuminate the statue with an electric light but unfortunately this could not be made to work. The statue itself met with widespread approval. Drake stands on a pedestal of local granite in a posture that, in the words of the *Western Daily Mercury*, 'strikes the observer as easy and unconstrained'.[16] The attitude is certainly one of complete self-possession and

PLATE 9. Joseph Edgar Boehm, *Sir Francis Drake*, 1883, Tavistock, Devon.

confidence. Drake, dressed in the ordinary clothing of a wealthy Elizabethan, stands with his left arm akimbo while his right hand holds a compass over a globe, which is supported by a delicately wrought stand. The semiotic emphasis is firmly on Drake's identity as a navigator. Just in case there should be any doubt, bronze lettering on the front of the pedestal reads 'Sir Francis Drake, one of ye first who in his voyages put a girdle round the world.' The treatment of Drake's head and torso suggests that Boehm was familiar with the engraving by Robert Boissard or an image taken from it such as that by Vaughan (see PLATE 3). Drake certainly wears the same sash knotted at the right shoulder. Around his neck is the Drake jewel.

Three bronze bas-reliefs portraying moments from Drake's career were displayed on the pedestal. On the front was a representation of Drake receiving his knighthood on the deck of the *Golden Hinde*. Drake bends before the Queen who regally rests the sword on his shoulder. The relief perpetuates the belief that Elizabeth herself performed the knighting – it would not do for the English hero to receive the honour from a foreigner. Looking on is a collection of courtiers including Robert Dudley (second left), Walter Raleigh (second right) and to his left, Francis Russell, second Earl of Bedford. The image of Russell is taken from a portrait in the family collection at Woburn Abbey and acknowledges the connection between Tavistock, the Drakes and the Bedfords. The inclusion of his ancestor was also, no doubt, a mark of thanks for the ninth Duke's generosity in paying for the statue. On the south side of the pedestal is Drake's game of bowls. The influence of Seymour Lucas's *The Armada in Sight* is very clear. As the news is delivered, Sir Francis holds out a restraining arm to Charles Howard who anxiously clutches Drake's wrist. It is, perhaps, difficult to agree with a contemporary description of the bas-relief that claimed 'the concentration which evidently marks his action shows he is not disturbed by the news just being delivered by a breathless messenger'.[17] Drake actually appears to be rather distracted by the intelligence. The final relief depicts Drake's burial at sea. Contrary to contemporary accounts that claim Drake was lowered overboard in a leaden coffin, Boehm prefers the romanticized image of Drake's body being carefully lowered into the sea sewn inside a sail. Three burly mariners carry out their sorrowful task while Mr Bride, the ship's chaplain, oversees the burial. To the right a trumpeter and cannon provide a sombre final salute.

The town was so proud of its new statue that bronze commemorative medals were struck to mark the occasion. The obverse depicted the statue of Drake and read 'First English statue to Francis Drake unveiled at Tavistock September 29 1883.' The reverse was inscribed 'Presented to his birthplace, Tavistock, by Hastings, IX Duke of Bedford.' As we have seen, this was not the first statue of Francis Drake in England; there was also the figure standing on Plymouth's guildhall. Nor was it the first European statue to represent Drake. In 1854 a statue of Sir Francis by Andreas Friedrich had been erected in the small town of Offenburg in western Germany. The designer of the medal obviously knew of this work even if he was unaware of the Plymouth guildhall Drake. The Offenburg statue represented Drake holding a potato stalk in his left hand and a map of America in his right. Festoons of potato leaves decorated the base. An inscription read 'To God and Francis Drake, who brought to Europe for the everlasting benefit of the poor the potato.' In Germany, it seems, Drake and Raleigh had become confused, Raleigh's actions being attributed to his more famous compatriot. The statue was destroyed prior to the outbreak of the Second World War.

Plymouth finally raised its own memorial to Drake in 1884. Lacking funds for anything more ambitious, the memorial committee decided to commission Boehm to produce a replica of the Tavistock statue – without the bas-reliefs – and this was unveiled on 14 February 1884. But what Plymouth lacked in terms of originality it made up for in the location of the statue and in the celebrations that accompanied its unveiling. According to the *Western Daily Mercury*,

> The statue stands on the only possible site for such a memorial: for no other place than the Hoe, overlooking the spot whence he set out on so many of his expeditions, and whence he set out with his comrades to thrash the proud Spaniard – commanding also a view of the far away hills from whence he brought to Plymouth her precious possession of a good and abundant water- supply – no other than this historic spot would have been appropriate for a statue of Sir Francis Drake.[18]

Gazing commandingly across Plymouth Sound, Sir Francis retains a dignity that the Tavistock Drake, marooned on a traffic island, certainly lacks. The unveiling ceremony was a demonstration of great civic and naval pride, as befitted Plymouth's most famous (if adopted) son and the figure believed to have been responsible for the establishment of British maritime power. It is likely that Plymouth in the 1880s felt it had better reason than most towns to be grateful to Drake: the prosperity of the rapidly expanding town depended heavily upon the imperial navy. During this decade the dockyard built twenty-three ships for the Royal Navy, almost all over 700 tons – a figure staggering by modern standards. Plymouth had, of course, been a major military centre since Drake's day; the great natural harbour made it the obvious western port for the Queen's navy. But after the first naval dock was opened in 1693, the town's economic well-being depended primarily upon ship-building and upon maintaining and provisioning the fleet. Plymouth was, of course, the port that guarded the Western Approaches. Plymouth Dock[19] grew steadily over the years but it was the advent of steam power that saw the greatest expansion of the yard. By 1837 a quarter of the Royal Navy's vessels were powered by steam and special dockyards were required to maintain them. The newly renamed Devonport Dockyard was chosen along with Portsmouth and Malta as a yard that would be extended to cope with the needs of the new ships. The Keyham Steam Yard, a huge complex of docks, basins, machine shops and stores that adjoined Devonport to the north, was opened in 1853.

On the day of the unveiling activities began with a huge procession of 3000 schoolchildren making its way from the Guildhall Square, through the principal and suitably decorated streets to the Hoe. The mayor and corporation, joined by the local fire brigade, soon followed. On the Hoe the Royal Marines formed a guard of honour and all Royal Navy ships in the Sound were dressed with flags in 'rainbow fashion'. The band of the Royal Marines provided musical accompaniment and when all the specially invited spectators were seated the children sang the national anthem. The vicar of St Andrew's said a prayer and the chairman of the Memorial Committee, Mr Burnard, presented the statue to the mayor and the people of Plymouth. The statue was finally unveiled by Lady Elizabeth Elliot-Drake (a descendent of Drake's brother Thomas) who, during the course of the ceremony, was seated on the chair purportedly made from the timbers of the *Golden Hinde*. This had been borrowed from the Bodleian Library for the occasion. Immediately after Sir Francis was unveiled, men and boys from the gunnery ships *HMS Cambridge* and *HMS Foudroyant* fired a seventeen-gun salute from the Royal Citadel, the imposing fort on Plymouth Hoe. Before the sound had died away W. H. K. Wright, a principal member of the Demonstration Committee, led the cheering.

The extent to which the shop assistants and others who had been given time off to watch the unveiling of the statue were conscious of Sir Francis as an empire-builder is difficult to ascertain. Indeed, the whole question of how far the notion of empire permeated the working-class consciousness is an area of some debate. Certainly the empire was pervasive in the material fabric of late nineteenth-century culture; we need look no further than Home and Colonial Stores or the Imperial Tobacco Company for evidence of this. Yet as suggested above, for the majority of the population the empire was of no great significance. True, there were occasional moments of imperial celebration such as Victoria's Jubilee or the unveiling of the Drake statue but the economic pressures of everyday life ensured that the empire was not a preoccupation. It is possible, however, that Plymouth was something of an exception and that awareness of imperial matters was relatively high. The town was, of course, a busy port and received vessels from all corners of the empire. Moreover, a large proportion of the inhabitants of Devonport were employed building ships for the Royal Navy. Of course, we cannot know to what degree this consciousness extended to the events that purportedly made up the imperial past. But even if specific knowledge of Drake's attempts at expanding the British 'empire' was limited, it is probable that, as the founder of the navy, he was identified as the figure responsible for the town's economic well-being so dependent as it was upon the fleet.

If the Drake tercentenaries received little national attention, the same cannot be said of the three hundredth anniversary of the defeat of the Spanish Armada in 1888. The *Illustrated London News* and the *Graphic*, both of which were widely read by a middle-class audience, devoted a great deal of space to lengthy and well-illustrated accounts of the conflict.[20] Curiously, neither publication paid much attention to the construction of Drake as Armada victor in their tercentennial articles. The *Illustrated London News* in particular seems to have adopted an anti-Drakean stance. Indeed, the narrative by Charles N. Robinson was keen to overturn the popular cultural construction of Drake as sole victor.

> Of the four [English commanders], Sir Francis Drake has by some writers been made the central figure of the defeat of the Armada. His chief exploit was the taking of *Our Lady of the Rosary*, the capitana of Pedro de Valdez. Drake's conduct on the Hoe at Plymouth, if the story is true, was hardly that of a zealous subordinate, wishful to give a good example to the men under him. Disobedience is generally charged to him also in the matter of carrying a light on the night of the fight off the Start. His conduct in the action off Gravelines was that of an impetuous, brave, and an intrepid officer, and he was indisputably a capital seaman; but he appears possibly from old associations, to have allowed his lust for dollars to detract from the duty he owed his chief and his country.[21]

What Robinson fails to recognize is that the capture of prizes was an accepted part of sixteenth-century naval warfare; even Drake's chief, Charles Howard, had gone in pursuit of a stranded galleass. But Drake's self-serving action obviously did not conform to late Victorian notions of duty. A week later the *Illustrated London News* renewed the assault on Drake's reputation, this time in an article titled 'The Plymouth Statue of Drake'.

> It may be questioned indeed, whether the town of Plymouth should not have preferred, as the first object of its local honours, in connection with the defeat of the Armada, to erect a statue of Sir John Hawkins, a Plymouth man, whose part in the series of conflicts that took place during ten days in the English Channel was actually more important than that of Drake, and by whose skill and industry, in his office as chief administrator of the Queen's navy, the most powerful ships engaged on this occasion had been constructed and fitted out.[22]

The points the article raises would be very relevant if the Plymouth statue of Drake was intended as an Armada memorial. Rather ironically, in seeking to overturn the tradition of Drake as Armada victor, the piece actually reinforces the myth. The Plymouth statue was, of course, a memorial to Drake and all his actions, not just the defeat of the Spanish fleet. Yet for the author, Drake signifies the Armada, his statue must, therefore, be an Armada memorial.

Unsurprisingly the Armada tercentennial celebrations were centred on Plymouth. Even less surprising was the fact that – despite the efforts of the *Illustrated London News* – Drake figured very prominently. The first event took place on 18 July when the mayor of Plymouth, H. J. Waring, opened an exhibition of Armada and Elizabethan relics in the Western Law Courts. The amount of Drake material far surpassed that connected with the other figures. Sir Francis was represented in paintings, engravings, and in photographs of images. Also included was an iron chest supposedly removed from the *Rosario* and a giant bust of Drake probably cast from a ship's figurehead. Items purportedly possessed by Drake formed a large part of the collection. The *Western Antiquary* noted: 'It is somewhat singular that, as in the case of the portraits, so in that of relics, there were more specimens of the personal property of Drake than all other Armada heroes put together.'[23] Many of the items were of dubious authenticity, but the fact that their owners should *want* them to be connected with Drake is a further demonstration of his popularity. A silver tankard loaned by a Mrs Owen, for example, was supposedly given by Sir Francis to one of her ancestors. It *was* given by Francis Drake, but Sir Francis Henry Drake, fourth baronet. The visitor to the exhibition was able to cast their gaze over a silver plate with the Drake arms and crest, a silver spoon similarly marked, two swords, Drake's dagger, his walking stick – which, the viewer was assured, had circuited the world with him – and the eighteenth-century snuff boxes by John Obrisset.

The main tercentennial event in Plymouth was the laying of the foundation stone of the Armada Memorial. This took place on 19 July, the three hundredth anniversary of the sighting of the Spanish fleet off the Lizard, and was performed, once more, by Waring. The scheme for some form of Armada memorial had actually come into being even before the Drake statue was raised in Plymouth. Again there was disagreement as to the form the memorial should take. A 'Drake Institute' for retired merchant sailors and an insurance company for fishermen were suggested. But the preferred option was for a rather more visible expression of the English victory, a column or tower. The scheme managed to secure the patronage of the Queen and, in January 1883, an advertisement inviting competitive designs was published. The winning entry was that of Herbert Gribble, a locally trained architect primarily famous for designing the Brompton Oratory. The monument comprises a huge granite pillar surmounted by Britannia, trident in hand, accompanied by the British lion. Medallion portraits of the principal commanders are positioned on the fours sides of the column (Drake facing Plymouth), along with their arms. A panel on the front of the base depicts the destruction of the Armada, and beneath this are the crown and arms of Elizabeth. Above the Armada panel is the wording 'He blew with his winds and they were scattered,' a reference to the so-called 'Protestant Wind' that had dispersed the Spanish fleet. On the opposite side of the column, beneath the Drake medallion, are inscribed Nelson's words before the battle of Trafalgar, 'England expects that every man will do his duty.' Below this is a bronze panel depicting late nineteenth-century warships, and beneath this the arms and crown of Victoria. In this way the Armada Memorial not only commemorates the defeat of the Armada but also celebrates the Royal Navy of the 1880s. The Victorian present becomes the natural and inevitable product of a smooth historical process that began in the sixteenth century. The north face of the column, which signifies the three great ages of English maritime prowess, demonstrates this line of continuity. It moves from Drake and the Elizabethan past to Nelson and Trafalgar and then to the Victorian present. The south-facing side with the Armada panel and Elizabeth's crown balances the north with its bas-relief of modern cruisers. The connection with Nelson and Trafalgar was re-established when Prince Alfred, the Duke of Edinburgh (himself an accomplished naval officer and Commander-in-Chief at Devonport Naval Base), unveiled the completed Memorial over two years later on 21 October 1890. The date was not coincidental: it was Trafalgar day. Beneath the two figures are the arms of the towns that contributed to the defence of the country in 1588. Notably, the Memorial did not perpetuate the myth of Drake as the single-handed Armada victor.

The same was not true of the other events held in Plymouth to celebrate the supposed signal victory. On the same day as the laying of the foundation stone an estimated 20,000 people crowded on to Plymouth Hoe to watch a costumed re-enactment of the mythical game of bowls. The railways struggled to cope with the numbers heading for Plymouth. The game was contested between bowling clubs from Torrington and Leeds and was played on a specially prepared green inside the Royal Citadel. That evening a grand historical procession made its way through the principal streets of Plymouth, preceded by the band of the Royal Marines. The pageant was designed and planned by one Leslie Morton, Master of Revels, and represented all the sovereigns of England from William I to William IV. There was also a cavalcade of deputations of all the nations that contained Queen Victoria seated beneath a giant triumphal arch. Among the other tableaux were several scenes from the Elizabethan past including the knighting of Raleigh and, of course, Drake's game of bowls. The *Western Daily Mercury* jovially noted that the tableau was not without its problems: 'the balls showed a decided tendency to part company with the car'.[24] No doubt Sir Francis remained characteristically unperturbed. Like the stained-glass windows in Plymouth's guildhall, the pageant represented English history condensed into a series of narrative episodes. These episodes culminated in the imperial present represented by Victoria seated beneath her triumphal arch. Those who had visited Plymouth to watch the events could return home with mementoes of the occasion: a cast iron statuette of the Drake statue or perhaps a transfer-printed handkerchief depicting Drake in the act of bowling and with the Armada just visible in the distance. The *Graphic* thought the Armada events important enough to include engravings of the game of bowls and the historical procession on its front page.

In May 1888 the *Western Antiquary* also published a special 'Armada edition'.[25] This contained material celebrating Drake as the principal player in the conflict. W. H. K. Wright contributed an article on the game of bowls from which I quoted at the beginning of this chapter. The piece is entitled 'The Historical Game of Bowls' and argues that the story is actually 'based upon solid fact'.[26] The evidence for this assertion is rather shaky and rests, firstly, on the belief that many traditions can be traced back to historical incidents and, secondly, on the tract *Vox Populi*. This was published less than forty years after the incident – still within living memory, reasons Wright – and was not refuted by anyone at the time. Historical veracity did not concern the poets whose work was included in the 'Armada edition'. 'The Armada off Devon' subtitled 'A Sketch for a Poem after Tennyson's "Revenge"'[27] by Douglas Sladen is, perhaps, the best of a none-too skilful collection. Sladen was practically involved with the poetry of the empire – with poetry of the colonial present as well as that constructing the imperial past. He lived for five years in Australia where he published poems by Australian writers. The second stanza deals with the now familiar events on Plymouth Hoe.

> 'To sea!
> And fight the Spaniards free!'
> Cried the Admiral, Lord Howard; but our sturdy Francis Drake
> Cried, 'We will not quit our noble game for any Spaniard's sake.
> I pray, you Sirs, play on:
> We have time enough I trow
> To see who wins this now
> And afterwards to settle with the Don.' (12–19)

To fully understand Sladen's construction we need to take account of the public school games ethic that had gradually emerged during the second half of the century. The emphasis the public schools placed on team games was an attempt at producing robust, stoic and preferably not over-read young imperialists. The connection between the public schools and the empire cannot be overlooked. 'Once the Empire was established', claims J. A. Mangan, 'the public schools sustained it.'[28] Team sports, it was believed, inculcated manliness. They were used to foster vigorous athleticism but also to instil courage, assertion, loyalty and a sense of duty – the quintessential English virtues deemed essential for those set for a life defending and administering the British Empire. The relationship between militarism and sport had been perceived since the beginning of the century but by the 1880s organized games had become an essential part of the curriculum. There existed 'an absolute belief that Anglo-Saxon training for conquest took place on the football pitches and the cricket squares of the English public schools'.[29] This conviction finds its most famous expression in Newbolt's poem 'Vitaï Lampada' (1898). Fulfilling one's duty often involved self-sacrifice but life was not to be taken too seriously: death should be faced in the same light-hearted fashion as a game of cricket – or, perhaps, bowls. Projecting this stoicism and regard for duty back in time naturalizes it. Thus Sladen is able to write:

> *And we pray when it comes once more*
> *For England to hold her breath,*
> *In the struggle of life and death,*
> *That men may be many to die*
> *With the smile on the lip and eye,*
> *Which has made these Armada heroes*
> *A proverb the wide world o'er.* (24–30)

By the end of the 1880s, 'the foremost image of the public schoolboy in Empire was defined, and constant: the warrior-patriot'.[30] Sir Francis Drake, an exemplary warrior-patriot, was frequently constructed as a precursive model for the public school games ethic. This is certainly how he appears in 'A Ballad of the Armada'[31] by Edward Capern, which was also printed in the 'Armada edition' of the *Western Antiquary*. Drake laughs in the face of danger as if the forthcoming battles were an extension of the game he was already playing.

> *So, with a loud laugh, out he spake,*
> *'Thou cock of courage true,*
> *We've time my lad to win the game*
> *And thrash the Spaniards too my boys,*
> *And thrash the Spaniards too'.* (129–33)

The dividing line between war and sport becomes blurred: John Hawkins claims "'Our ships must be the players now,/ Our cannon shot the bowls'" (112–13). Capern, the 'postman poet' who lived and worked in Bideford, was one of the 'untutored geniuses' much loved by the Victorians. His poetry was widely read, particularly in the South West – James Anthony Froude was an admirer. Obviously Capern did not attend public school, but the fact that he is able to draw on a construction of Drake so heavily influenced by the games ethic demonstrates its literary currency, and perhaps its wider class dissemination.

The public schools were not the only means of transmitting imperial ideology to the nation's male children. Fiction was an important tool in disseminating those qualities believed to be responsible for creating and maintaining the British Empire. As J. S. Bratton observes, 'Fiction had the advantage of a much more nearly universal availability: anyone educated to the level of basic literacy was accessible through a story.'[32] Boys' novels concentrated heavily on the world of action, and the privateering exploits of the Elizabethan era provided the ideal setting for a fictional adventure that sought to mould the character of the young imperialist. The prolific writer George Alfred Henty produced the first Drake novel specifically intended for a juvenile audience: *Under Drake's Flag: A Tale of the Spanish Main*[33] (1883) but several others appeared in the 1890s and after.[34] Henty weaves the adventures of his young hero, Ned Hearne, around the narratives of the 1572 Panama raids and the circumnavigation. Ned and his comrades display admirable stoicism and leadership as they live among the natives and battle against the Spaniards. Superior British daring and seamanship is stressed throughout. Henty reproduces some of the most

action-packed passages from the accounts of the voyages including the wounding
of Drake during the raid on Nombre de Dios, the capture of the treasure ship
Cacafuego, and the fight with the natives on Mocha Island.

It is worth noting that *Under Drake's Flag* corresponds to the pattern of nautical
adventure stories identified by Bratton. According to this reading, the young
protagonist rises from obscurity to a position of wealth and power through his own
exertions. Physical prowess, natural leadership and practical intelligence together with
a keen moral sense see Ned promoted from a ships' boy to a third officer and finally
to a knight. This elevation provides a very bourgeois lesson for the potential empire-
builder and one that is addressed to a middle-class audience. In Bratton's words,

> The social objective of these stories is to set forth a model for behaviour
> which offers the middle- or lower middle-class youth a path to the highest
> distinction, a way in which he can prove himself a gentleman equal to the
> highest in the land.[35]

Although rising from relatively humble beginnings, the hero in the sea-faring
adventures is almost always a displaced middle-class boy who is separated from
those around him by some easily identifiable trait such as accent or dress. Ned
Hearne is no exception; when he first appears we are told he is dressed differently
from the fisher lads who are gathered on the shore. We later learn that he is the
schoolmaster's son, a man believed to have once been wealthy. Having helped defeat
the Armada, Ned is rewarded with a comfortable retirement in the shires.

In the year after the Armada tercentennial celebrations John Seymour Lucas
exhibited another Drake painting at the Royal Academy. This was titled *The
Surrender* and dealt with the capture of the *Rosario* (PLATE 10). Again, a short
explanatory narrative accompanied the painting.

> Whereupon Pedro (de Valdez) hearing that it was the fiery Drake (ever
> terrible to the Spaniards) who held him in chase, with forty of his
> followers, came on board Sir Francis his ship, where first giving him the
> conge, he protested that he, and all his, were resolved to die in defence,
> had they not fallen under his power, whose valour was so great that Mars
> and Neptune seemed to attend him in his attempts.

In the painting a slender de Valdez proffers his sword to a rather chunky-looking
Drake in a display of great chivalry. The contrasting physical appearance of the two
figures is important. Drake represents the robust muscular Englishness so prized by
Charles Kingsley; de Valdez, although stately, represents a certain Latin effeminacy. He
is the Other that defines the desired version of Englishness. The surrender of de
Valdez's sword is also the symbolic surrender of Spanish naval power. A contemporary
audience familiar with Froude and Kingsley would be well aware of this. The fact that
priests are seen among the sorrowful-looking Spaniards suggests the victory is also
that of Protestantism. The positioning of the viewer is crucial to the painting's success.
We are located behind and to the left of Drake so that while the surrendered sword
is offered to Drake it is also offered to us – or the late nineteenth-century English

PLATE 10. John Seymour Lucas, *The Surrender*, 1889. Not only the surrender of the *Rosario* but also the surrender of Spanish maritime power.

viewer. This provided a reassuring reminder of the nation's supposed long history of naval dominance. Coming in 1889, the year that government opted for the 'two-power standard' of naval strength (the belief that the fleet should always outnumber the navies of the next two strongest powers combined), the image can be seen as a further response to the anxieties Britain was feeling about her position in the world. In the years leading up to the First World War, this anxiety would be a constant underlying motive when constructing Sir Francis Drake.

Notes

[1] 'The Historical Windows in the New Guildhall', *Smith's Plymouth Almanac* (Plymouth, 1876–7), unpaginated.

[2] W. H. K. Wright, 'The Historical Game of Bowls', *Western Antiquary*, vol. 7 (1887- 8), 317.

[3] Heaton, Butler and Bayne were one of the major stained-glass studios operating during the second half of the nineteenth century. Their work was at its most popular during the High Victorian phase of the Gothic Revival, particularly in the early 1860s. By the 1870s they had adapted to integrate new approaches. The Armada Window was one of their later works. For a detailed account of their output, see Martin Harrison, *Victorian Stained Glass* (London, 1980).

[4] The five surviving fragments of cartoons for the windows are reproduced in Simone Bayne-Dupaquier, *Heaton, Butler and Bayne: A Hundred Years of the Art of Stained Glass* (Montreux, 1986), 68–72. No representation of Drake survives but images of Sir Walter Raleigh and Lord Sheffield from the Armada Window are reproduced.

[5] 'The Historical Windows', unpaginated.

[6] Fouracre and Watson were among the number of small stained-glass firms that emerged in the 1870s. Their work (and that of many of the other new firms) was a reaction against the heavy approach of the Gothic Revivalists. See Harrison, *Victorian Stained Glass*.

[7] 'The Historical Windows', unpaginated.

[8] 'Account of the Plymouth New Guildhall and Municipal Offices', *Smith's Plymouth Almanac* (Plymouth, 1876–7), unpaginated.

[9] See, for example, John Seeley, *The Expansion of England* (London, 1883).

[10] H. D. Rawnsley, 'Sir Francis Drake, the Hoe', *Western Antiquary*, vol. 8 (1888–9), 29–30.

[11] *Western Daily Mercury*, 17 September 1881, 2.

[12] W. S. Lach-Szyrma, letter, *Western Antiquary*, vol. 3 (1883–4), 70.

[13] 'The Drake Commemoration at Plymouth', *Western Daily Mercury*, 15 February 1884, 2

[14] Bernard Porter, *The Lion's Share: A Short History of British Imperialism 1850–1983* (1975; London, 1984), 340.

[15] 'The Proposed Memorial to Sir Francis Drake', *Western Daily Mercury*, 27 January 1882, 3.

[16] 'The Drake Memorial at Tavistock', *Western Daily Mercury*, 28 September 1883, 3.

[17] 'The Drake Memorial at Tavistock', *Western Daily Mercury*, 28 September 1883, 3.

[18] 'The Drake Commemoration', *Western Daily Mercury*, 15 February 1884, 3.

[19] The town that grew up around the dockyard was known as Plymouth Dock or simply Dock. In 1824 Plymouth Dock obtained its incorporation as an independent town and became known as Devonport. The three towns that made up the conurbation known as Plymouth – Devonport, Stonehouse and Plymouth – were finally merged in 1914.

[20] See Charles N. Robinson, 'The Spanish Armada', *Illustrated London News*, 14 July 1888, 41–50. William Laird Clowes, 'The Tercentenary of the Defeat of the Spanish Armada', *Graphic*, 21 July 1888, 65–8, 74.

[21] Robinson, 'Spanish Armada', 42.

[22] 'The Plymouth Statue of Drake', *Illustrated London News* 21 July 1888, 76.

[23] W. H. K. Wright, 'The Armada Tercentenary Exhibition', *Western Antiquary*, vol. 8 (1888–9), 34.

[24] 'The Armada Tercentenary', *Western Daily Mercury*, 20 July 1888, 3.

[25] *Western Antiquary*, vol. 7 (1887–8), 273–326.

[26] Wright, 'The Historical Game of Bowls', 316.

[27] Douglas Sladen, 'The Armada off Devon', *Western Antiquary*, vol. 7 (1887–8), 315.

[28] J. A. Mangan, *The Games Ethic and Imperialism: Aspects of the Diffusion of an Ideal* (London, 1986), 21.

[29] Mangan, 45.

[30] Mangan, 60.

[31] Edward Capern, 'A Ballad of the Armada', *Western Antiquary*, vol. 7 (1887–8), 323–4.

[32] J. S. Bratton, 'Of England, Home and Duty: The Image of England in Victorian and Edwardian Juvenile Fiction', in John M. Mackenzie, ed., *Imperialism and Popular Culture* (Manchester, 1986), 76.

[33] George Alfred Henty, *Under Drake's Flag: A Tale of the Spanish Main* (London, 1883).

[34] See also Charles Henry Eden, *At Sea with Drake on the Spanish Main* (London, 1899); William Murray Graydon, *The Fighting Lads of Devon: Or, In the Days of the Armada* (London, 1900); William Gordon Stables, *Old England on the Sea: The Story of Admiral Drake* (London, 1900).

[35] Bratton, 'Of England, Home and Duty', 85.

CHAPTER EIGHT

'Gun to Gun he'll Challenge us'

See that ye hold fast the heritage we leave you.
(Louis Napoleon Parker, 1912)[1]

The construction of Sir Francis Drake that emerged in the period between the 1888 Armada tercentenary celebrations and the outbreak of the First World War clearly reflects the anxieties of a nation whose long economic and naval hegemony was facing serious challenges from both within and without Europe. In the previous chapter it was mentioned that the rapid spread of industrialization – particularly in Germany and the United States – led to a dramatic shortening of Britain's commercial and industrial lead over the rest of the world. Statistics expose this worrying trend. In 1880 Germany's share of world trade stood at 9.7 per cent but by 1898 this had steadily increased to 11.8 per cent. Meanwhile Britain's share had dropped significantly from 23.2 per cent in 1880 to 17.1 per cent in 1898.[2] One consequence of industrial expansion was that rival powers were able to construct threateningly powerful navies. France, Russia and Japan as well as Germany and the United States embarked on large-scale shipbuilding programmes. Although no fleet could yet challenge the supremacy of the Royal Navy, agitation for increased naval expenditure commenced in the press and was rapidly taken up by organizations such as the Navy League, which was particularly vocal in its demands for rearmament. In the face of extensive foreign armament, the 1889 Naval Defence Act, which introduced the two-power standard – and which provided £21.5 million for new vessels including ten battleships – soon appeared inadequate. Finance for an additional seven battleships had been found by 1893. The issue of naval expenditure lay behind much of the Drake material produced during the first years of the century.

In 1890 Sir Julian Corbett published *Sir Francis Drake*,[3] a robust and immensely readable life of the great seafarer. A novelist and war correspondent, *Drake* was Corbett's first attempt at an historical work. The biography was one volume in a series titled *English Men of Action*, which also included works on such exemplary figures as Henry V, Nelson and Wellington. The lives of these heroes provided historical validity for the activities of the modern empire-builders; both those included in the series – General Gordon, Henry Havelock and David Livingstone

– and those still actively engaged in expanding Britain's possessions. Corbett's Drake is a man of action *par excellence* whose restless spirit is only restrained by the political manoeuvrings of the Court and the not infrequent need to assuage Spain. Sir Francis's exploits are presented as the result of a lifelong quest for vengeance following the treacherous attack on Hawkins's slaving fleet in the harbour at San Juan d'Ulua. From that incident in 1567 until the time of the Armada 'he had never ceased a day to do and dare against Spain'.[4] But the battle at San Juan was not only a turning point in the life of Francis Drake; it was also a crucial moment in the history of England. With a reference to Froude's version of the Elizabethan past, Corbett writes that the battle 'may fairly be said to mark the opening of a new book in the great epic of the Reformation'.[5] The hero of this epic is unequivocally Drake. Corbett admits that the romantic allure of the Drake story can still excite the most scientific and unemotional mind. '[E]ven now the most chastened explorer of pay-sheets and reports cannot save his imagination from the taint of the same irrational exultation that possessed the Admiral's contemporaries.'[6] The author's skill as a novelist as well as a naval historian ensures that the Drake narrative is rendered with a great deal of imagination and empathy. For example, the young Drake living in Kent 'must have seen Wyatt ride into Rochester and establish his headquarters in the castle. He must have heard him call on all true Englishmen to rally to his standard to save the country from the Pope and Spain.'[7] In such moments Corbett often resorts to colourful prose. Of the Spanish Armada he claims, 'Into the midst he [Drake] pictured himself bursting like a thunder-clap, and in a storm of fire and iron completing the ruin which Heaven had begun.'[8]

Corbett begins his biography by drawing attention to the body of myths that obscure the 'real' Drake. 'Of all the heroes whose exploits have set our history aglow with romance,' he writes, 'there is not one who so soon passed into legend as Francis Drake. He was not dead before his life became a fairy tale, and he himself as indistinct as Sir Guy of Warwick or Croquemitaine.'[9] (The foregrounding of the Drake myths and particularly the reference to Guy of Warwick suggests that Corbett was familiar with Southey's life of the admiral.) Corbett's version of Drake grew from contemporary ideas about naval power. If Froude had located the origins of British naval mastery in the sea-faring activities of the late sixteenth century, then Corbett was responsible for popularizing the notion of Drake as the founder of modern naval strategy. A book published in 1890 by an American naval captain was undoubtedly a major influence on Corbett's ideas. This was A. T. Mahan's *The Influence of Sea Power Upon History 1660–1783*,[10] which concluded that 'the great power rivalries between 1660 and 1815 had their outcomes decided chiefly by maritime campaigns'.[11] In a Britain already anxious about its naval strength, Mahan's work reinforced the argument for increased naval expenditure. Indeed, *The Influence of Sea Power* was regarded as expressing indisputable truths about the role of navies in the modern era and Mahan himself came to be revered. From Mahan it was gathered that control of the oceans should be the ultimate goal of a maritime power. Paul Kennedy provides a neat summary of the major implications for naval strategy contained within Mahan's work.

[L]arge battlefleets, and a concentration of force, decided control of the
oceans, whereas a *guerre de course* strategy was always ineffectual; that the
blockade was a very effective weapon which would sooner or later bring
an enemy to its knees; that the possession of select bases on islands or
continental peripheries was more valuable than control of large land
masses.[12]

These ideas, crucial to naval thought up until the First World War, are clearly
discernible in Corbett's treatment of Francis Drake. The Descent on the Indies
becomes the nation's first attempt at bringing together a powerful battle-fleet. The
extent to which Corbett is preoccupied with contemporary naval theory is revealed
by his use of anachronistic terms when describing Drake's fleet: 'It consisted of two
battle-ships and eighteen cruisers.'[13] But not until preparations were well in hand for
the Cadiz raid did Drake begin to comprehend the central idea that emerges from
Mahan's research. In Corbett's words, 'He was beginning to dimly grasp that
command of the sea was the first object for a naval power to aim at.'[14] Carthagena
had been lost in 1585 because Sir Francis did not secure control of the sea: he learnt
from this lesson. For Corbett, the Cadiz expedition represented Drake's first use of
modern naval strategy. Drake takes the fight to the enemy; 'He knew that in attack
lay England's best defence.'[15] The idea of gaining control of the seas, if Corbett is to
be believed, was still occupying Drake in 1588. Awaiting the arrival of the Spanish
Armada, Drake begins to appreciate the full significance of this new naval objective.

> During his impatient striding up and down the Hoe, the true theory of
> naval warfare, of which he had already a dim perception, had been growing
> clearer in his teeming mind ... for the first time [he] distinctly formulates
> the idea of getting command of the sea. He fully grasped that the invasion
> was to come from Parma in the Netherlands; but no less perfectly he
> perceived that its feasibility hung upon the possession of the four seas.[16]

The Armada, when it finally came, was not the great battle-fleet that Sir Francis was
beginning to perceive as necessary to accomplish its aims. Instead it was 'a convoy of
an unwieldy mass of transports and storeships'[17] that, according to Mahan's theory,
was unlikely to succeed. But Corbett's Drake is far more than the pioneer of a new
naval strategy; he is also an unconventional leader and a tactical genius. He abolished
the system which, according to Corbett, 'paralysed the Spanish navy'.[18] In the
Spanish fleet a ships' master was compelled to take orders from any army officer or
gentlemen adventurer being conveyed. In Drake's navy the seaman was firmly in
control. Drake also developed tactics that horrified more conservative naval
commanders. At Cadiz, for example, he sailed into the harbour and confronted a
small fleet of galleys, perhaps the most feared vessels in the Spanish navy.

> In a few minutes the English Admiral had taught the world a new lesson
> in tactics. Galleys could only fire straight ahead; and as they came on line
> abreast, Drake, passing with the Queen's four battle-ships athwart their
> course poured in heavy broadsides.[19]

Perhaps the most intriguing aspect of Corbett's reassessment of Drake's strategic and tactical awareness is his construction of Sir Francis as a forerunner of Nelson. As we will see later, by the end of the First World War, this representation had undergone a transformation that resulted in Nelson being projected as a 'reincarnation' of Drake, and this construction, in turn, being presented as an example of West Country folklore. Of course, Corbett the historian does not concern himself with such romantic fancies; he is, nevertheless, keen to align the two greatest figures in the history of English naval endeavour. In a passage that dwells upon the tactics adopted by Drake during the course of the Armada battle off Portland, he writes:

> [T]he Spanish officers had been shown the mobility of a fleet formed line-ahead, and its power of concentration on weak points. It was the dawn of those modern tactics which Blake and Monck were to develop and Nelson to perfect, and both sides recognized the great fact.[20]

The victory over the Armada is, of course, Drake's and Corbett takes the opportunity to re-establish the link with Nelson. '[T]he honour belongs to Drake no less rightly than the laurels of Copenhagen are Nelson's.'[21]

With Mahan and his emphasis upon the necessity of naval dominance such a major influence, it is hardly surprising that Corbett's work should reflect the contemporary naval expenditure debate. Britain's anxiety about maintaining her maritime hegemony meant that the annual estimated costs of expenditure on the Royal Navy, the so-called naval estimates, were increasing dramatically: £11 million in 1883, they had risen to £18.7 million in 1896, and £35.9 million in 1903.[22] For Corbett, and many others, this was a price worth paying. In *Sir Francis Drake* he highlights the vital importance of a large fleet: during his time on the Spanish coast in 1587, we are told, Drake had informed Walsingham that 'he ought to have at least six more cruisers to do his work properly'.[23] In the later work *Drake and the Tudor Navy* (1898) Corbett dwells on the lessons that were drawn from the Armada conflict: that the Royal Navy needed to be increased from 30 to 50 large ships; for a ratio of two men to every three tons of shipping (instead of one man to every two tons); and for an improvement in the design of ships specifically for fighting. The modern navy, he implies, must not be neglected, and technological advances must be utilized.

Concern about maintaining high levels of spending was not confined to Corbett, however. Froude also makes frequent allusions to the subject in what was to be his final work on the Elizabethan maritime past: *English Seamen in the Sixteenth Century*.[24] Although forty years had passed since the publication of 'England's Forgotten Worthies', Froude continued to propound his version of English naval history in a series of lectures delivered at Oxford in 1893–4. These were published in 1895 under the title *English Seamen*. Despite the great enthusiasm for Drake that he and Kingsley had engendered (and which Corbett had sought to keep vigorously alive), Froude was still not satisfied that the significance of the English Reformation had been adequately appreciated.

> [A] time will come when we shall see better than we see now what the Reformation was, and what we owe to it, and these sea-captains of Elizabeth will then form the subject of a great English national epic as grand as the 'Odyssey'.[25]

Sir Francis Drake, as we might expect, takes a prominent place in this exposition of sixteenth-century history: over half the lectures are concerned with Drake's exploits or events in which he played a major part. If the Elizabethan past was directly responsible for the maritime present, then it could also be used to illustrate the contemporary need for increased naval spending. Of the treasure taken from the captured carrack *San Felipe* Froude claims 'I doubt if such a naval estimate was ever presented to an English House of Commons.'[26] Like Corbett, Froude uses the Armada as a dire warning against neglecting the Royal Navy. During the early part of 1588 Elizabeth was reluctant to spend money on preparations for a threat that might yet dissolve.

> She found fault with Drake's expenses. She charged him with wasting her ammunition in target practice. She had it doled out to him in driblets, and allowed no more than would serve a day and a half's service. She kept a sharp hand on the victualling houses. April went, and her four finest ships … were still with sails unbent, 'keeping Chatham Church.' She said they would not be wanted and it would be a waste of money to refit them.[27]

And yet the threat did materialize and only with good fortune was the English victory secured. Froude is not explicit about where any modern challenge may lie, but it may be noted that the very first lecture begins with a reference to German expansionism. In recent years, writes Froude, 'The wings of France have been clipped; the German Empire has become a solid thing; but England still holds her watery domain; Britannia does still rule the waves.'[28] But the tone has none of the certainty that we encountered in the 'Forgotten Worthies'. Froude, it seems, is hopeful that England can maintain her maritime hegemony in a rapidly changing world but is far from convinced. Echoing Tennyson's warning in 'Epilogue to the Queen'[29] (1873) that a failure to recognize Britain's imperial destiny – no matter what the economic cost of that destiny – would leave the nation 'Some third-rate isle half-lost amongst her seas' (25), Froude writes 'Take away her merchant fleets, take away the navy that guards them: her empire will come to and end … and Britain will become once again an insignificant island in the North Sea.'[30]

Drake, by now synonymous with the defeat of the Armada, was the ideal figure to call upon in times of anxiety about England's vulnerability. This is precisely what Henry Newbolt does in the poem 'Drake's Drum'[31] first published in the *St. James's Gazette* on 15 January 1896. The poem gave rise to the second of the great Drake myths: that of the Elizabethan warrior returning to save embattled England whenever his drum was struck. The notion of the returning hero had literary currency. Tennyson incorporates a West Country folk-tradition concerning the return of King Arthur into the epilogue of 'The Epic' framework for *Morte d'Arthur*[32] (1842). In the West Country version of the folk-tale Arthur sleeps in a cavern beneath Cadbury Castle waiting to be summoned to save his kingdom.[33] In Tennyson's poem Arthur appears not as a seventh-century king but 'like a modern gentleman' (345). In the 'Dedication' (1862) added to *Idylls of the King*[34] in 1873, Tennyson suggests that the late Prince Albert could have been a new Arthur figure to deliver the country from its perceived ills.

In the first chapter I discussed the appropriation of secular figures, including Francis Drake, to fulfil the imaginative need that resulted from the abandonment of the practice of invoking mediating saints. 'Drake's Drum' suggests that even in late nineteenth-century England, Drake was still acting as a mediating figure to be invoked at times of national anxiety. He will guarantee the empire and the nation's security. The act of invocation is suggested very clearly by the following lines: 'Call him on the deep sea, call him up the Sound,/ Call him when ye sail to meet the foe' (21–2). In his autobiography Newbolt reveals how the poem came to be published.

> The Kaiser Wilhelm had made a threatening move, and it was announced that as a proof of our readiness to meet a serious challenge, a Special Service Squadron would be sent to sea at once. I had in my drawer some verses which I had written with the title 'Drake's Drum' more than a month before – early in December, 1895. I posted them to the editor … as possibly appropriate to the present moment, and on the evening of 15th January I had the singular pleasure of seeing in every street as I walked home from Lincoln's Inn, the placards of the St. James's Gazette bearing two words only, in enormous capitals: as it were the beat of the Drum made visible.[35]

The poem depicts Sir Francis sleeping (the parallel with King Arthur is noticeable) in his watery grave in the Caribbean Sea; like Boehm's bas-relief on the pedestal of the Tavistock Drake statue, Newbolt favours the romanticized image of the admiral sewn inside a sail weighted with shot.

> *Drake he's in his hammock an' a thousand mile away,*
> *(Capten, art tha sleepin' there below?)*
> *Slung atween the round shot in Nombre Dios Bay,*
> *An' dreamin' arl the time o' Plymouth Hoe.* (1–4)

Dying for Queen and country in an exotic foreign place, never to see England again, Drake becomes an exemplary self-sacrificial hero of empire. Sir Francis is left to dream of home; of Plymouth Hoe, purportedly the scene of the game of bowls, and of an idealized version of ship-board life 'Wi' sailor lads a dancin' heel-an'-toe' (6). In Drake's dying moments Newbolt has him giving a final instruction that acknowledges the very real anxiety that England was feeling about her position in the world.

> *'Take my drum to England, hang et by the shore,*
> *Strike et when your powder's runnin' low;*
> *If the Dons sight Devon, I'll quit the port o' Heaven,*
> *An' drum them up the Channel as we drummed them long ago'.* (13–16)

There had, of course, been exaggerated invasion scares in the 1850s and 1860s prompting fears about England's maritime strength, but not since the Napoleonic Wars had the nation faced a serious challenge to her naval hegemony. Newbolt mobilizes the maritime past to counter this threat. When invoked, Sir Francis will return in person, or perhaps embodied in a new naval hero (the poem's deliberate ambiguity allows both readings), to deliver England from her present danger.

Newbolt's poem was instantly popular and elevated the drum to an iconic status. Indeed, a silver replica of the drum was presented to *HMS Devonshire* in 1929.[36] Perhaps through constant repetition or the romantic nature of the subject and undoubtedly aided by the poet's attempt at local dialect, 'Drake's Drum' was quickly taken to be a literary expression of local folklore. This suggested an organic continuity between the late sixteenth century and the present (rather than a constructed continuity working in reverse, or linking the present with the past). The idea of the hero returning to save England when summoned by the beating of his drum is almost certainly an invention of Newbolt's. The drum, as we saw earlier, was displayed for visitors to Buckland Abbey but no early guide-books seem to have attributed any special powers to the instrument. There is, however, some evidence, which predates the poem, for a belief in the drum's ability to summon Sir Francis not for military service but for merrymaking. In 1865 Robert Hunt, a scientific writer who was born in Plymouth Dock, published *Popular Romances of the West of England*,[37] a collection of Cornish folk-tales. This collection provides the first indication that, in the Buckland Monachorum area at least, Drake's Drum may have been associated with special powers. He writes, 'Even now, – as old Betty Donithorne, formerly the housekeeper at Buckland Abbey, told me, – if the warrior hears the drum which hangs in the hall of the Abbey and which had accompanied him around the world, he rises and has a revel.'[38] Whether Newbolt was aware of this myth we cannot know.

In 1883 a serious attempt was made to return Drake's body to England. The *Graphic* reported that

> A search for the body of Sir Francis Drake is to be made by the British squadron belonging to the West Indies and North American stations, which during its cruise will visit Puerto Cabello. Off this spot nearly three centuries ago the gallant explorer was buried at sea in a leaden coffin, and every effort will be made to recover the coffin.[39]

Drake was actually buried off Porto Bello in Panama and not Puerto Cabello, Venezuela. If the *Graphic* was reporting accurately, the mission was doomed to failure. We can only speculate as to where Drake would have been interred had his coffin been recovered. St Paul's Cathedral is the obvious choice, being the resting place of both Nelson and Wellington, but without doubt this would have been challenged by the city of Plymouth, keen to claim Drake as its own. The attempt at locating his remains suggests the continuing existence of the cult of secular relics discussed in the second chapter. The successful recovery of Drake's body would have provided a point of focus for all those who revered Sir Francis. Just as the founders of the early Church were elevated to sainthood and worshipped at shrines, so Drake – a figure so often constructed as a founder of early empire – seems to have been endowed with an imperial sanctity. His remains, if only they could they be found, would be a great imperial relic. But the notion of the relic was not confined to Drake's body. Medieval relics were both saints' remains and objects connected with saints. Drake's drum, with its supposed miraculous power to 'cure' England's troubles, was the most important tangible relic connected with Drake.

The myth of the returning hero so successfully developed in 'Drake's Drum' could also be mobilized in the colonial theatre, and this is precisely what Newbolt does in 'Waggon Hill'.[40] First published in 1900, the poem takes its title from a battle that took place during the Boer War. Wagon-Hill Ridge was a key position in the defences of the town of Ladysmith. On 6 January 1900 Boer forces attempted to take the ridge and the town that they had besieged since November 1899. The attack was successfully repelled largely through the efforts of the Devonshire Regiment. Newbolt's poem is obviously a product of the intense patriotism engendered by the event. Strikingly, however, the poem begins not in South Africa but in the North Sea, and not in the nineteenth century but in the sixteenth century, with Drake pursuing the shattered and fleeing Armada.

> *Drake in the North Sea grimly prowling,*
> *Treading his dear Revenge's deck,*
> *Watched, with the sea-dogs round him growling,*
> *Galleons drifting wreck by wreck.* (1–4)

Apparently unrelated, both Drake's defeat of the Spanish Armada and the successful defence of Wagon-Hill Ridge provided examples of the potent and by now familiar image of plucky Britons defending themselves from foreign aggression. Newbolt, of course, avoids locating the battle in its full context. That the Boer War was fought in a less than glorious attempt to expand Britain's economic interests had no part in the mythology of empire. That the besieging force was not a professional army but a hastily gathered collection of farmers is similarly elided. Having established a link with the Elizabethan past, the poem swiftly shifts to one of Newbolt's familiar motifs: the dying hero. Drake's last words to the Devon seamen gathered around him are a 'sign' of his intention to deliver England once more. The reference to the storm is almost certainly an allusion to the so-called Protestant Wind that ended the invasion attempt in 1588. Drake or his spirit can be invoked not by the beating of his drum but by calling to the storm.

> *'Pride of the West! What Devon hath kept*
> *Devon shall keep on tide or main;*
> *Call to the storm and drive them flying,*
> *Devon, O Devon, in wind and rain!'* (13–16)

For Newbolt, the men of the Devonshire Regiment who had blunted the Boer attack at Wagon-Hill Ridge are the descendents of Drake's Elizabethan sea-dogs. The Devons have, it seems, inherited the courage and determination of the county's most famous son; these qualities will ensure victory. But Drake is also a presence on Wagon-Hill, summoned from his sleep, when the 'Valour of England' was 'Locked in a death-grip all day tightening' (19).

> *Battle and storm and the sea-dog's way!*
> *Drake from his long rest turned again,*
> *Victory lit thy steel with lightening,*
> *Devon, O Devon, in wind and rain!* (22–5)

If Devon's soldiers firmly on the back foot had inherited Drake's spirit, then it also lived on in England's naval commanders. Newbolt explored this idea in the poem 'Admirals All'[41] published in 1896. Again we can see the poem as a response to the nation's concerns about her maritime dominance. England's naval strength throughout the nineteenth century meant that she had not fought a major naval engagement since Trafalgar in 1805. With rival nations beginning to construct powerful navies, it was reassuring to celebrate past maritime glories and England's seemingly unending line of unrivalled naval commanders who are invoked *en masse*. In 'Admirals All' Newbolt constructs an unbroken line of continuity connecting Drake with Nelson, or sixteenth-century naval enterprise with nineteenth-century endeavours.

> *Effingham, Grenville, Raleigh, Drake,*
> *Here's to the bold and the free!*
> *Benbow, Collingwood, Byron, Blake,*
> *Hail to the Kings of the Sea!*
> . . . .
> *And honour, as long as waves shall break,*
> *To Nelson's peerless name!* (1–4, 7–8)

The skilled seamanship that had founded English greatness had survived throughout the eighteenth century and was still very much alive in the early 1800s. Sir Francis Drake and Horatio Nelson share the same independent spirit, tactical awareness and attitude to authority that separated them from lesser mortals. Here is the literary fruition of the connection Corbett draws repeatedly in *Sir Francis Drake* and *Drake and the Tudor Navy*.

> *He was playing at Plymouth a rubber of bowls*
> *When the great Armada came;*
> *But he said, 'They must wait their turn, good souls,'*
> *And he stooped, and finished the game.*
>
> *The Admiral's signal bade him fly,*
> *But he wickedly wagged his head,*
> *He clapped the glass to his sightless eye*
> *And 'I'm damned if I see it,' he said.* (25–8, 41–4)

The final lines of the poem look forward to continuing British naval dominance. What had been won by Drake and defended by Nelson, the poem suggests, would not be lost in the 1890s: the maritime present (and future) was equal to the nautical past. The conclusion is hopeful rather than certain.

> *But they left us a kingdom none can take,*
> *The realm of the circling sea,*
> *To be ruled by the rightful sons of Blake*
> *And the Rodneys yet to be.* (49–52)

Admirals All was also the title of Newbolt's first collection of poetry published in October 1897. Containing both 'Admirals All' and 'Drake's Drum', its popularity – four editions in two weeks – provides further evidence of a deep anxiety that Newbolt's patriotism helped soothe but also tacitly acknowledged.

The relationship between Drake and Nelson was reinforced by one of Newbolt's later poems, 'The Little Admiral'[42] (1908). Both naval commanders – neither of whom were of great physical stature – are present in the figure of the Little Admiral. To fully understand the poem it is important to locate 'The Little Admiral' in its immediate context, that of the naval arms race that was taking place in the years leading up to the First World War. With other nations rapidly arming it was becoming clear that Britain's position as the world's greatest maritime power was not unassailable. This realization led to another major shipbuilding programme distinct from that of the 1890s. Between 1904 and 1907, under the First Sea Lord, Sir John Fisher, the Royal Navy underwent a dramatic reorganization. The main thrust of Fisher's reform was to reduce the number of obsolete gunboats and small cruisers stationed around the world and to concentrate naval forces in home waters. To replace the multitude of outdated vessels a new class of battleship was created: the all-big-gun dreadnought, the first of which was launched in 1906. With a company of around 800 men, and carrying a massive concentration of firepower (*HMS Dreadnought*, the vessel after which the class was named, carried ten twelve-inch guns), the dreadnoughts were the most awesome vessels in the Royal Navy's possession. By 1914 Britain had 19 dreadnoughts at sea with another 13 under construction. In the same year Germany had 13 dreadnought-type ships at sea, and America eight.

The opening lines of Newbolt's poem are addressed to the rival powers but might well be applied to Britain. 'Stand by to reckon up your battleships-/ Ten, twenty, thirty, there they go' (1–2). Yet what value are such vessels, Newbolt asks, without 'the mighty will that shows the way to them'? (16). The implication is that Britain's rivals do not possess such commanders. But what evidence was there that Britain's untested naval officers were up to the task? Like 'Admiral's All', 'The Little Admiral' invokes the past to reassure the present. Modern naval commanders, Newbolt assures us, have inherited the spirit of those great signifiers of English naval supremacy, Francis Drake and Horatio Nelson. But it is not simply the spirit of the two admirals that guides the modern navy. The little Admiral is also a presence aboard ship, only perceivable – although not fully understood – by 'sailormen' in visionary moments. There is no mistaking his identity. The poem is spoken by an ordinary seaman who claims 'I could swear that he had stars upon his uniform,/ And one sleeve pinned across his breast' (31–2). Yet Nelson is also Francis

Drake. Heavily influenced by Corbett's account of the development of naval strategy, Newbolt is fully aware of Nelson's debt to the Elizabethan admiral. The final stanza anticipates the challenge of an unnamed enemy: the little Admiral who meets the foe is identified not as Nelson but as his predecessor, Drake.

> Keel to keel and gun to gun he'll challenge us
> To meet him at the great Armada game.
> None knows what may be at the end of it,
> But we'll give all our bodies and our souls
> To see the little Admiral a-playing him
> A rubber of the old Long Bowls. (39–44)

Sir Charles Villiers Stanford, Professor of Music at Cambridge, set five of Newbolt's poems to music in a song cycle for baritone, male chorus and orchestra titled *Songs of the Sea*. This was first performed at the Leeds Festival in 1904. In order the songs are 'Drake's Drum', 'Outward Bound', 'Devon, O Devon, in Wind and Rain' (actually 'Waggon Hill' but renamed to maintain an explicit nautical feel), 'Homeward Bound' and 'The Old Superb', named after a ship in Nelson's fleet. The stirring march of 'Drake's Drum' helped to further popularize an already well-known poem. Beginning with Drake and moving through an outward journey, an episode of intense action, a return journey, and concluding with Nelson, the song cycle has the feel of a voyage, perhaps even a circumnavigation. The rousing chorus of 'The Old Superb' confirms this circularity: 'Round the world if need be, and round the world again.' Because Newbolt had popularized the idea of Nelson as a 'reincarnation' of Drake, the cycle seems to return to its beginning. Six years later Stanford set another five of Newbolt's poems to music in a song cycle titled *Songs of the Fleet*. Rather more reflective than *Songs of the Sea*, this never achieved the popularity of the earlier work. Nelson rather than Drake is the central figure of the cycle, although the fourth song, 'The Little Admiral', makes Sir Francis's presence clear. The chorus of the opening song, 'Sailing at Dawn', calls on the maritime past to assist the present, 'Admirals of the old time, bring us on the bold ways!/ Soul of all the sea-dogs, lead the line today!' But the jaunty conclusion of *Songs of the Sea* is not repeated. Perhaps the cycle can be seen as a product of the emergent anxieties about Britain's maritime hegemony. 'Fare Well' is a meditation on the human cost of naval supremacy – and, indeed, empire – which seems to eclipse the evocation of Drake and Nelson.

Drake's cultural presence was not confined to words and music, however. In 1899 Thomas Davidson exhibited *The Burial of Admiral Drake* at the Royal Academy (PLATE 11). Davidson had previously exhibited several paintings concerning Nelson, including his mortal wounding at Trafalgar. Given the contemporary emphasis on the connection between the two admirals, an image of Drake's burial at sea must have seemed a natural progression. The text of an accompanying explanatory note was taken from Corbett's *Drake and the Tudor Navy*: 'Next day Sir Thomas Baskerville bore the admiral's body in a leaden coffin a league from shore, and there, amidst a lament of trumpets and the thunder of the guns, the sea received her own again.' The way Drake was represented in Academy art had clearly changed

PLATE 11. Thomas Davidson, *The Burial of Admiral Drake*, 1899. The influence of Newbolt's poem *Drake's Drum* and an increasing anxiety about maintaining British hegemony.

since Seymour Lucas produced the (on the surface, at least) self-confident canvases *The Armada in Sight* and *The Surrender* in the 1880s. Three bare-footed sailors are engaged in tipping the leaden coffin over the side of the *Defiance*; Mr Bride, the ship's chaplain, says a prayer; Sir Thomas Baskerville, commander of land forces during the expedition, stands beside him head bowed. Trumpeters and musketeers provide a salute while a ship in the distance fires a broadside. In the left foreground two drummers provide an accompaniment to the burial. The side drums in the foreground are an obvious reference to the returning hero myth.

The single greatest contribution to the mythology of Sir Francis Drake to appear during the first decade of the twentieth century was the work of Alfred Noyes. This was the epic biographical poem *Drake*,[43] serialized in *Blackwood's Magazine* between 1906 and 1908. Noyes was a prolific writer – and an outspoken critic of modernism – whose work although little-read today was very popular during the early decades of the century. Many of his poems are on nautical themes and one of these, 'The Admiral's Ghost'[44] (1910), develops the construction of Nelson as a 'reincarnation' of Drake. The poem is spoken by an old sea-dog who freezes the blood of his listener with 'the things that he seemed to know' (12). According to Noyes's mariner, Nelson was not a man at all but a ghost, the patch and missing arm merely a disguise. Nelson, he reveals, was actually the shade of Sir Francis Drake. If Newbolt had taken Corbett's interpretation of Drake as a

forerunner of Nelson and turned it into a literary creation, then Noyes began the
process of turning the literary into the 'folk'.

> Ask of the Devonshire men!
>   They know, and they'll tell you true;
> He wasn't the pore little chawed-up chap
>   That Hardy thought he knew. (21–4)

Noyes's version of the returning hero myth draws very heavily on 'Drake's Drum'.
The details of Sir Francis's final instruction to his comrades and his burial at sea are
clearly taken from Newbolt.

> 'You must take my drum,' he says,
>   'To the old sea-wall at home;
> And if ever you strike that drum,' he says,
>   'Why, strike me blind, I'll come!' (64–7)

> 'They sewed him up in his shroud
>   With a round-shot top and toe,
> To sink him under the salt sharp sea
>   Where all good seamen go'. (72–5)

Given that Newbolt's poem was already regarded as a literary expression of regional
folklore, then the incorporation of the drum myth into 'The Admiral's Ghost' may
well have led to Noyes's construction of Drake-as-Nelson being viewed in the same
way. This is a conscious effort to suggest an organic continuity between past and
present. Instead of the drum being used to summon Sir Francis, the instrument
seems to herald his arrival in England's hour of peril. For the sea-dog speaker, Drake
is the real victor of Trafalgar. The drum sounded, he claims, as 'Sir Francis' sailed to
meet Villeneuve's fleet. The men of Devon 'heard in the dead of night/ The roll of
a drum, and they saw *him* pass/On a ship all shining white' (102–4).

  Comprising twelve books of blank verse, Noyes's *Drake* is undoubtedly a
response to J.A. Froude's idea in *English Seamen in the Sixteenth Century* for a national
epic on the exploits of the Elizabethan mariners. Noyes draws his information from
many sources, but Froude is clearly the greatest influence: Drake's story is that of the
rise of the English empire. With its fantastic treasures, grizzled sea-dogs and
adventure in tropical seas, *Drake* presents a highly romanticized version of
Elizabethan sea-faring life. In sharp contrast to the admirably uncomplicated figure
created by Kingsley (and later, Corbett), Noyes's Francis Drake is a visionary whose
acts are impelled by prophetic dreams of an English empire secured by naval power.
He is given the opportunity to commence the realization of his vision when
Elizabeth sanctions the circumnavigation as a means of annoying Spain without
initiating a full-scale conflict. At several points in the voyage Drake goes into a
reverie on England's future empire. Having generously freed the prisoners removed
from a vessel captured off Cape Blanco, for example (the timing is not coincidental),
Drake sets out his vision of a new, benevolent and liberating empire in the west.

Oh, in the new Atlantis of my soul
There are no captives: there the wind blows free;
And, as in sleep, I have heard the marching song
Of mighty peoples rising in the West,
Wonderful cities that shall set their foot
Upon the throats of all old tyrannies;
And on the West wind I have heard a cry,
The shoreless cry of the prophetic sea
Heralding through that golden wilderness
The Soul whose path our task is to make straight,
Freedom, the last great saviour of mankind.
. . . .
                    Why should we drag
Thither this Old-World weight of utter gloom,
Or with the ballast of these heavy hearts
Make sail in sorrow for Pacific Seas?
Let us leave chains and prisoners to Spain;
But set these free to make their own way home!
                    (Book 2, 917–27, 932–6)

Noyes and the majority of his Edwardian audience did not, it seems, find the notion of an empire liberating the world paradoxical. The natives of conquered territories, it was believed, were being liberated from their savagery by the civilizing effect of British rule. In contrast to the other great empires – particularly that of Spain, which Noyes goes to great lengths to portray as especially cruel and intolerant – the future English empire will not be secured by force. Like Hakluyt over three hundred years earlier, Noyes uses the story of Drake's encounter with the Coast Miwok Indians to demonstrate that English expansionism was not only a peaceful process but also one welcomed by native peoples. This, of course, ignored the imperial reality of the 1880s and 1890s. The wonderful cities that appear in his vision are those of the empire but also perhaps those of the United States. The myth of English racial superiority is clearly detectable here. The success of Modern America – where Noyes had toured lecturing in Modern English Literature – can be attributed to the racial origins of the early settlers. As Drake and his crew laugh with the natives on the coast of the newly named (and claimed) Nova Albion the imperial vision reappears.

And the vision of the great
Empire of Englishmen arose and flashed
A moment round them, on that lonely shore.
. . . .
An Empire that should liberate the world;
A Power before the lightening of whose arms
Darkness should die and all oppression cease;
A Federation of the strong and weak.
                    (Book 6, 255–7, 261–4)

We can read Noyes's blank verse as betraying an uncertainty about England's imperial role. *Drake* attempts (perhaps rather too enthusiastically) to stir the patriotism of its readers and remind them of the nation's hard-won maritime supremacy at a time when the concept of empire was beginning to lose its gloss. The Boer War had done much to undermine imperial rhetoric. Fought in a blatant attempt at expanding Britain's economic interests and only ended by brutal repression and the introduction of concentration camps, it highlighted the hollowness of imperialism's higher moral claims and the shortcomings of England's military commanders. The war was also extremely costly. And it was the economic cost of empire that lay behind the increasing scepticism. The roots of the problem were located in the middle years of the nineteenth century when the colonies of white settlement were granted responsible government or legislative independence. As Lance Davis and Robert Huttenback observe in *Mammon and the Pursuit of Empire*, 'with the advent of responsible government, the self-governing colonies lost British subsidies for internal administration, but they were, in return, able to refuse aid on matters of "imperial" as opposed to local concern'.[45] Inevitably the costly area of defence would be identified as an imperial concern. Davis and Huttenback again: 'The self-governing colonies saw little advantage in supporting an Imperial defence establishment. They were convinced the British tax-payer would assume that responsibility if they did not, and in large measure they were correct.'[46] The middle-class taxpayer found himself responsible for financing both the Royal Navy – with its huge dreadnought-building programme – and its far-flung Squadrons. During the early years of the twentieth century this was placing a huge strain on the national economy. In short, the empire was failing to pay.

A familiar construction of Sir Francis Drake was provided by Louis Napoleon Parker in *Drake: A Pageant Play*,[47] first performed at His Majesty's Theatre, London, in 1912. In this production Drake was played by the foremost actor of the time, Sir Herbert Beerbohm Tree, who was also the play's dedicatee. Less well known than Noyes, Parker was a prolific playwright whose work was much in demand from the 1880s onwards. In 1905 he turned from theatre work to producing large-scale historical pageants. This transition was probably achieved with some ease; after all, the historical pageant represented episodes from the past as theatre. Parker's reference to 'Pageant' in the title of the play relates to the contemporary popularity of pageant as an entertainment; this will be discussed presently. *Drake* is a colourful and fast-moving romp through a pre-industrial merrie Englande inhabited by homely fisher folk and robust sea-dogs. Plotting and villainy at Court complete the picture. The play comprises three acts all of which have titles: 'Drake's Drum', 'The World Encompassed' and 'The Fortunate and Invincible Armada'. The plot is not complex: Drake is given permission to raid the Spanish Americas as a reprisal for the treachery at San Juan d'Ulua. Having seen the Pacific Ocean, he vows to make it 'the English Sea'. To fulfil his vow Drake embarks upon the circumnavigation together with the Doughty brothers who, unbeknown to Sir Francis, are devout Catholics and plotting the overthrow of the Queen. Thomas Doughty also has instructions from Burghley to raise a mutiny that will prevent Drake's piracy from

dragging England into a costly war with Spain. Doughty's mutiny is discovered and
he is executed as a traitor; Drake returns triumphantly to be knighted on board his
ship. In the final act the English commanders play bowls while awaiting the arrival
of the Spanish Armada; during the battles Drake captures the *Rosario*. At the
thanksgiving service held at St Paul's following the victory, John Doughty attempts
to stab Drake but is unsuccessful. The play closes with a speech by Sir Francis that
is meant to rally his contemporaries and make them aware of their new position in
the world. It also reminds the modern audience during the tense years leading up
to the First World War that they must live up to their 'heritage'.

> We have opened the gates of the Sea, we have given you the keys of the
> World. This little spot ye stand on has become the centre of the earth. …
> Our labour is done: yours is to begin. Men pass away, but the People
> abide. See that ye hold fast the heritage we leave you. Yea, and teach your
> children its value: that never in the coming centuries their hearts may fail
> them, or their hands grow weak. Men of England! Hitherto we have been
> too much afraid! Henceforth we will fear only God! (3.3)

Despite Parker's manipulation of events (Sir Francis, for example, is wounded in
a fight with a Spanish officer during the mule train raid), *Drake* reveals a close
reading of historical texts. Following the defeat of the Armada, a ballad-monger
moves among the cheering crowds crying 'Thirty-nine verses, setting forth the
birth, life, and heroic deeds of Francis Drake, Knight, with his true presentment
done from life. One groat. Buy! Buy! Buy!' – a detail most likely derived from
Edmund Howes's *Annales, or General Chronicall of England*, which records that,
following Drake's return from the circumnavigation, 'Books, pictures and ballads
were produced in his praise.' But it is not only historical narratives to which Parker
turns: he is fully aware of the Drake folk-tales. Of the Spanish Armada, a Plymouth
inhabitant declares: 'He'll play at bowls with em, I warrant! Do you but look at his
fleet! Do seem's though he'd split his wood up, and every splinter had a-turned into
a ship!' (3.1). In the hundred years since Robert Southey and Anna Eliza Bray first
recorded versions of this tale as an example of genuine oral culture, it had become
an almost indispensable part of the Drake mythology. The play, of course, makes use
of the drum myth (an image of the instrument is actually printed on one of the
preliminary pages of the text). The drum first appears in the second scene of the
first act when Drake appoints Diego, a Cimarrone, his drummer. The significance
of Drake's drum is widely known by the characters. The people of Plymouth
understand that the sound of the drum will announce Drake's return – both from
a voyage and to save England. In Drake's words, 'It shall thunder again in England's
need' (2.3). Mother Moone, wife of Tom Moone, one of Drake's most trusted sea-
dogs, claims 'For when you least expect you'll hear a girt roll o'thunder, and that'll
be Drake's drum, and there'll be Drake hisself, wi' Tom beside him all dressed up in
gold and diamonds' (1.3). Sure enough, moments later, the drum is used to
announce Drake's return from Panama, an event that caused the congregation of St
Andrew's church to abandon the service. The stage instructions read:

DIEGO beats a long roll. The psalm and the laughter stop abruptly. Intent
pause. At a motion from DRAKE, DIEGO beats another roll, fiercer and
louder. A great shout is heard from the Church and from the Inn:– 'Drake!'
[At once the doors are burst open and the people tumble out wildly, crying
'Drake! – Drake's Drum – Drake's Drum! – Drake's come back!'] (1.3)

The play was revived by Herbert Beerbohm Tree in August 1914, two years after
its initial performance. *Drake* struck the right patriotic note during the early stages
of the First World War. The scenery in this production appears to have been very
realistic and included ships with tattered sails, a cabin, the deck of an English warship
and a Devon cottage.[48] Special emphasis was placed on Drake's lines quoted above
on the necessity of living up to the past. Once again Tree played Sir Francis, and he
and Parker gave all the profits made from the play to war charities. Drake, one of the
initiators of the Chatham Chest, would have undoubtedly approved.

It was during the First World War, when the threat to Britain's hegemony had
finally been realized, that the patriotic potential of the new Drake myths – those of
the drum and of Nelson as a 'reincarnation' of Sir Francis – were fully exploited.
On 28 August 1916 the *Times* printed an article by Alfred Noyes titled 'The Silent
Hand'.[49] This was actually about the fleet of 3000 trawlers whose crews were being
trained to employ steel 'cages' to trap German submarines off the Channel coast.
Noyes introduces the article through the story of Drake's drum.

> There is a tale in Devonshire that Sir Francis Drake has not merely
> listened for his drum, during the last 300 years but has also heard and
> answered it on more than one naval occasion. It was heard, as the men of
> the Brixham trawlers can testify, about a hundred years ago, when a little
> man under the pseudonym of Nelson (for all Devonshire knows that
> Nelson was a reincarnation of Sir Francis) went sailing by to Trafalgar.[50]

He continues with the most recent occasion on which the drum was heard to beat.

> It was only a little before the great naval action in the North Sea –
> perhaps the greatest British victory since Trafalgar – that the word came
> from the Brixham trawlers again. They had 'heard Drake's drum beat' and
> were now assured that the ghost of Sir Francis Drake was inhabiting the
> body of Sir John Jellicoe.[51]

The battle to which Noyes refers is the Battle of Jutland, the only full-scale
engagement between the two major battle-fleets fought on 31 May 1916. The
engagement proved indecisive and Jellicoe, who had command of the Grand Fleet,
was later criticized for not winning an outright victory. (Noyes's reference to the
greatest victory since Trafalgar is, of course, patriotic rhetoric.) The Royal Navy's
losses were substantial: three cruisers, three battle-cruisers and eight destroyers. But
despite these losses Britain was able to maintain numerical superiority in the North
Sea and the German fleet never again sought a full-scale engagement.

Linking Drake with Nelson was one thing, but in time of war a modern
embodiment was required and, for Noyes, Jellicoe seemed the obvious choice. Not

only did Drake inhabit the body of Jellicoe, but the fleet of submarine-ensnaring trawlers was also a recreation of the Elizabethan maritime past.

> In this host of auxiliaries England has, in fact, brought to life again and organized on a huge scale, with certain modern improvements, the men and the fleets of Drake and Hawkins; and it is these fleets and men that have struck terror into German submarines and driven them from the seas.[52]

A volunteer force mobilized in defence of the country and manned, in large measure, by men from Devon ports; the connection, for Noyes, was obvious.

While Noyes suggested that Drake's ghost inhabited the body of John Jellicoe, *Punch* was keen to link him with another contemporary naval commander: Sir Roger Keyes. On 1 May 1918 the magazine carried a cartoon titled 'Drake's Way' depicting Drake's shade hailing Keyes on the quayside at Zeebrugge. This followed a successful raid on the port on 22–23 April 1918 that Keyes had planned and directed. To prevent Zeebrugge being used as a base by German submarines two ships were scuttled in the entrance to the harbour, effectively blocking it. This greatly reduced the incidence of submarine predation in the Straits of Dover. A daring strike against the enemy in his own (or rather, occupied) port, *Punch* clearly saw a parallel with Drake's raid on Cadiz. The raid provided excellent propaganda and was used by *Punch* to show that the spirit of the Elizabethan admiral had been inherited by his modern counterpart. Appropriately, the raid had taken place on St George's Day; England's patron saint had recently been revived as a patriotic figurehead. Drake congratulates Keyes: 'Bravo, Sir! Tradition holds. My men singed a king's beard and yours have singed a kaiser's moustaches.'

A month after the *Times* printed Noyes's article it carried a short story, 'Heard at Sea',[53] also dealing with the drum myth. The story tells of a strange encounter in a remote coastal village and develops the drum myth in an inventive but rather grim way. The narrator recalls being joined by an old man as he sat smoking his pipe on a small hill overlooking the sea. He commented on the sound of the artillery coming to them across the water from France, but the old man assured him that he was mistaken. '"Guns?" he said smilingly; "they're not guns. It's the drum rolling – Frankie's drum, as he said it would. He's afloat again and away up Channel."'[54] The drum, of course, carries all the associations of the returning hero but here it has a new function: it becomes a rallying call for all true Englishmen.

> 'It's a sign for all of England's enemies, but mostly it's a sign for us, so I take it. That's as he meant it I think. When we hear it we are to remember all we fight for. Some say we fight for the present, some for the years to come. Both be right, but I have a mind we fight for the past as well. It is not every nation that can say that, for many of them be upstarts.'[55]

Success, in other words, can only be achieved by living up to the traditions of the past. The upstart is, of course, Germany whose states did not achieve real unity until 1871. Towards the end of the narrative the old man is revealed to be the ghost of an Elizabethan sailor who, according to his headstone in the local churchyard, 'Died on Hys Shippe When Fighting the Spaniard'. Drake's supposed return during the Great War – and the encounter with the ghostly interpreter of the 'drum' – is an extension of the mythology of the Western Front of which the most famous example is, perhaps, the story of the Angels of Mons. This myth emerged after the Battle of Mons (August 1914), the first major engagement between British and German troops. The story had its origins in a short story by Arthur Machen called 'The Bowmen'[56] in which the archers of Agincourt are invoked to help repel a German advance. The story became very well known and gradually, through oral transmission, the archers were transformed into angels.

The construction of Sir Francis Drake as a hero of empire survived the First World War. Perhaps this is surprising when we consider that the more elevated mythology of empire – of which Drake was such a celebrated embodiment – hardly accorded with the reality of trench warfare. War was not a game when fought on the battlefields of the Somme or Ypres; there was clearly nothing blessed or glorious about dying for one's country. Perhaps professional soldiers had always known this, but now it was apparent to all those who fought on the Western Front. We might expect Drake, a figure so heavily burdened with imperial ideology, to receive scant attention in the years following the war, and it is true that Sir Francis never recovered the widespread appeal that he exerted in the 1880s and 1890s. But although Sir Francis's popularity had fluctuated over the three hundred years between his death and the end of the Great War, he had never faded into historical obscurity. Nor would he in the twentieth century. One of the most resilient of historical characters, he remains a celebrated figure both in Devon – especially in the Plymouth area – and in the Royal Navy. In the final chapter I shall investigate the directions in which the construction of Sir Francis Drake has developed during the twentieth century.

Notes

1 Louis Napoleon Parker, *Drake: A Pageant Play* (London, 1912), Act 3, Scene, 3.
2 Statistics quoted in Paul M. Kennedy, *The Rise and Fall of British Naval Mastery* (London, 1983), 190.
3 Julian Corbett, *Sir Francis Drake* (1890; London, 1901).
4 Corbett, *Sir Francis Drake*, 132.
5 Corbett, *Sir Francis Drake*, 16.
6 Corbett, *Sir Francis Drake*, 1.
7 Corbett, *Sir Francis Drake*, 5.
8 Corbett, *Sir Francis Drake*, 144.
9 Corbett, *Sir Francis Drake*, 1.
10 A. T. Mahan, *The Influence of Sea Power Upon History 1660–1783* (London, 1890).
11 Kennedy, 182.
12 Kennedy, 182.
13 Corbett, *Sir Francis Drake*, 99.
14 Corbett, *Sir Francis Drake*, 117.
15 Corbett, *Sir Francis Drake*, 114.
16 Corbett, *Sir Francis Drake*, 138.

[17] Corbett, *Sir Francis Drake*, 151.

[18] Corbett, *Sir Francis Drake*, 67.

[19] Corbett, *Sir Francis Drake*, 120.

[20] Corbett, *Sir Francis Drake*, 159.

[21] Corbett, *Sir Francis Drake*, 172.

[22] Statistics quoted in Kennedy, 193.

[23] Corbett, *Sir Francis Drake*, 128.

[24] James Anthony Froude, *English Seamen in the Sixteenth Century* (1895; London, 1926).

[25] Froude, 104.

[26] Froude, 237.

[27] Froude, 256–7.

[28] Froude, 1.

[29] Alfred Tennyson, 'Epilogue to the Queen', in Christopher Ricks, ed., *The Poems of Tennyson*, 3 vols (London, 1969), vol. 3, 561–3.

[30] Froude, 2.

[31] Henry Newbolt, 'Drake's Drum', in *Collected Poems 1897–1907* (London, 1907), 15–17.

[32] Alfred Tennyson, *Morte d'Arthur*, in Ricks, ed., *The Poems of Tennyson*, vol. 2, 19.

[33] See Roger Sherman Loomis, 'Arthurian Tradition and Folk-Lore', *FolkLore*, vol. 69 (1958), 1–25.

[34] Alfred Tennyson, *Idylls of the King*, in Ricks, ed., *The Poems of Tennyson*, vol. 3, 263–5.

[35] Henry Newbolt, *My World as in My Time: Memoirs of Sir Henry Newbolt* (London, 1932), 186.

[36] Strangely, the silver drum came to be associated with bad luck. On her maiden voyage *HMS Devonshire* hit a harbour wall and on her second trip she caught fire. Both officers and ratings blamed these misfortunes on the drum. In 1936 the offending instrument was handed over to the safekeeping of the chapel of St Nicholas at Devonport naval base. See Cynthia Gaskell Brown, *The Battle's Sound: Drake's Drum and the Drake Flags* (Tiverton, 1996), 34–5.

[37] Robert Hunt, *Popular Romances of the West of England: or, The Drolls, Traditions and Superstitions of Old Cornwall*, 2 vols (London, 1865).

[38] Hunt, vol. 1, 261.

[39] *Graphic*, 17 February 1883, 171.

[40] Henry Newbolt, 'Waggon Hill', in *Collected Poems 1897–1907* (London, 1907), 141–3.

[41] Henry Newbolt, 'Admirals All', in *Collected Poems 1897–1907*, 22–6.

[42] Henry Newbolt, 'The Little Admiral', in *Selected Poems of Henry Newbolt* (London, 1940), 21–2.

[43] Alfred Noyes, *Drake*, in *Collected Poems*, 2 vols (London, 1914), vol. 2, 1–201.

[44] Alfred Noyes, 'The Admiral's Ghost', in *Collected Poems*, vol. 2, 232–5.

[45] Lance E. Davis and Robert Huttenback, *Mammon and the Pursuit of Empire: The Economics of British Imperialism* (Cambridge, 1988), 114.

[46] Davis and Huttenback, 113.

[47] Parker, *Drake: A Pageant Play*.

[48] Details of the scenery are given in Madeleine Bingham, *The Great Lover: The Life and Art of Herbert Beerbohm Tree* (London, 1978), 239.

[49] Alfred Noyes, 'The Silent Hand', *The Times*, 28 August 1916, 5.

[50] Noyes, 'Silent Hand', 5.

[51] Noyes, 'Silent Hand', 5.

[52] Noyes, 'Silent Hand', 5.

[53] 'Heard at Sea', *The Times*, 29 September 1916, 9.

[54] 'Heard at Sea', 9.

[55] 'Heard at Sea', 9.

[56] Arthur Machen, *The Bowmen and Other Legends of the War* (London, 1915).

CHAPTER NINE

'a pirate, and a good one'

Historians have long been at work to erode the reputation of that
quasi-mythological figure Sir Francis Drake. His tactics have been
criticized, his sense of strategy impugned and his contribution
to the defeat of the Armada belittled.
(*The Times*, 24 January 1996)[1]

In the years between the world wars, the late Victorian and Edwardian consensus
of opinion on Drake began to break down. As we have seen, from the middle
of the nineteenth century right up until the Great War, 'high' and popular
culture had usually been united in fervent hero-worship of the great empire-
building mariner. Academics such as Froude and Corbett were as fulsome in their
praise of Sir Francis as popular poets like Newbolt and Noyes. But this convergence
did not survive the First World War. It is generally accepted that, in the aftermath
of the war, 'the literary culture of at least some parts of the intelligentsia had begun
seriously to diverge from the common causes of the period before the First World
War'.[2] Although we cannot link those historians – particularly those naval
historians – writing on Drake with the literary avant-garde, the huge disruption of
the war appears to have had a marked effect on the practice of history-writing.
Scholarly work concerned with Sir Francis Drake reveals a disengagement with
empire or, at least, with the more elevated claims of the mythology that sustained
it. During the 1920s there was a shift away from the epic scope of the nineteenth-
century narrative of causation exemplified by Froude's *History of England*. Few
accounts from this period dwell on the defeat of the Spanish Armada as the
moment from which England's rise as an imperial power could be charted.
Similarly, the hero-worship so characteristic of late nineteenth-century treatments
of Drake was abandoned.

The move away from the metanarrative of England's rise to pre-eminence by
many academic historians did not, however, result in a lacuna in the production of
Drake material. Freed from his familiar role as a guarantor of empire, Sir Francis
became the focus for renewed scholarly attention. But instead of manipulating the
past to reinforce the grand narrative, historians began to seek out undiscovered
documentary evidence and construct detailed narratives of individual voyages or

single episodes from Drake's career. Between the wars dozens of journal articles
dealing with Drake were published. Their titles reflect a self-conscious concern
with re-examining the past. The journal of nautical research, the *Mariner's Mirror*,
for example, published 'Fresh Light on San Juan de Ulua', 'Fresh Light on Drake'
and 'A Forgotten Life of Sir Francis Drake'.[3] Journal articles were soon joined by
full-length books that reproduced previously undiscovered – or, perhaps, ignored –
contemporary Spanish documents. The voices silenced by English hegemony were,
it appears, beginning to be heard. The first of the new works to delve into this mass
of largely unexplored material was Zelia Nuttall's influential collection *New Light
on Drake*[4] published in 1914. In a move away from the triumphalism that usually
accompanied pre-war accounts of the circumnavigation, Nuttall suggests that the
voyage was undertaken not to raid Spanish ships and ports but to find a site suitable
for colonization on the western coast of America. Nuttall's work was followed by
Henry Wagner's *Sir Francis Drake's Voyage Around the World*[5] (1926). Wagner suggests
that the famous voyage was specifically intended to initiate trade with the Spice
Islands. Perhaps the most thoroughly researched collection to appear before the
Second World War was Irene Wright's *Documents Concerning English Voyages to the
Caribbean and Spanish Main 1569–80*[6] (1932). Wright reproduces a great number of
texts from the Spanish state papers including John Oxenham's deposition before the
Inquisition. A second section is devoted to contemporary English documents and
includes the 1626 narrative of the Panama raids, *Sir Francis Drake Revived* and the
account of Oxenham's voyage taken from Hakluyt.

The huge amount of material generated in the inter-war period is a clear
demonstration of the interest that Sir Francis Drake continued to generate. Despite
the shift away from the construction of Drake as a hero of empire, he remained a
fascinating historical character. In 1921, however, an article was published that
seems to pre-empt the antipathy towards Drake that began to emerge in the 1980s.
Gregory Robinson's 'A Forgotten Life of Sir Francis Drake'[7] attempts a vilification
of Drake that hardly seemed possible before 1914. 'I never liked Sir Francis,' writes
Robinson in a good-natured introduction, 'nor believed much in his Drum.'[8] The
forgotten life to which the title refers is that presented by George Anderson (see
Chapter Three), one of Drake's most vociferous detractors, in *A New, Authentic, and
Complete Account of Voyages Round the World* (1784). Robinson returns to the
Doughty affair, the bloodiest and most persistent stain on Drake's reputation, and
finds him guilty of murder. He also seeks to overturn the construction of Drake as
a forerunner of Nelson that was initiated by Corbett some twenty years earlier. To
this end the article concludes with a list of Drake's failings as a naval officer: his
abandonment of Hawkins on the return voyage from San Juan, his abuse of power
in the Doughty affair, his lust for treasure that saw him capture the *San Felipe* and
go in search of the *Rosario*, and his failure to meet Norris at Lisbon. A reply to
Robinson's article was not long in coming – it was not only among his crews, it
seems, that Drake could command loyalty. 'Drake and his Detractors'[9] by Geoffrey
Callender – very much a traditionalist in his view of Drake – seeks to undermine
Robinson's argument by exposing the discrepancies between the two main sources

used by Anderson in his account of the circumnavigation, the Fletcher manuscript and Cooke narrative. By mounting an unsubstantiated attack on the character of the little-known chaplain Francis Fletcher, Callender attempts to discredit his evidence. The quarrel rumbled on, with Robinson clearly irritated by Callender's claim that the circumnavigation was actually a training exercise for the 'educated privateers' who Drake perceived as essential for the nation's maritime well-being. Robinson writes sarcastically,

> I suspect Drake will in future appear as the father of a sound system of naval education, the inventor of the sea-going training ship, and perhaps the father of a rational system of discipline. There will hardly be a department at the Admiralty that will not look to Sir Francis Drake as its founder.[10]

The argument provides perhaps the clearest evidence that although the details of the Drake narrative were available for minor reinterpretation, the climate was not yet right for a revisionist questioning of Drake's heroic status. An attempt – no matter how jocund – at throwing fresh light into the shadier regions of the Drake narrative was not welcome. Callender, in fact, summarizes the fate of rediscovered documentary evidence that ran counter to the accepted version of the past.

> It is a commonplace in the history of criticism that newly discussed documents seem for a while to change our whole conception of man, until the documents themselves and their writers are put upon the dissecting board and pathologically examined. Then a revulsion takes place; healthy opinion reasserts itself; and it is found that the new facts serve to confirm and support the very beliefs which at first they seemed to shatter and destroy.[11]

The influence of the high cultural disengagement with imperialism on the dominant bourgeois culture during the inter-war years was, as we might expect, negligible. As Stephen Constantine has observed,

> the prevailing preoccupation of those who governed Britain in the 1920s and 1930s [was] with maintaining, utilizing and developing Empire links and resources. The preservation of imperial control over India, the Middle East and the Colonial Empire remained a priority.[12]

Constructing the imperial past and providing ideological justification for empire continued to be an important cultural project. Sir Francis Drake remained the founder of the Royal Navy and an adventurous pioneer of English expansionism. Two of the full-length biographies to appear between the wars, Walter Harte's *Sir Francis Drake* (1920) and Edward Frederic Benson's work of the same name (1927) – both of which were intended for a popular readership – demonstrate that Drake's name was still inextricably bound up with the formation of empire. Harte's uninspiring narrative claims to 'offer a reasonable estimate of his position as one of the Pioneers of the British Empire'.[13] His reasonable estimate is, however, limited to a reiteration of the belief that Drake's treaty in the Spice Islands had laid the foundation of British rule in India. A novelist and biographer, Edward Benson was the brother of Christopher Benson who added 'Land of Hope and Glory' to Elgar's first *Pomp and Circumstance* march. His unashamedly pro-Drake account is revealing in terms of its continuity – the interpretation of Sir Francis that is offered is little different from that developed by Corbett. The introduction claims that 'as a group, they [the Elizabethan explorers] invested themselves and their age with an aura of grandeur which made them unique in the annals of the sea, of exploration, and of the extension of Empire'.[14] He writes of the political situation 'which led, so largely through him [Drake], to the defeat of the Spanish Armada and the foundation of English sea-power'.[15] Intriguingly, Benson dismisses the game of bowls – that great signifier of English superiority – as a fiction and, with refreshing rationality, terms Drake's supposed response to the news of the sighting of the Armada 'lunatic behaviour'. According to Benson, it was much more likely that 'Sailors were lounging about the quay, and Drake came bawling in among them.'[16] But this is undoubtedly a product of Benson's well-documented contempt for the absurd rather than a conscious attempt at subverting imperial ideology. The game of bowls remained an important image for bourgeois culture. Indeed, the event was woven into the very fabric of bourgeois culture and was found represented in a great number of unexpected places. For instance, in the early 1930s Burgess and Leigh, one of the Staffordshire potteries, produced a decorative bowl for a series titled *Merrie England* that depicted the game. The image, which was transfer printed, was by the popular artist Cecil Aldin.

In historical accounts intended for a juvenile audience, Drake was still presented as the archetypal English man of action. Arthur Mee's *Heroes of the Flag*, published in 1935, provides a concise life of Sir Francis along with other great patriots such as Walter Raleigh, Captain Cook, and, in a chapter titled 'Men who Saved the World', the heroes of the First World War. Drake's importance for Mee lies in the fact that he was the first Englishman to appreciate what could be achieved with sea-power. In short, he paved the way for empire:

> He was born into an age when the inhabitants of the British Isles were prisoners in the sea. He set them free, and took their ships around the world; he terrified and broke their enemies; and when he died there was no man on earth who dare flout a British ship at sea.[17]

Like Charles Kingsley eighty years earlier, Mee is keen to contrast Drake's world of action with that of the Court.

> Drake had brought home the keys of the earth, and our dilly-dally Court, packed with spies and plotters and cravens, would have let them rust for a thousand years if the movement of events had not been too strong for them.[18]

The 'movement of events' hints at the inevitability of empire. The episode in which Drake climbs a tree and sees, for the first time, the Pacific Ocean is given prominence. This is a symbolic moment, the point at which England in the figure of Drake began to look west. The episode was evidently so important that it was chosen as the jacket illustration for *Heroes of the Flag*.

This enthusiasm for Drake was maintained in children's – or more specifically boys' – literature. The pattern set by George Alfred Henty in *Under Drake's Flag: A Tale of the Spanish Main* was taken up by Robert Sargent Holland in *Drake's Lad* (1929). A tale of adventure on the high seas, *Drake's Lad* aimed at promoting those quintessential English qualities, courage, loyalty and a sense of fair play. Evidently influenced by Alfred Noyes's visionary Drake, Holland's Sir Francis implores Elizabeth to sanction the circumnavigation.

> 'There is the ocean-sea, there is that world of the deep stretching from pole to pole, that empire of great waters that may be England's own! Let us but hold that empire, and we may send our argosies to shores of untold wealth, carry the flag of England to lands yet unmapped, dare the might of Spain or any other kingdom! There lies our heritage. Oh, claim it my queen!'[19]

Similarly, it was the action-filled version of the Elizabethan past that was projected to a popular audience on the cinema screen. Whether led by supply or demand, the imperial epics of the 1930s suggest that, contrary to received opinion, the working class (which made up the bulk of the cinema audience) was not indifferent to empire. With huge weekly audiences in the 1930s, the cinema was a powerful disseminator of imperial ideology. Films such as Alexander Korda's trilogy of imperial epics – *Sanders of the River* (1935), *The Drum* (1938) and *The Four Feathers* (1939) – all of which were set in the nineteenth century, continued to portray colonial possession as both desirable and natural.[20] The distant imperial past was represented by Arthur Woods's swash-buckling adventure *Drake of England*,[21] first screened in 1935. In this production Matheson Lang plays Sir Francis Drake while Jane Baxter takes the role of Elizabeth Sydenham. The film is undoubtedly adapted from Louis Napoleon Parker's *Drake: A Pageant Play*. The great numbers of historical characters that process through the film certainly maintain the feel of Parker's original 'Pageant'. A lengthy sequence is devoted to the mule train ambush while the defeat of the Spanish Armada provides an explosive climax. Reviewing the film, *Variety* noted that 'The routing of the Spanish Armada by a handful of ships under the bold, shabby Devon pioneer; the looting of the enemy's treasure by bravado and cunning makes for exciting entertainment.'[22]

In 1940 Drake's exploits provided the inspiration for an American feature film, Michael Curtiz's *The Sea Hawk*.[23] Originally adapted from Rafael Sabatini's novel of the same name (1915), which was concerned with the adventures of a Cornish pirate not unlike Drake, the screenplay went through numerous drafts that eventually removed all trace of the novel except for the title. Several episodes from the Drake story were manoeuvred into the script.[24] These include the Panama raid and the knighting of the Drakean hero Geoffrey Thorpe played by Errol Flynn. The film closes with a shot of the masts of the English fleet that dissolves to the steel bridge of a modern warship and then to the English fleet under full steam. The notion of English naval power originating in the activities of the Elizabethan sea-dogs was still being presented to a popular audience. Perhaps we should not be surprised at the ending when we learn that among the books consulted in the course of research[25] were Froude's *English Seamen in the Sixteenth Century* and Corbett's *Drake and the Tudor Navy*.

During the Second World War the qualities that Sir Francis embodied were called upon once again: Drake provided an inspiration for Britons on the defensive just as he had in the conflicts of the previous centuries. With a German invasion anticipated during the early stages of the war, the narrative of the Spanish Armada made excellent patriotic propaganda. Winston Churchill made reference to the sixteenth-century conflict in a speech broadcast on 11 September 1940. The present, claimed Churchill, 'ranks with the days when the Spanish Armada was approaching the Channel, and Drake was finishing his game of bowls; or when Nelson stood between us and Napoleon's Grand Army at Boulogne'.[26] Yet the narrative of the Armada, powerful as it was, was eclipsed by the myth of Drake's drum. On 16 August 1940 – two months after the evacuation of Dunkirk and with the Battle of Britain being fought in the skies over southern England – the BBC's Overseas Transmission sent out a broadcast titled *Drake's Drum*, which was part of a series called *This Land of Ours*. The broadcast was by Isaac Foot – a Plymouthian, one-time Labour MP for Bodmin and a distinguished orator – who was very keen to develop the drum myth. Foot's text was later printed in the journal *Prediction* under the title 'Drake's Drum Beats Again'.[27] It was afterwards incorporated into a leaflet distributed to Plymouth schoolchildren when Foot became Lord Mayor of the city in November 1945. Foot repeated the story of the drum beating at the surrender of the German Fleet in 1918 and went on to list other figures from history who had also heard the sound. All of these had some connection with Plymouth: the citizens of the town when Cromwell came to thank them for their support during the Civil War, Admiral Blake who returned to Plymouth 'sick unto death', Nelson when made a freeman of the Borough, and Wellington who had sailed from Plymouth to 'defeat an earlier tyranny'. Claimed Foot,

> Here in the West Country, 'we are never surprised to hear the beating of Drake's Drum. Our fathers heard it when the *Mayflower* made its way out of the Sound. When Drake from his place on the Hoe watched it sail, that ship was to him like another *Golden Hinde*.[28]

As several commentators have pointed out, Drake died twenty-four years before the Pilgrim Fathers set out on their voyage.[29] It is possible that Foot was referring to the Drake statue – he mentioned it standing 'always on guard' – which ignores the fact that it was not erected until 1884. Yet Foot was engaged upon a mythopoeic process in which Drake reference points were synthesized and historical distinctions elided. The purpose of this 'alternative history' was to create a sense of an heroic past for a city that was losing its identity as well as its architecture through severe enemy bombing.

Instead of Drake's drum being used to summon the sleeping hero or to herald the arrival of Sir Francis in England's hour of need, Foot used it in the wider sense:

to hear the drum was to feel Drake's presence and to become infused with his spirit. Francis Drake's courage and determination were made available not only to the great figures of the past but also to the ordinary people of the present. Foot gave contemporary examples of those who had heard the drumming. They included crews of the ships that had taken the British Expeditionary Force off the beach at Dunkirk and the civilians who had watched the arrival of the troopships from the empire. Foot's construction of Drake was a model of egalitarianism, 'He insisted that on his ship ... there should only be a fellowship of common service and the brotherhood of common sacrifice.'[30] This allowed Foot to claim that '[W]hen the Prime Minister the other day said that this was a war of the Unknown Warriors, Drake beat his drum again.'[31] Using the myth of the Drake's drum to connect the ordinary Englishman with the figures and events of the nation's past was skilful and intensely patriotic rhetoric.

Shortly after the war restoration work began on St Andrew's church in Plymouth, which had been badly damaged by bombing. On the ledge of the window by the south door, a rough scratching was found in the plaster. This appears to represent the divinely guided ship crest from Drake's coat of arms and is thought to date from the late sixteenth century. Presumably a workman created the scratching, which is now known as the 'Drake graffiti', at the height of Sir Francis's popularity soon after his return from the circumnavigation. Isaac Foot's conception of Drake as a key presence during Plymouth's most dramatic episodes seemed to be confirmed by the freshly uncovered inscription. Incredibly, here amid the rubble at the heart of the old city, Drake's crest emerged as a sign of continuity.

The use of Drake as an inspirational figure during the war led to the creation of an important new strand in the Drake mythology. On 20 November 1939 a letter titled 'The True Glory'[32] by the Reverend E. Stogdon appeared in *The Times*. The letter drew attention to a dispatch written from Drake to Walsingham on 17 May 1587, shortly before the raid on Cadiz. *The Times* rendered Drake's prose in modern English:

> There must be a beginning of every great matter but the continuing unto the end yields the true glory. If we can thoroughly believe that this which we do is in defence of our religion and country, no doubt our merciful God for Christ our Saviour's sake is able and will give us victory, though our sins be red.

Clearly Stogdon thought Drake's pious words appropriate for the present moment. In 1941 Drake's prose was converted into a prayer by Eric Milner-White and G. W. Briggs.

> O Lord God, when thou givest to thy servants to endeavour any great matter, grant us also to know that it is not the beginning, but the continuing of the same unto the end, until it be thoroughly finished, which yieldeth the true glory; through him who for the finishing of thy work laid down his life, our Redeemer, Jesus Christ.[33]

The fact that the words were merely *after* Drake was soon elided and the text became 'Drake's Prayer'. This was certainly how it was termed in the official leaflet that accompanied the National Day of Prayer on 23 March 1941. Intriguingly, Drake's Prayer provides another link to the idea of Drake as an intercessor figure. Although the prayer is not addressed to Drake, his supposed words are part of the intercessory process. In the absence of the old saints, Sir Francis maintains his quasi-religious role.

Although victorious in the war, Britain's post-war self-image was (and, perhaps, continues to be) that of a nation in decline. There are manifold reasons for this perception but the gradual withdrawal from the colonies in the 1950s and 1960s has had a great yet largely unexplored impact on national self-esteem. As the British Empire was gradually transformed into the British Commonwealth of Nations, the old mythology of empire was slowly abandoned. One strategy for negotiating Britain's decline as an imperial power has been to play down the significance of empire and, ultimately, to reappraise the reputations of the men who built it. Inevitably a figure woven so tightly into the mythology of empire as Sir Francis Drake would find his achievements reassessed. This process was very gradual and began, as we might expect, in historical works. In 1941 Alfred Edward Mason published *The Life of Sir Francis Drake*,[34] the only Drake biography to appear during the war. A writer of imperial adventure stories, Mason was the author of the bestseller *The Four Feathers* (1902), which was subsequently made into a film by Korda in 1939. Given Mason's literary output, it is not surprising to find Drake constructed as a hero of empire. But his largely unremarkable biography of Drake is most notable for the way it adheres very rigidly to the construction of Sir Francis initiated by Julian Corbett. He writes,

> The two most outstanding voyages were the circumnavigation of the world and the attack upon Cadiz. This last one flawless in its execution, marked the beginning of naval strategy as practiced in England. Up to then we hugged our own coasts. He first of sailors said: 'Seek out the enemy on his own coasts, bring him to action, and there destroy him.'[35]

While attempting to overturn the popular notion of Drake as the father of the Royal Navy, James Williamson's *Sir Francis Drake* (1951) also portrays him as a pioneer of offensive naval strategy. 'He made English sea power great and feared. He did not create it – no one man did that – but he used it for ends before unthought of.'[36] By the time Christopher Lloyd came to publish his biographical account, also titled *Sir Francis Drake*, in 1957, a rather more dispassionate approach to Drake and his achievements was in evidence. Lloyd claims that his life of Drake 'is not written in the spirit of hero-worship, because Drake's achievements are great enough to make an uncritical account of them impertinent as well as misleading'.[37] He continues that 'we can no longer regard Drake simply as the Protestant Hero, or the Devon Sea Dog of drawing-room ballads'.[38] And, sure enough, there is no mention of Drake's drum – Stanford's setting of which had been performed in many a drawing room. In an effort to subvert the construction of Drake as a forerunner of

Nelson, Lloyd claims that Drake's 'true disciples' were not the great naval commanders such as Blake and Vernon but the buccaneers of the seventeenth century.

The departure from the old Drake mythology is, perhaps, best illustrated by Garrett Mattingly's *The Defeat of the Spanish Armada*[39] (1959), which remains one of the most highly regarded accounts of the conflict. The work certainly represents a pivotal moment in the construction of the Armada. As an American with less of a cultural investment in the Drake story, it is possible that Mattingly found it easier to subvert the traditional narrative. Instead of the defeat of the Armada heralding the arrival of England as a maritime power, Mattingly suggests that the entire Anglo-Spanish conflict proved indecisive. He writes:

> English sea power in the Atlantic had usually been superior to the combined strengths of Castile and Portugal, and so it continued to be, but after 1588 the margin of superiority diminished ... in the war of Elizabeth nobody commanded the seas.[40]

Written during the Cold War, Mattingly's interpretation of events was almost certainly influenced by the tense stand-off between the US and USSR during which neither side could claim the ascendancy. The defeat of the Armada is not Drake's alone; he is merely one player, albeit a very important one, in the conflict. The popular cultural tradition of Drake as the single-handed victor and the academic interpretation of events, which had converged in the later years of the nineteenth century, were now drawing apart once more. When it comes to Sir Francis Drake, Mattingly presents us with a figure possessing immense self-belief but obsessed with traitors – real or imaginary – at Court who, he believed, sought to frustrate his plans. Great emphasis is placed upon the rather quixotic notion of a private war between Drake and the King of Spain, and Mattingly suggests that Sir Francis may have actually believed such a state of war existed: 'On more than one occasion he sent King Philip his personal defiance.'[41] The game of bowls is not dismissed outright; it *might* have happened, Mattingly insists. 'The words are like Drake; they have his touch of swagger and his flair for the homely jest to relieve a moment of tension.'[42] But the game has become divorced from its imperial ideological function; it is an historical curiosity rather than a signifier of English superiority.

In the 1950s Drake's voyages continued to provide an ideal setting for juvenile adventure stories. Douglas Bell's *Drake was My Captain*[43] (1953) and Peter Dawlish's *He Went with Drake*[44] (1955) both adhere to the familiar formula: the young protagonist is sent to sea in the company of the great admiral and learns the value of duty and service. But this trend slackened in the 1960s when works such as Jean Latham's *The Man they Called a Pirate*[45] (1961) and Frank Knight's *The Young Drake*[46] (1962) marked the end of the tradition of setting boys' adventure stories at sea with Captain Drake. Perhaps the reality of space exploration in the 1960s coupled with Britain's diminished world role made the high seas redundant as the location for adventure. The nautical stories that aimed at inculcating imperial ideology certainly fell out of fashion.[47]

In terms of the amount of material produced, the 1960s represent a low point in scholarly interest in Drake. Two lengthy accounts of the Spanish Armada appeared in the first half of the decade: Michael Lewis's *The Spanish Armada*[48] (1960) and Robert Marx's *The Battle of the Spanish Armada*[49] (1965). Both draw heavily on Mattingly and both regard Drake as just one combatant among many. In 1963 *The Silver Circle* by Lewis Gibbs was published. This was a new account of the circumnavigation that sought to distance itself from the old myths:

> Drake was not an empire-builder, but the imperial spirit [of the Victorians] found much in his character that was congenial to it, to say nothing of the fact that the empire rested upon sea-power. He therefore took his place naturally among the great admirals.[50]

A biography published by Ernle Bradford[51] in 1965 reveals the striking way in which Drake was repositioned at a crucial historical moment. Three years after the Cuban Missile Crisis Drake became the prototypical Cold Warrior. In Bradford's narrative Drake is a master of 'brinkmanship', Elizabeth's instrument in her 'Cold War'. Perhaps Drake's cultural neglect in the 1960s is best symbolized by the withdrawal of the halfpenny piece, which since 1936 had depicted an image of the *Golden Hinde* by T. H. Paget on the reverse. During the middle decades of the century millions of Britons had come into contact with Sir Francis on a daily basis. The coin ceased to be legal tender on 1 August 1969 as Britain prepared to adopt the decimal system.

Perhaps the finest work to emerge from this period of neglect is Kenneth Andrews *Drake's Voyages: A Re-Assessment of their Place in Elizabethan Maritime Expansion*,[52] which appeared in 1967. This is a thoughtful and genuinely unbiased attempt at revising the Drake narrative. For Andrews, the Spanish Armada was not the great turning point when control of the seas passed from Spain to England; it provides the point from which the decline of Spain's commercial empire can be traced. With England still able to supply the rebels in the Netherlands, the United Provinces – a vital economic interest for Spain – could not be subdued satisfactorily. Similarly, continuing English privateering in the Atlantic meant that trade with the Indies needed constant and expensive protection. Drake's greatest contribution to the defeat of the attempted invasion was not the destruction of shipping and supplies at Cadiz but the fact that Santa Cruz's Portuguese galleons pursued him to the Azores on a three-month voyage that wasted supplies and wearied men. 'But for this the Armada might well have set forth in the autumn. In sum, Drake's decision to leave the coast could hardly have been bettered. Yet it was taken for reasons that had little to do with strategy.'[53] Needless to say, Corbett's construction of Drake as the father of modern naval strategy receives a reappraisal: 'Few students of the subject today would attempt to justify the comparison of Drake and Nelson in Corbett's terms, and a detached survey, even of the campaigns of 1585–8, provides insufficient grounds for regarding Drake as a great strategist.'[54] For Andrews, Corbett completely misinterprets the nature of the Elizabethan navy. The Royal Navy, he argues, was not a distinct entity in the late sixteenth century.

Although it seemed to be moving in that direction in the period 1585–8, the usual form of maritime warfare, privateering, re-established itself when the danger of invasion had passed.

The decline in the production of Drake material was, however, short-lived. The four hundredth anniversaries of Drake's exploits in the 1970s and 1980s saw a revived interest in the seafarer. Yet Drake's significance had been reassessed. The emphasis had shifted away from Sir Francis as the founder of English naval power and, of course, colonial expansion, and was placed very firmly upon Drake as a navigator. The construction of Sir Francis had thus come full circle; we should not forget that the sixteenth-century engravings discussed in the first chapter also foregrounded Drake's identity as an expert navigator. This repositioning is best illustrated by the exhibition in celebration of the circumnavigation held at the British Library in 1977. The exhibition was, to a large extent, made up of Elizabethan navigational equipment, and contemporary maps and manuscripts. The accompanying booklet drew careful attention to Drake's geographical discoveries.[55] Importantly, the exhibition made no reference to the nineteenth-century Drake myths. (Nor were there any snuff-boxes, walking sticks or other dubiously attributed items, as there had been in the 1888 Armada tercentenary exhibition.) The construction of Drake as a hero of empire had no place in a country still struggling to come to terms with its colonial past. Drake's privateering, an essential part of the narrative, was similarly played down. Navigation provided a suitably neutral element of the Drake story, untainted by triumphalism or imperial ideology, on which to dwell. The move away from the representation of Drake as a founder of empire was pre-empted by the inclusion of Sir Francis and Sir Walter Raleigh in a set of commemorative stamps issued by the Royal Mail five years earlier. Also pictured were David Livingstone and Henry Stanley. Tellingly, the title of the set was *British Explorers* – exploration obviously being less of a contentious issue than empire building.

In the West Country the anniversary of the circumnavigation was marked by a series of events titled *Drake 400*, which was held over a four-year period. Although an illustration of pride in the local hero, there was more behind the celebrations than simply a desire to commemorate an epic voyage. *Drake 400* was also about bringing visitors to Plymouth and establishing the city as the primary tourist centre in the South West. This reflects the increasing importance of tourism – and the notoriously indeterminate concept of heritage – to the economy both locally and nationally in the final quarter of the twentieth century. In Plymouth the desire to encourage tourism was a direct result of the slump in ship-building, the city's traditional industry. Inevitably the decline of the primary industry had a great impact on a city that had relied for so long on the dockyards and where 50 per cent of manufacturing output was geared towards marine engineering. But if the maritime present was in the doldrums, Plymouth's vibrant maritime past, its heritage, could be packaged and sold. As Robert Hewison has suggested, the whole heritage industry has, in fact, grown from the perception of Britain as a nation in decline (the withdrawal from empire has undoubtedly contributed to this) and from the insecurities that this perception carries with it. In Hewison's words, heritage 'exploits the economic potential of our culture'[56] by presenting us with an idealized version of the past, which helps assuage present anxieties and doubts. Of course, an obsession with the past is a tacit acknowledgement of the inferiority of the present. The anniversary of the circumnavigation provided an ideal opportunity to capitalize on Plymouth's past. As we shall see, it also anticipated the marketing of the city's past that occurred in the late 1980s. Drake, it appears, was still capable of bringing benefits to the town he had served as mayor four hundred years earlier.

The events encompassed by *Drake 400* were extremely varied (many were entirely unrelated to Drake but were nevertheless assimilated into the celebration) and included an exhibition of Drake relics, concerts at Buckland Abbey, commemorative dinners, and a *son et lumière* display held in St Andrew's church. In July 1980 a 'pageant' was held at the Royal Citadel on Plymouth Hoe. Episodes from Drake's life – including the game of bowls – were re-enacted against a projected image of the *Golden Hinde*. The arrival of a replica *Golden Hinde* in Plymouth Sound having completed a six-year circumnavigation of the globe marked the climax of *Drake 400*. Since 1963 one replica *Hinde* has been a tourist attraction permanently moored at Brixham at the western end of Torbay. Here, among the ever-diminishing trawlers, she seems to symbolize the decline of the traditional fishing industry and the growth of the tourist trade. A further copy of the ship is moored on the River Thames not far from the recreated Globe Theatre. In Southwark, it seems, the Elizabethan past is more real (and more profitable) than the present.

The next great Drake anniversary to be celebrated was the quadricentenary of the defeat of the Spanish Armada in 1988. A large number of historical accounts appeared during the 'Armada' year as publishers sought to exploit the occasion. Probably the finest was Mattingly's *Defeat of the Spanish Armada*, which illustrates how little scholarship had changed in thirty years. Other notable works were Felipe Fernandez-Armesto's *The Spanish Armada: The Experience of War in 1588*[57] and *The Spanish Armada*[58] by Colin Martin and Geoffrey Parker. No serious historical work sought to construct the Armada as a turning point in history or Drake as the single-handed victor. Fernandez-Armesto, for example, calls the conflict a 'typical example of sixteenth-century warfare'.[59] Yet it is noticeable that Martin and Parker seek to position Drake at the centre of the victory. They suggest that Drake was the first to appreciate the inadequacies of the gun carriages used by the Spaniards – the poor design of which did not allow for rapid reloading. Drake, the authors claim, may have made this discovery aboard the prize the *Rosario*. Thus the capture of de Valdez's ship 'was in retrospect one of the most significant episodes in the conflict'.[60]

While the circumnavigation festivities were largely uncontroversial, the same could not be said of the events organized in commemoration of the defeat of the Spanish Armada. It was rumoured that *Armada 1588–1988*, the major exhibition to be held at the National Maritime Museum, intended to relegate Drake to a peripheral role in the defeat. This was not in fact the case and a great deal of Drake material was displayed; this included portraits by Gheeraerts and Hilliard and a replica of Drake's drum. Yet the exhibition was revisionist, in seeking to strip away the old myths and present a historically accurate version of the conflict. There would be no game of bowls, no Protestant storm, and no personal duel between Sir Francis and King Philip. This rewriting of 'history' was not welcome in Plymouth, which was organizing its own celebrations. In *The Times* a former Lord Mayor of Plymouth blamed political correctness and Spain's recent entry into the Common Market for Drake's 'omission'.[61] Matters were not helped when it was discovered that the Spanish ambassador was on the exhibition's Committee of Honour. No wonder Sir Francis was being demoted! As *The Times* noted, 'Spain, once England's enemy, was by the 1980s a new partner in the EC, and Drake's shadow was not to be allowed to fall across delicate negotiations'.[62] The Armada was tricky territory indeed. Stephen Deuchar, one of the organizers of *Armada 1588–1988*, observed that even exhibitions that questioned the notion of a glorious English victory masterminded by Drake were problematic. They may 'promote the popular notion that Spain's ignominious failure was actually England's finest hour, for they also pay tribute to the existence of a 400-year-old store of collective relief that a small island was not after all overrun by a mighty foreign aggressor'.[63]

Plymouth had its own reasons for resenting the repositioning of Drake. An article in *The Times* on Plymouth's *Armada 400* celebrations revealed the real purpose of the events. 'The city's Armada celebrations in July are intended to give a further impetus to its strategy of creating new job opportunities.'[64] According to Plymouth's then director of marketing and leisure,

> It's really about the idea of Plymouth as a nice place to visit, a place where things happen ... [and raising] the profile of the city in the mind of people who want to come and spend money, whether they spend money as tourists or by putting up factories.[65]

The need to promote Plymouth was even more pressing than it had been in the late 1970s when *Drake 400* attempted to raise the city's profile. After privatization in 1987 Devonport Dockyard, the city's largest employer, came under control of Devonport Management Limited (now Babcock Marine). Substantial job losses were an immediate result as the new management sought to keep the yard competitive. (By 1992 the workforce had been reduced from 11,200 to 3600 full-time staff.) With rising levels of unemployment, Plymouth was ready to welcome any strategy for encouraging new investment.

In a continuing effort to promote tourism, the city was intent on preserving and selling the old, well-known Drake traditions. Although Drake's Victorian signifying function had been lost, *Armada 400* continued to project the nineteenth-century representation to a mass audience. Drake and the game of bowls had, in fact, acquired a new signification: Drake *was* Plymouth. If the National Maritime Museum wanted to play down Drake's role, the complete opposite was true of Plymouth. The city's *Armada 400* celebrations bore a remarkable similarity to the events that had taken place in 1888. They included 'Elizabethan revelries', a tea dance and, inevitably, a re-enactment of Drake's game of bowls. The discrepancy between the 'official' and the popular representation of the defeat (or to use the official and rather more neutral term, the destruction) of the Spanish fleet is well illustrated by ephemera produced at the time. The commemorative Armada stamps issued by the Royal Mail, for example, simply depict the Channel engagements, but the first-day cover as issued in Plymouth has Drake's identity quite literally stamped all over it – the postmark is an image of the Drake statue.

Although in many ways a problematic character, Sir Francis continues to generate great interest. In Britain biographical accounts continue to appear at the rate of about one every two years. One of the more recent accounts to be published chooses, once again, to emphasize Drake's identity as a pirate. Harry Kelsey's *Sir Francis Drake: The Queen's Pirate*[66] (1998) is intent on overturning the old chivalric construction of Drake. In Kelsey's hands Sir Francis becomes a ruthless and manipulative thief entirely lacking conventional morality: 'He was a pirate, and a good one, largely because he was untroubled by a conscience that in most men would murmur against theft or murder.'[67] The desertion of comrades such as Hawkins on their return from San Juan and the wounded Le Testu during the raid on the Panama mule train provides Kelsey with evidence of Drake's 'character flaws'. Contradicting almost every account of Drake's life, Kelsey claims that Sir Francis 'treated the ordinary sailors with contempt and punished them for the slightest infraction'.[68] Drake's oft-quoted statement on the equality of shipboard life – 'I must have the gentleman to haul and draw with the mariner' – is merely a means of securing loyalty. Although the publishers market the book as a radical new interpretation of the past, we should remember that there were many Englishmen in Drake's own day who condemned him as a pirate.

Kelsey's version of Drake is the 'right sort of Englishman', according to Mr Kant, the Russian Mafia boss in Edward Thomas's movie *Rancid Aluminium* (2000).[69] The film is actually rather poor and finally collapses into itself, but the frequent references to Drake provide evidence of an underlying idea that is never fully developed. Sir Francis Drake is held up as the ideal entrepreneurial figure, ruthless, self-motivated and not above murder when necessary. Kant despises the archetypal stiff upper-lipped, fair-playing English gentleman – the very construction of public school Englishness that Drake came to embody at the height of empire. Perhaps the film deliberately attempts to subvert this traditional construction. In a cricket pavilion – the perfect symbolic location – the English protagonist Pete Thompson is warned that the children of the weak (those, we must assume, who play up and play the game) do not inherit 'hard currency'. He is instructed to kill his cheating business associate: 'Think of your Francis Drake,' urges Kant as he wields a cricket bat with which he dubs Thompson on the shoulders. 'Drake!' he exclaims, having heard that Thompson has killed his rival. Later, when subjected to a mock execution, Thompson is warned 'Remember what Sir Francis Drake did to men who betrayed him.' Whether the producers were aware that Drake used simulated hangings is unclear but the mock execution was more characteristic of Drake than the straightforward beheading of Doughty to which the film presumably alludes. Importantly, both Kelsey's biography and *Rancid Aluminium* construct Drake as cut-throat (quite literally) entrepreneur. This fits very neatly with the late twentieth-century commercialization of Drake: the only use a consumerist culture can find for Sir Francis is as a means of economic exploitation. While appearing to radically deconstruct past mythologies and offer a 'real' Francis Drake, the Kelsey/*Rancid Aluminium* construction merely puts together another version, its economic rapacity providing covert historical validation for the primacy of money-making in our own culture.

Notes

[1] Peter Davies, 'A Lie on the Ocean Wave?', *The Times*, 24 January 1996, 37.

[2] John M. MacKenzie, 'Introduction', in John M. MacKenzie, ed., *Imperialism and Popular Culture* (Manchester, 1986), 7.

[3] Michael Lewis, 'Fresh Light on San Juan de Ulua', *Mariner's Mirror*, vol. 23 (1937), 295–315. Geoffrey Callender, 'Fresh Light on Drake', *Mariner's Mirror*, vol. 9 (1923), 16–28. Gregory Robinson, 'A Forgotten Life of Sir Francis Drake', *Mariner's Mirror*, vol. 7 (1921), 10–18.

[4] Zelia Nuttall, ed., *New Light on Drake* (London, 1914).

[5] Henry Wagner, *Sir Francis Drake's Voyage Around the World* (San Francisco, 1926).

[6] Irene Wright, *Documents Concerning English Voyages to the Caribbean and Spanish Main 1569–80* (London, 1932).

[7] Robinson, 'Forgotten Life', 10–18.

[8] Robinson, 'Forgotten Life', 10.

[9] Geoffrey Callender, 'Drake and his Detractors', *Mariner's Mirror*, vol. 7 (1921), 66–74, 98–105, 142–52.

[10] Gregory Robinson, 'The Trial and Death of Thomas Doughty', *Mariner's Mirror*, vol. 7 (1921), 272.

[11] Callender, 'Drake and his Detractors', 67.

[12] Stephen Constantine, '"Bringing the Empire Alive": The Empire Marketing Board and Imperial Propaganda, 1926–33', in MacKenzie, ed., *Imperialism and Popular Culture*, 192.

[13] Walter Harte, *Sir Francis Drake* (London, 1920), iii.

[14] Edward Benson, *Sir Francis Drake* (London, 1927), viii.

[15] Benson, 18.

[16] Benson, 242.

[17] Arthur Mee, *Heroes of the Flag* (London, 1935), 11.

[18] Mee, 27.

[19] Robert Sargent Holland, *Drake's Lad* (London, 1929). Quoted in John Cummins, *Francis Drake: The Lives of a Hero* (1995; London, 1997), 299.

[20] For a survey of the cinema of empire, see Jeffrey Richards, *Visions of Yesterday* (London, 1973). For a specific discussion of the 1930s cinema of empire including Korda's trilogy, see Jeffrey Richards, 'Boy's Own Empire: Feature Films and Imperialism in the 1930s', in MacKenzie, ed., *Imperialism and Popular Culture*, 140–64.

[21] *Drake of England*, dir. Arthur Woods, British International Pictures, 1935.

[22] Review of *Drake of England*, *Variety*, 29 May 1935, 34.

[23] *The Sea Hawk*, dir., Michael Curtiz, Warner Brothers, 1940.

[24] See Rudy Behlmer, ed., Introduction, *The Sea Hawk* (Madison, WI, 1982), 18–25.

[25] Behlmer, 43.

[26] Guy Boas, ed., *Winston S. Churchill: A Selection from his Writings and Speeches* (London, 1952), 194.

[27] Isaac Foot, 'Drake's Drum Beats Again', *Prediction*, vol. 5 (1940), 326–7.

[28] Foot, 'Drake's Drum', 326.

[29] Notably E. M. R. Ditmas in *The Legend of Drake's Drum* (Guernsey, 1973), 13.

[30] Foot, 'Drake's Drum', 327.

[31] Foot, 'Drake's Drum', 327.

[32] E. Stogdon, 'The True Glory', *The Times*, 20 November 1939, 7.

[33] Eric Milner-White and G.W. Briggs, compilers, *Daily Prayer* (London, 1941), 5.

[34] Alfred Edward Mason, *The Life of Sir Francis Drake* (London, 1941).

[35] Mason, 424.

[36] James Williamson, *Sir Francis Drake* (London, 1951), 158–9.

[37] Christopher Lloyd, *Sir Francis Drake* (London, 1957), 11.

[38] Lloyd, 12.

[39] Garret Mattingly, *The Defeat of the Spanish Armada* (1959; London, 1988).

[40] Mattingly, 354.

[41] Mattingly, 87.

[42] Mattingly, 242.

[43] Douglas Bell, *Drake was My Captain* (London, 1933).

[44] Peter Dawlish, *He Went with Drake* (London, 1955).

[45] Jean Latham, *The Man they Called a Pirate* (London, 1961).

[46] Frank Knight, *The Young Drake* (London, 1962).

[47] Children's literature aimed at supporting the National Curriculum does still send young protagonists to sea with Drake. For example, in Karen Wallace's *Captain Drake's Orders* (London, 1997), a boy rises through the ranks to become Drake's secretary. This is the result of his ability to translate Spanish, which allows Drake to interrogate de Valdez and discover that the Spanish are using inferior cannon. Thus the Armada is defeated not through pluck and daring but by an ability to learn. It is a far cry from Kingsley's version of not-too-educated manliness.

[48] Michael Lewis, *The Spanish Armada* (London, 1960).

[49] Robert Marx, *The Battle of the Spanish Armada* (1965; London, 1968).

[50] Lewis Gibbs, *The Silver Circle* (London, 1963), 137.

[51] Ernle Bradford, *Drake* (London, 1965), 8.

[52] Kenneth R. Andrews, *Drake's Voyages: A Re-assessment of their Place in Elizabethan Maritime Expansion* (London, 1967).

[53] Andrews, 125.

[54] Andrews, 184

[55] *Sir Francis Drake: An Exhibition to Commemorate Sir Francis Drake's Voyage Around the World 1577–1580* (exh. cat., London, 1977).

[56] See Robert Hewison, *The Heritage Industry: Britain in a Climate of Decline* (London, 1987).

[57] Felipe Fernandez-Armesto, *The Spanish Armada: The Experience of War in 1588* (Oxford, 1988).

[58] Colin Martin and Geoffrey Parker, *The Spanish Armada* (London, 1988).

[59] Fernandez-Armesto, vii.

[60] Martin and Parker, 213.

[61] See Alan Hamilton and Ruth Gledhill, 'Plymouth Defends Drake Against New Armada', *The Times*, 17 September 1987, 1.

[62] 'Modern Age Singes Free Booting Hero's Beard', *The Sunday Times*, 22 January 1995, section 3, page 3.

[63] Stephen Deuchar, 'The English Image of the Spanish Armada', *Apollo*, vol. 127 (1988), 467.

[64] Malcolm Brown and Anthony Cox, 'Flying the Flag for Jobs', *The Times*, 27 April 1988, 18.

[65] Quoted in Brown and Cox, 'Flying the Flag', 18.

[66] Harry Kelsey, *Sir Francis Drake: The Queen's Pirate* (New Haven, 1998).

[67] Kelsey, 136.

[68] Kelsey, 278.

[69] *Rancid Aluminium*, dir., Edward Thomas, Fiction Factory, 2000.

CHAPTER TEN

The Future

A lthough interest in Sir Francis Drake has fluctuated in the four hundred years since his leaden coffin slipped beneath the waves of the Caribbean Sea, his reputation as one of England's greatest heroes has survived largely intact. Only in very recent years has his heroic status been subjected to revision, and even now there is little evidence that Drake will be relegated to the role of a peripheral historical character. Yet there is no single reason why Sir Francis has been held in such high regard for so long. Each age has identified and emphasized what it has found desirable in the Drake narrative. The many ways in which Drake has been constructed reflect the broad historical and cultural developments of the time of production. Sir Francis has found himself represented as a great navigator, the Protestant champion, a hero of commerce, a moral exemplum, a pioneer of English expansionism and empire, the single-handed victor over the Spanish Armada, the founder of the Royal Navy and, just occasionally, a pirate. No doubt each transformation has appeared to disclose the 'real' Sir Francis Drake. I have tried to show that there is no 'authentic' Drake to be discovered but rather a series of interpretations that are determined by the dominant culture of the day. But what can we expect from the future?

Commercial exploitation is one of the reasons for the high profile Sir Francis maintains in his native Devon, and it is almost certain that this will continue on a popular cultural level. The myths that came to prominence in the nineteenth century are still widely disseminated; games of bowls will continue to be re-enacted on Plymouth Hoe. More generally, what I have termed the commercialisation of Drake shows no sign of abating. In 2007 a PlayStation computer game titled *Uncharted: Drake's Fortune* was released. Players seek a treasure that Drake has supposedly hidden on the fabled island of El Dorado. Clearly, the prospect of acquiring gold in exotic locations continues to excite the imagination just as it did for the audiences of Davenant's *The History of Sir Francis Drake* or the readers of *Sir Francis Drake Revived*. For those requiring more than a 'virtual' experience, it is now possible to book a package holiday to Panama and walk Las Cruces Trail where the location of Drake's raid on the mule trains will be pointed out. These are but two examples of the way in which Drake has been exploited for commercial gain; there are, of course, many more.

It is tempting to think that Drake may have approved of this rapacity; he did, after all, try numerous means to secure his fortune. With consumerism and its ideology dominant in modern Britain, the notion of Drake-as-entrepreneur has currency (in both senses) and, as shown, has already been presented to a popular audience on the cinema screen. Similarly, it is no coincidence that a recent piece of research seeks to situate the seventeenth-century revival of Drake within a framework of changing financial models.[1] Drake's lust for wealth and fame and the ways in which he set about obtaining them are likely to feature in future representations. When discussing the possibility (and desirability) of locating Drake's coffin and 'repatriating' the Elizabethan admiral, the founder of the Sir Francis Drake Exploration Society is recorded as stating

> Vainglorious, social climber and attention seeker that he was, he would have wanted a resting place in St. Paul's like Nelson or in Westminster Abbey, near his sovereign. He would have adored the adulation of visitors to his tomb.[2]

Revealingly, the speaker is untroubled by this less than flattering description of Drake. Sir Francis has become a product of the late twentieth/early twenty-first century cult of celebrity in which amoral or immoral behaviour, social climbing and attention seeking seems to be a guarantee of celebrity status.

In contrast to the exhibitions of the 1970s that celebrated Drake as an explorer and a skilled navigator, a more recent exhibition held in Plymouth emphasized a different aspect of Drake's commercial activities. *Human Cargo* was concerned with Devon's role in the slave trade and had the task of reintroducing slavery into the Drake narrative This is, perhaps, the least comfortable aspect of the story to acknowledge and has often be elided completely. Held in 2007 and so timed to coincide with the two-hundredth anniversary of the Slave Trade Act, the exhibition acknowledged that the local hero had taken part in a slaving voyage but fell short of taking full account of pervasiveness of slavery in his story. It could have shown how his country seat at Buckland Abbey and the elaborate costumes that he wears in his portraits were paid for from the treasure captured on his voyages. Much of this treasure was produced through the Spanish enslavement of Native Americans. This is one aspect of the Drake story that remains largely unrecognized and is little discussed. Future Drake studies may seek to develop this 'contrapuntal' reading and explore the connection between Spanish slaves in Central and South America and the tangible remains of an Elizabethan sailor in a far-off corner of the world. Thus the silenced players in the great drama that was Drake's career would begin to gain recognition.

Confronting the part that slaving played in the story of the sixteenth-century mariners is, of course, necessary in modern multicultural Britain, and it seems likely that the reputations of Drake and John Hawkins will undergo further revision in the light of contemporary sensitivity to the subject. Just as the Victorians created Others who defined the desired version of Englishness, so anxiety about the nation's colonial past has resulted in Drake, at times, becoming an historical Other whose actions contrast with and so help define an acceptable version of modern Englishness. We should perhaps note that the Victorians, with the firmly held but paradoxical belief that conquering other peoples would guarantee their freedom, faced a similar problem when dealing with Drake and the slave trade. Most chose to exclude the subject from their biographies. Froude touches on slavery briefly but makes it clear that Drake had been led into the trade. 'It was not until he was five-

and-twenty that he was tempted by Hawkins into the negro-catching business, and of this one experiment was enough.'[3] And while it may no longer be possible to dismiss the subject is such a casual manner, another aspect of the narrative is sometimes given prominence in an attempt to redeem Drake's reputation: his good relationship with escaped Spanish slaves. John Sugden writes:

> Drake had turned to the Cimarrones as tools to his ends, but from the relationship he learnt a respect for Negroes and coloured peoples generally that was in advance of most of the empire builders of his time ... He relied upon them as he relied upon his Plymouth lads, saw qualities in them as sterling as those he found in any whites, and they did not let him down.[4]

Here Drake is reconstructed in a way that addresses very modern concerns. Rather than being vilified as a slave trader, it is almost possible that Drake's encounters with Native Americans and escaped slaves will see him constructed as an early English exponent of multiculturalism.

While we may speculate on the new directions the construction of Drake may take, it is also worth noting continuities in the way he is used. Perhaps surprisingly, the tradition of setting children's stories at sea with Captain Drake continues. For the most part these works of fiction are written with the intention of supporting the 'Tudors' component of the National Curriculum. There are, of course, no attempts at portraying England as a racially or morally superior nation, as we saw in nineteenth-and early twentieth-century works, but the pattern of gaining advancement through one's own energies is evident. For example, as noted in the previous chapter, the young protagonist of Karen Wallace's *Captain Drake's Orders*[5] rises to become Sir Francis's secretary through his ability to speak Spanish, with significant results. Instead of inculcating imperial ideology, this work aims at instilling the importance of education, specifically foreign languages. In this way the book represents an unintentional subversion of Kingsley's hugely important *Westward Ho!* with its scorn for 'book learning'.

In the twenty-first century the Victorian construction of Drake has been subverted and overturned in many ways. But it is the ability of the Drake narrative to be continually reshaped by ever-changing cultural, economic and ideological determinants that ensures the survival of Sir Francis. Despite the peaks and troughs in his popularity over the last four hundred years, the time has not yet come to sound Drake's drum to summon the old warrior for, in truth, he has never left the popular consciousness.

Notes

[1] Mark Netzloff, 'Sir Francis Drake's Ghost: Piracy, Cultural Memory, and Spectral Nationhood', in Claire Jowitt, ed., *Pirates? The Politics of Plunder, 1550–1650* (Basingstoke, 2007), 137–50.
[2] Michael Turner, 'New Resting Place for Drake', *The Times*, 2 February 1995, 19.
[3] James Anthony Froude, *English Seamen in the Sixteenth Century* (London, 1926).
[4] John Sugden, *Sir Francis Drake* (London, 1990). 62–3.
[5] Karen Wallace, *Captain Drake's Orders: A Tale about the Armada* (London, 1997).

Bibliography

'Account of the Plymouth New Guildhall and Municipal Offices', *Smith's Plymouth Almanac* (Plymouth, 1876–7), unpaginated.

Adamson, J. S. A., 'Chivalric and Political Culture in Caroline England', in Kevin Sharpe and Peter Lake, eds, *Culture and Politics in Early Stuart England* (London, 1994), 161–98.

Addison, William, *Worthy Dr. Fuller* (London, 1951).

Allen, Michael J., 'Charles Fitzgeffrey's Commendatory Lamentations on the Death of Drake', in Thrower, ed., *Sir Francis Drake*, 99–111.

Anderson, Adam, *An Historical and Chronological Deduction of the Origin of Commerce*, 4 vols (1764; London, 1787).

Anderson, George, *A New Authentic, and Complete Collection of Voyages Round the World* (London, 1784).

Andrews, Kenneth R., *Drake's Voyages: A Reassessment of their Place in Elizabethan Maritime Expansion* (London, 1967).

——, *Trade, Plunder and Settlement: Maritime Enterprise and the Genesis of the British Empire 1480–1630* (Cambridge, 1984).

Anon., 'Eighty Eight, or Sir Francis Drake', in T. W. H. Crosland, compiler, *English Songs and Ballads* (London, 1907), 117–18.

Anon., *History of the Spanish Armada* (London, 1759).

Anon., *A Sermon Preached on October 19th 1803, the date appointed for a National Fast. To which is added an account of the destruction of the Spanish Armada* (London, 1803).

Anon., *Sir Francis Drake Revived. Calling Upon this Dull or Effeminate Age to Follow his Noble Steps for Gold and Silver* (London, 1626).

Anon., *Sir Francis Drake Revived. Who is or may be a Pattern to Stirre up all Heroicke and Active Spirits of these Times, to Benefit their Country and Eternize their Names by Like Noble Attempts* (London, 1653).

Anon., *The World Encompassed by Sir Francis Drake being his Next Voyage to that to Nombre de Dios* (London, 1628).

Appleby, John C., 'War, Politics and Colonisation 1558–1625', in Nicholas Canny, ed., *The Origins of Empire: British Overseas Enterprise to the Close of the Seventeenth Century* (Oxford, 1998), 55–78.

'Armada Tercentenary', *Western Daily Mercury*, 20 July 1888, 2–3.

'Armada Tercentenary Memorial', *Illustrated London News*, 21 July 1888, 60.

Armitage, David, *The Ideological Origins of the British Empire* (Cambridge, 2000).

Ayling, S. E., *The Georgian Century 1714–1837* (London, 1966).

Barber, Chips, *The Lost City of Exeter* (Exeter, 1982).

Baring-Gould, Sabine, *The Lives of the Saints*, 16 vols (Edinburgh, 1914).

Barnfield, Richard, *The Encomium of Lady Pecunia: or, The Praise of Money*, in Edward Arber, ed., *Richard Barnfield: Poems 1594–1598* (Birmingham, 1882), 81–93.

Barrow, John, *The Life, Voyages, and Exploits of Admiral Sir Francis Drake, Knight* (London, 1843).

'Barrow's *Life, Voyages, and Exploits of Sir Francis Drake, Knight*', review, *Edinburgh Review*, vol. 80 (1844), 376–406.

Bawlf, Samuel, *The Secret Voyage of Sir Francis Drake* (London, 2004).

Bayne-Dupaquier, Simone, *Heaton, Butler and Bayne: One Hundred Years of the Art of Stained Glass* (Montreux, 1986).

Behlmer, Rudy, ed., *The Sea Hawk* (Madison, WI, 1982), 43.

Behrman, Cynthia Fansler, *Victorian Myths of the Sea* (Athens, OH, 1977).

Bell, Douglas, *Drake was My Captain* (London, 1953).

Benson, Edward Frederic, *Sir Francis Drake* (London, 1927).

Bingham, Madeleine, *The Great Lover: The Life and Art of Herbert Beerbohm Tree* (London, 1978).

Birch, Thomas, *The Heads and Characters of Illustrious Persons of Great Britain, with their Portraits Engraved by Mr. Houbraken and Mr. Vertue*, 2 vols (London, 1743).

Black, Jeremy and Donald M. MacRaid, *Studying History* (London, 1997).

Blaen, Angela, *The Mystery of Michael* (Guernsey, 1987).

Boas, Guy, ed., *Winston S. Churchill: A Selection from his Writings and Speeches* (London, 1952).

Booth, Michael R., *English Melodrama* (London, 1965).

Bradford, Ernle, *Drake* (London, 1965).

Bratton, J. S., 'Of England, Home and Duty: The Image of England in Victorian and Edwardian Juvenile Fiction', in Mackenzie, ed., *Imperialism and Popular Culture*, 73–93.

Bray, Anna Eliza, *The Borders of the Tamar and Tavy*, 2 vols (London, 1874). Reprint of *A Description of the Part of Devonshire Bordering on the Tamar and Tavy* (London, 1836).

——, ed., *Poetical Remains, Social Sacred, and Miscellaneous of the Late Edward Atkyns Bray*, 2 vols (London, 1859).

Brimacombe, Peter, *Drake's Drum: A History of the Devonport Naval Base and Dockyard* (Plymouth, 1998).

'British Naval History', *Penny Magazine of the Society for the Diffusion of Useful Knowledge*, vol. 7 (1838), 157–9.

Brooks, Chris, *The Gothic Revival* (London, 1999).

——, 'Historicism and the Nineteenth Century', in Vanessa Brand, ed., *The Study of the Past in the Victorian Age* (Oxford, 1998), 1–19.

Brown, Malcolm and Anthony Cox, 'Flying the Flag for Jobs', *The Times*, 27 April 1988, 18.

Bryan, Michael, *Bryan's Dictionary of Painters and Engravers*, 5 vols (London, 1926–4).

Buck, Philip W, *The Politics of Mercantilism* (New York, 1964).

Burke, Edmund, *Reflections on the Revolution in France*, 1790, ed. Conor Cruise O'Brien (London, 1976).

Burton, Anthony, and Pip, *The Green Bag Travellers: Britain's First Tourists* (London, 1978).

Burton, Robert, *The English Hero: or, Sir Francis Drake Revived: Being a full Account of the Dangerous Voyages, Admirable Adventures, Notable Discoveries, and Magnanimous Atchievements of that Valiant and Renowned Commander* (1687; London, 1706).

Butterfield, Herbert, *The Whig Interpretation of History* (1931; London, 1951).

Cabinet Portrait Gallery of British Worthies, 15 vols (London, 1845).

Callender, Geoffrey, 'Drake and his Detractors', *Mariner's Mirror*, vol. 7 (1921), 66–74, 98–105, 142–52.

——, 'Fresh Light on Drake', *Mariner's Mirror*, vol. 9 (1923), 16–28.

——, 'The Greenwich Portrait of Sir Francis Drake' *Mariner's Mirror*, vol. 18 (1932), 359–62.

Camden, William, *The Historie of the Most Renowned and Victorious Princess Elizabeth Late Queen of England* (London, 1630).

Campbell, John, *The Lives of the British Admirals, Containing a New and Accurate Naval History From the Earliest Periods*, 4 vols (1742; London, 1779).

Campbell, Lorne, *Renaissance Portraits: European Portrait Painting in the 14th, 15th and 16th Centuries* (New Haven, 1990).

Carlyle, Thomas, *Chartism* (London, 1840).

———, *History of Frederick II of Prussia, Called Frederick the Great*, 6 vols (London, 1858-65).

———, *Oliver Cromwell's Letters and Speeches with Elucidations*, 2 vols (London, 1845).

———, *On Heroes, Hero-Worship and the Heroic in History* (1841; London, 1928).

———, *Past and Present* (1843; London, 1928).

Carrington, Henry, *The Plymouth and Devonport Guide with Sketches of the Surrounding Scenery* (London, 1828).

Chapman, George, 'De Guiana, Carmen Epicum', in Phyllis Brooks Bartlett, ed., *The Poems of George Chapman* (New York, 1962), 353–7.

Clark, Samuel, *The Life and Death of the Valiant and Renowned Sir Francis Drake, His Voyages and Discoveries in the West Indies, and About the World, with his Noble and Heroick Acts* (London, 1671).

Clarke, Edward, *A Tour Through the South of England, Wales and Part of Ireland made during the Summer of 1791* (London, 1793).

Clarke, George, 'Grecian Taste and Gothic Virtue: Lord Cobham's Gardening Programme and its Iconography', *Apollo*, vol. 97 (1973), 566–71.

Clowes, William Laird, 'The Tercentenary of the Defeat of the Spanish Armada', *Graphic*, 21 July 1888, 65–8, 74.

Colley, Linda, *Britons: Forging the Nation 1707–1837* (London, 1996).

Constantine, Stephen, '"Bringing the Empire Alive": The Empire Marketing Board and Imperial Propaganda, 1926–33', in MacKenzie, ed., *Imperialism and Popular Culture*, 192–231.

Corbett, Julian, *Drake and the Tudor Navy with a History of the Rise of England as a Maritime Power*, 2 vols (1898; London, 1899).

———, *Sir Francis Drake* (1890; London, 1901).

Cowper, William, 'Boadicea', in Robert Aris Willmott, ed., *The Poetical Works of William Cowper* (London, 1895), 180.

Creasy, Edward, *The Fifteen Decisive Battles of the World: From Marathon to Waterloo* (1851; London, 1862).

Cressy, David, *Bonfires and Bells: National Memory and the Protestant Calendar in Elizabethan and Stuart England* (London, 1989).

Cummins, John, *Sir Francis Drake: The Lives of a Hero* (1995; London, 1997).

Davenant, William, *The History of Sir Francis Drake. The First Part*, 1659, in *Three Centuries of English Drama: English 1642–1700* (New York, 1960), Microcard 9.

Davies, Peter, 'A Lie on the Ocean Wave?', *The Times*, 24 January, 1996, 37.

Davis, Lance E. and Robert Huttenback, *Mammon and the Pursuit of Empire: The Economics of British Imperialism* (Cambridge, 1988).

Dawlish, Peter, *He Went with Drake* (London, 1955).

Defoe, Daniel, *A New Voyage Around the World by a Course Never Sailed Before*, 1725, in *The Novels and Miscellaneous Works of Daniel Defoe*, 7 vols (London, 1910), vol. 6, 191–459.

Deuchar, Stephen, 'The English Image of the Spanish Armada', *Apollo*, vol. 127 (1988), 244–51.

Dibdin, Charles, 'Naval Victories', in *The Professional Life of Mr. Dibdin, Written by Himself*, 4 vols (London, 1803), vol. 4, 197–8.

Dibdin, John, 'This Snug Little Island', in *Dibdin's Sea Songs* (London, 1841), 228–31.

Dictionary of National Biography.

Disher, Maurice Willson, *Blood and Thunder: Mid-Victorian Melodrama and its Origins* (London, 1949).

Ditmas, E. M. R., *The Legend of Drake's Drum* (Guernsey, 1973).

Donkin, Andrew, *Sir Francis Drake and his Daring Deeds* (London, 2006).

'Drake Commemoration at Plymouth', *Western Daily Mercury*, 15 February 1884, 2–3.

'Drake Memorial at Tavistock', *Western Daily Mercury*, 28 September 1883, 3.

Drake of England, dir. Arthur Woods, British International Pictures, 1935.

Drake of England, review, *Variety*, 29 May 1935, 34.

'Drake's Leat', *South Devon Monthly Museum*, vol. 4, no. 22 (1834), 157–68.

Drayton, Michael, *Poly-Olbion*, 1612 and 1622, in J. William Hebel, ed., *The Works of Michael Drayton*. 5 vols (Oxford, 1931–41), vol. 4.

Dunn, Waldo Hilary, *James Anthony Froude: A Biography*, 2 vols (Oxford, 1961).

Eden, Charles Henry, *At Sea with Drake on the Spanish Main* (London, 1899).

Edmond, Mary, *Rare Sir William Davenant, Poet Laureate, Playwright, Civil War General, Restoration Theatre Manager* (Manchester, 1987).

Effra, Helmut von and Allen Staley, *The Paintings of Benjamin West* (New York, 1986).

Elliot-Drake, Elizabeth, *The Family and Heirs of Sir Francis Drake*, 2 vols (London, 1911).

Emsley, Clive, *British Society and the French Wars 1793–1815* (London, 1979).

Faber, Geoffrey, *Oxford Apostles: A Character Study of the Oxford Movement* (London, 1933).

Fernandez-Armesto, Felipe, *The Spanish Armada: The Experience of War in 1588* (Oxford, 1988).

Finkelpearl, Philip J., *Court and Country Politics in the Plays of Beaumont and Fletcher* (Princeton, 1990).

'Fishing Feast of the Plymouth Town Council', *Illustrated London News*, 30 August 1856, 219.

Fletcher, John, *Rule a Wife and Have a Wife*, in *The Works of Francis Beaumont and John Fletcher* 10 vols (Cambridge, 1906), vol. 3, 169–235.

Foot, Isaac, 'Drake's Drum Beats Again', *Prediction*, vol. 5 (1940), 326–7.

Freeman, Edward, *History of the Norman Conquest of England*, 6 vols (Oxford, 1867).

Freeman, Rosemary, *English Emblem Books* (London, 1948).

Froude, James Anthony, 'England's Forgotten Worthies', *Westminster and Foreign Quarterly Review*, new series, vol. 2 (1852), 32–67.

——, *English Seaman in the Sixteenth Century* (1895; London, 1926).

——, *History of England from the Fall of Wolsey to the Defeat of the Spanish Armada*, 12 vols (London, 1856–70).

——, 'Scientific Method Applied to History', in *Short Studies on Great Subjects*, 4 vols (London, 1894), vol. 2, 563–98.

'Froude's *History of England*', review, *Edinburgh Review*, vol. 119, pt 1 (1864), 243–79.

'Froude's History of Queen Elizabeth', review, *Edinburgh Review*, vol. 131, pt 1 (1870), 1–39.

'Froude's *Queen Elizabeth*', review, *Quarterly Review*, vol. 128 (1870), 506–44.

Fuller, Thomas, *The History of the Worthies of England*, 2 vols (1662; London, 1811).

——, *The Holy and Profane State* (1642; London, 1840).

Gaskell Brown, Cynthia, *The Battle's Sound: Drake's Drum and the Drake Flags* (Tiverton, 1996).

Gerassi-Navarro, Nina, *Pirate Novels: Fictions of Nation Building in Spanish America* (Durham, NC, 1999).

Gibbs, Lewis, *The Silver Circle* (London, 1963).

Gill, Crispin, 'Drake and Plymouth', in Thrower, ed., *Sir Francis Drake*, 78–89.

——, *The Pageant of Plymouth Hoe* (Plymouth, 1953).

——, *Plymouth: A New History* (1966; Tiverton, 1993).

Gilpin, William, *A Dialogue Upon the Gardens of the Right Honourable the Lord Viscount Cobham at Stowe*, 1748, in *The Gardens at Stowe: Six Descriptions* (London, 1982), 1–60.

Graves, Algernon, *The Royal Academy of Arts: A Complete Dictionary of Contributors and Their Work from its Foundation in 1769 to 1904*, 4 vols (London, 1905).

'Grand Naval Obelisk to be Erected on Portsdown', *Gentleman's Magazine*, vol. 68 (1798), 24–7.

Graphic, 17 February 1883, 171.

Graydon, William Murray, *The Fighting Lads of Devon: Or, In the Days of the Armada* (London, 1900),

Grosart, Alexander, ed., *The Complete Works in Verse and Prose of Abraham Cowley* (1881; Hildesheim, n.d.).

——, ed., *The Poems of the Reverend Charles Fitzgeffrey 1593–1636*, (Manchester, 1881).

Hackett, Helen. *Virgin Mother, Maiden Queen: Elizabeth I and the Cult of the Virgin Mary* (New York, 1995).

Hakluyt, Richard, *Divers Voyages Touching the Discovery of America and the Islands Adjacent*, 1582, ed. John Winter Jones (London, 1850).

——, *The Principal Navigations, Voyages, Traffiques and Discoveries of the English Nation*, 1589 and 1598–1600, 8 vols (London, 1907).

Hamilton, Alan and Ruth Gledhill, 'Plymouth Defends Drake Against New Armada', *The Times*, 17 September 1987, 1.

Harrison, Martin, *Victorian Stained Glass* (London, 1980).

Harte, Walter, *Sir Francis Drake* (London, 1920).

Hawkins, David J., *Water From the Moor: An Illustrated History of the Plymouth, Stonehouse and Devonport Leats* (Newton Abbot, 1987).

'Heard at Sea', *The Times*, 29 September 1916, 9.

Henty, George Alfred, *Under Drake's Flag: A Tale of the Spanish Main* (London, 1883).

Hewison, Robert, *The Heritage Industry: Britain in a Climate of Decline* (London, 1987).

Heywood, Thomas, *If You Know Not Me, You Know Nobody*, 1606 and 1632, in *The Dramatic Works of Thomas Heywood*, 6 vols (London, 1874), vol. 1, 249–351.

Hill, Christopher, *A Nation of Change and Novelty. Radical Politics, Religion and Literature in Seventeenth-Century England* (London, 1990).

——, *Reformation to Industrial Revolution: A Social and Economic History of Britain 1530–1780* (London, 1967).

Hind, Arthur M., *Engraving in the Sixteenth and Seventeenth Centuries: A Descriptive Catalogue with Instructions*, 2 vols (Cambridge, 1952).

'Historical Windows in the New Guildhall', *Smith's Plymouth Almanac* (Plymouth, 1876–7), unpaginated.

Hodgkins, Christopher, *Reforming Empire, Protestant Colonialism and Conscience in British Literature* (Columbia, MI, 2002).

Horrocks, J. W., *A Short History of Mercantilism* (London, 1926).

Howes, Edmund, *Annales, or A General Chronicall of England Begun by John Stow, Continued and Augmented unto 1631 by Edmund Howes* (London, 1631).

Hughes, Ann, *The Causes of the English Civil War* (London, 1991).

Hunt, Robert, *Popular Romances of the West of England: or, The Drolls, Traditions and Superstitions of Old Cornwall*, 2 vols (London, 1865).

Hyde, Ralph, *A Prospect of Britain: The Town Panoramas of Samuel and Nathaniel Buck* (London, 1994).

Jewkes, W. T., 'Sir Francis Drake Revived: From Letter to Legend', in Thrower, ed., *Sir Francis Drake*, 112–20.

Johnson, Samuel, 'The Life of Admiral Drake', *Gentleman's Magazine*, vol. 10 (1740), 389–96, 443–7, 509–15, 600–3; vol. 11 (1741), 38–44.

——, 'London: A Poem', in *Samuel Johnson: The Complete English Poems*, ed. J. Fleeman (London, 1971).

Jonson, Ben, *Eastward Ho!*, 1605, in G. A. Wilkes, ed., *The Complete Plays of Ben Jonson*, 4 vols (Oxford, 1981–2), vol. 2, 351–531.

Jordan, Gerald and Nicholas Rogers, 'Admirals as Heroes: Patriotism and Liberty in Hanoverian England', *Journal of British Studies*, vol. 28 (1989), 201–24.

Keeler, Mary Frear, ed., *Sir Francis Drake's West Indian Voyage* (London, 1981).

Kelsey, Harry, *Sir Francis Drake: The Queen's Pirate* (New Haven, 1998).

Kennedy, Paul M, *The Rise and Fall of British Naval Mastery* (London, 1983).

Kingsley, Charles, 'Froude's History of England: Volumes VII and VIII', *Macmillan's Magazine*, vol. 9 (1863–4), 211–24.

——, *Westward Ho!* (1855; London, n.d.).

Kippis, Andrew, *Biographia Britannica: or, The Lives of the Most Eminent Persons who have Flourished in Great Britain and Ireland*, 5 vols (London, 1778–93).

Knight, Frank, *The Young Drake* (London, 1962).

Knight Hunt, F., ed., *The Book of Art, Cartoons, Frescos, Sculpture and Decorative Arts, as Applied to the New Houses of Parliament* (London, 1846).

Latham, Jean, *The Man they Called a Pirate* (London, 1961).

Lediard, Thomas, *The Naval History of England* (London, 1735).

Levine, Joseph M., *The Battle of the Books: History and Literature in the Augustan Age* (Ithaca, NY, 1991).

Lewis, Frederic, *The Scenery of the Tamar and Tavy* (London, 1823).

Lewis, Michael, 'Fresh Light on San Juan de Ulua', *Mariner's Mirror*, vol. 23 (1937), 295–315.

——, *The Spanish Armada* (London, 1960).

'Life of Admiral Blake', *Gentleman's Magazine*, vol. 10 (1740), 301–7.

Lingard, John, *A History of England from the First Invasion by the Romans*, 14 vols (Paris, 1826).

Lipscomb, George, *A Journey into Cornwall through the Counties of Southampton, Wiltshire, Dorset, Somerset and Devon* (Warwick, 1799).

Lloyd, Christopher, 'Drake's Game of Bowls', *Mariner's Mirror*, vol. 39 (1953), 144–5.

——, *Sir Francis Drake* (London, 1957).

Lloyd, T. O., *The British Empire 1558–1995* (Oxford, 1996).

Lockyer, Roger, *The Early Stuarts: A Political History of England 1603–1642* (London, 1989).

Lodge, Edmund, *Portraits of Illustrious Personages of Great Britain, Engraved from Authentic Portraits in the Galleries of the Nobility, and the Public Collections of the Country*, 4 vols (London, 1821).

Logie Robertson, J., ed., *The Complete Poetical Works of James Thomson* (London, 1963).

Loomis, George Sherman, 'Arthurian Tradition and Folklore', *Folklore*, vol. 69 (1958), 1–25.

Low, Rachael, *The History of the British Film 1906–1914* (London, 1949).

——, *The History of the British Film 1929–1939* (London, 1985).

Lowenthal, David, *The Past is a Foreign Country* (1985; Cambridge, 1987).

Lowes, John Livingston, *The Road to Xanadu: A Study in the Ways of Imagination* (New York, 1927).

Lyon, David, *The Sailing Navy: All the Ships of the Royal Navy, Built, Purchased and Captured 1688–1860* (London, 1993).

Macaulay, Thomas Babington, 'The Armada: A Fragment', in Lady Trevelyan, ed., *The Works of Lord Macaulay*, 8 vols (London, 1871), vol. 8, 587–8.

Machen, Arthur, *The Bowmen and Other Legends of the War* (London, 1915).

MacKenzie, John M., 'Introduction', in John M. MacKenzie, ed., *Imperialism and Popular Culture* (Manchester, 1986), 1–16.

Mackintosh, James, *The History of England*, 10 vols (London, 1831).

Mahan, A. T., *The Influence of Sea Power Upon History 1660–1783* (1890; London, 1918).

Mangan, J. A., *The Games Ethic and Imperialism: Aspects of the Diffusion of an Ideal* (London, 1986).

Martin, Colin and Geoffrey Parker, *The Spanish Armada* (London, 1988).

Marvell, Andrew, 'Bermudas', in Alexander Grosart, ed., *The Complete Works of Andrew Marvell*, 4 vols (1872; New York, 1966), vol. 1, 82–3.

Marx, Robert, *The Battle of the Spanish Armada* (1965; London, 1968).

Mason, Alfred Edward, *The Life of Sir Francis Drake* (London, 1941).

Mattingly, Garrett, *The Defeat of the Spanish Armada* (1959; London, 1988).

Mee, Arthur, *Heroes of the Flag* (London, 1935).

Milner-White, Eric and G. W. Briggs, compilers, *Daily Prayer* (London, 1941).

'Modern Age Singes Free Booting Hero's Beard', *The Sunday Times*, 22 January 1995, section 3, page 3.

Moir, Esther, *The Discovery of Britain: The English Tourists 1540–1840* (London, 1964).

Monson, William, *Naval Tracts*, in Awnsham Churchill, *A Collection of Voyages and Travels*, 8 vols (London, 1704), vol. 3, 154–560.

Netzloff, Mark, 'Sir Francis Drake's Ghost: Piracy, Cultural Memory, and Spectral Nationhood', in Claire Jowitt, ed., *Pirates? The Politics of Plunder, 1550–1650* (Basingstoke, 2007) 137–50.

Newbolt, Henry, *Collected Poems 1897–1907* (London, 1907).

——, *My World as in My Time: The Memoirs of Sir Henry Newbolt* (London, 1932), 186.

——, *Selected Poems of Henry Newbolt* (London, 1940).

'News of the Armada: Bowls on the Hoe', *The Times*, 1 August 1933, 9.

Nicoll, Allardyce, *The Development of the Theatre: A Study of Theatrical Art from the Beginnings to the Present Day* (1927; London, 1955).

——, *A History of English Drama 1660–1900*, 5 vols (Cambridge, 1952–9).

Noyes, Alfred, *Collected Poems*, 2 vols (London, 1914).

——, 'Silent Hand', *The Times*, 28 August 1916, 5.

Nuttall, Zelia, ed., *New Light on Drake* (London, 1914).

Oldys, William, 'Life of Sir Walter Raleigh', in Walter Raleigh, *The History of the World in Five Books* (London, 1736).

'On Admiral Vernon's Success in America', *Gentleman's Magazine*, vol. 11 (1741), 274.

Opie, John, *Lectures on Painting Delivered at the Royal Academy of Arts with a Letter on the Proposal for a Public Memorial to the Naval Glory of Great Britain* (London, 1809).

Pagden, Anthony, 'The Struggle for legitimacy and the Image of Empire in the Atlantic to c.1750', in Nicholas Canny, ed., *The Origins of Empire: British Overseas Enterprise to the Close of the Seventeenth Century* (Oxford, 1998), 34–54.

Paine, Thomas, *Rights of Man* (1791; London, 1985).

Parker, Louis Napoleon, *Drake: A Pageant Play* (London, 1912).

Parks, G. B., 'Tudor Travel Literature: A Brief History', in Quinn, ed., *The Hakluyt Handbook*, vol. 1, 97–132.

Parry, John H., 'Drake and the World Encompassed', in Thrower, ed., *Sir Francis Drake*, 1–11.

——, 'Hakluyt's view of British History', in Quinn, ed., *The Hakluyt Handbook*, vol. 1, 3–7.

Peele, George, 'A Farewell Intitled to the Famous and Fortunate Generals of Our English Forces by Land and Sea, Sir John Norris and Sir Francis Drake', in A. H. Bullen, ed., *The Works of George Peele*, 2 vols (London, 1888), vol. 2, 237–40.

Penny Cyclopaedia of the Society for the Diffusion of Useful Knowledge, 29 vols (London, 1833–46).

Pevsner, Nikolaus, *The Buildings of England: Buckinghamshire* (London, 1960).

——, *The Buildings of England: Devon*, rev. edn (London, 1989).

Phillips, Philip A. S., *John Obrisset: Huguenot, Carver, Medallist, Horn and Tortoiseshell Worker, and Snuff-box Maker, with Examples of his work dated 1705–1728* (London, 1931).

Pinkerton, John, *A General Collection of the Best and Most Interesting Voyages and Travels in all Parts of the World*, 17 vols (London, 1812).

'Plymouth Statue of Drake', *Illustrated London News*, 21 July 1888, 76.

Porter, Bernard, *The Lion's Share: A Short History of British Imperialism 1850–1983* (1975; London, 1984).

'Proposed Memorial to Sir Francis', *Western Daily Mercury*, 27 January 1882, 3.

Propp, Vladimir, *Morphology of the Folktale*, 1928, trans. Laurence Scott (Austin, TX, 1998).

Purchas, Samuel, *Hakluyt Posthumus, or Purchas his Pilgrimes containing a History of the World in Sea Voyages and Lande Travells by Englishmen and Others*, 1625, 20 vols (Glasgow, 1905–7).

Quinn, David B., 'Early Accounts of the Famous Voyage', in Thrower, ed., *Sir Francis Drake*, 33–48.

——, ed., *The Hakluyt Handbook*, 2 vols (London, 1974).

——, *Sir Francis Drake as Seen by his Contemporaries* (Providence, RI, 1996).

Rancid Aluminium, dir., Edward Thomas, Fiction Factory, 2000.

Richard, Henry, *Some Account of the Lives and Writings of Lope Felix de Vega Carpio and Guillen de Castro*, 2 vols (London, 1817).

Richards, Jeffrey, 'Boy's Own Empire: Feature Films and Imperialism in the 1930s', in MacKenzie, ed., *Imperialism and Popular Culture*, 140–64.

——, *Visions of Yesterday* (London, 1973).

Ricks, Christopher, ed., *The Poems of Tennyson*, 3 vols (London, 1969).

Ritchie, Robert C., 'Government Measures against Piracy and Privateering in the Atlantic Area, 1750–1850', in David J. Starkey, E. S. van Heslinga and J. A. De Moor, eds, *Pirates and Privateers: New Perspectives on the War on Trade in the Eighteenth and Nineteenth Centuries* (Exeter, 1997), 10–28.

Robarts, Henry, *A Most Friendly Farewell to Sir Francis Drake* (1585; Cambridge, 1924).

Robinson, Charles N., 'The Spanish Armada', *Illustrated London News*, 14 July 1888, 41–50.

Robinson, Gregory, 'A Forgotten Life of Sir Francis Drake', *Mariner's Mirror*, vol. 7, no. 1 (1921), 10–18.

Robinson, John Martin, *Temples of Delight: Stowe Landscape Gardens* (London, 1990).

Rodriguez-Salgado, M. J., et al., *Armada 1588–1988: An International Exhibition to Commemorate the Spanish Armada* (exh. cat., National Maritime Museum, London, 1988).

Rowe, Samuel, *The Panorama of Plymouth: or, Tourists Guide to the Principal Objects of Interest in the Towns of Plymouth, Dock, and Stonehouse* (Plymouth, 1821).

Sadler, John, 'Great News From Drake's and Raleigh's Ghosts', in *The Harleian Miscellany*, 12 vols (London, 1810), vol. 11, 32–9.

Samuel, Raphael, 'Grand Narratives', *History Workshop*, vol. 29 (1990), 120–33.

Sea Hawk, dir., Michael Curtiz, Warner Brothers, 1940.

Seeley, John, *The Expansion of England* (London, 1883).

Shannon, Richard Stoll, *The Arms of Achilles and Homeric Compositional Technique* (Leiden, 1975).

Sharpe, Kevin, *The Personal Rule of Charles I* (New Haven, 1992).

Sidney, Philip, *The Defence of Poesie* (1595; Cambridge, 1905).

Simons, John, ed., *Guy of Warwick and Other Chapbook Romances: Six Tales from the Popular Literature of Pre-industrial England* (Exeter, 1998).

Sinclair, John, *Thoughts on the Naval Strength of the British Empire* (London, 1782).

Sir Francis Drake: An Exhibition to Commemorate Sir Francis Drake's Voyage Around the World 1577–1580 (exh. cat., British Library, London, 1977).

Smith, Adam, *An Inquiry into the Nature and Causes of the Wealth of Nations*, 1776, ed. R. H. Campbell, A. S. Skinner and W. B. Todd, 2 vols (Oxford, 1979).

Smollett, Tobias, *The History of England*, 5 vols (1762; London, 1827).

Somerset, Fitzroy Richard, *The Hero: A Study in Tradition, Myth, and Drama* (1936; Westport, CN, 1975).

Southey, Robert, *Common Place Book*, 4 vols (London, 1851).

——, *The Lives of the British Admirals*, 5 vols (London, 1833–7).

——, 'Some Account of the Lives and Writings of Lope Felix de Vega Carpio, and Guillen de Castro, by Henry Richard, Lord Holland', *Quarterly Review*, vol. 18 (1817–18), 1–46.

Stables, William Gordon, *Old England on the Sea: The Story of Admiral Drake* (London, 1900).

Starkey, David J., *British Privateering and Enterprise in the Eighteenth Century* (Exeter, 1990).

Stogdon, E, 'The True Glory', *The Times*, 20 November 1939, 7.

Strong, Roy, *And when did you last see your father? The Victorian Painter and British History* (London, 1978).

——, *The Cult of Elizabeth: Elizabethan Portraits and Pageantry* (London, 1977).

——, *The English Icon: Elizabethan and Jacobean Portraiture* (London, 1969).

——, *The English Renaissance Miniature* (London, 1983).

Sugden, John, *Sir Francis Drake* (1990; London, 1996).

——, 'Sir Francis Drake: A Note on His Portraiture', *Mariner's Mirror*, vol. 70 (1984), 303–9.

Thrower, Norman J. W., ed., *Sir Francis Drake and the Famous Voyage, 1577–1580: Essays Commemorating the Quadricentennial of Drake's Circumnavigation of the Earth* (Berkeley, 1980).

Turner, Michael, 'New Resting Place for Drake', *The Times*, 2 February 1995, 19.

Vance, Norman, *The Sinews of the Spirit: The Ideal of Christian Manliness in Victorian Literature and Religious Thought* (Cambridge, 1985).

Vaux, William, ed., *The World Encompassed by Sir Francis Drake* (London, 1854).

Virgil, *The Aeneid*, trans. David West (London, 1990).

Wagner, Henry R., *Sir Francis Drake's Voyage Around the World: Its Aims and Achievements* (San Francisco, 1926).

Wallace, Karen, *Captain Drake's Orders* (London, 1997).

Walsh, W. H., 'The Constancy of Human Nature', in H. D. Lewis, ed., *Contemporary British Philosophy* (London, 1975), 274–91.

Walvin, James, *Black Ivory: A History of British Slavery* (London, 1993).

Welch, Edwin, 'The Origins of the Plymouth Fishing Feast', *Devon and Cornwall Notes and Queries*, vol. 30 (1965–7), 155–6.

Wells, Roger, *Insurrection: The British Experience 1795–1803* (Gloucester, 1983).

Westcote, Thomas, *A View of Devonshire in MDCXXX* (Exeter, 1845).

Western Antiquary, 12 vols (1881–93).

Western Daily Mercury, 17 September 1881, 2.

White, Hayden, *Tropics of Discourse: Essays in Cultural Criticism* (1978; Baltimore, 1995).

Whitney, Geoffrey, *A Choice of Emblemes*, 1586, ed. Henry Green (1866; Hildesheim, 1971).

Wightwick, George, 'The Old Town Conduit', *South Devon Monthly Museum*, vol. 15, no. 4 (1834), 89.

Williamson, James, *Sir Francis Drake* (London, 1951).

Wilson, Charles, *Mercantilism* (London, 1971).

Woodman, Thomas, *A Preface to Samuel Johnson* (London, 1993).

Worth, Richard Nicholls, *The History of Plymouth from the Earliest Period until the Present Time* (1870; Plymouth, 1890).

——, *Sir Francis Drake and the Plymouth Corporation; the History of the Plymouth Leat from the Municipal Records* (Plymouth, 1881).

——, 'Sir Francis Drake: His Origins, Arms and Dealing With the Plymouth Corporation', *Transactions of the Devonshire Association*, vol. 16 (1884), 505–52.

Wright, Irene, ed., *Documents Concerning English Voyages to the Spanish Main 1569–1580* (London, 1932).

Index

Page numbers in *italic* refer to an illustration. Sub-subheadings are arranged in ascending page number order.